FROM STUDENT TO SOLICITOR

The Complete Guide to Securing a Training Contract

Second Edition

By

Charlotte Harrison

SWEET & MAXWELL

THOMSON REUTERS

First Edition 2010
Second Edition 2015

Published in 2015 by Thomson Reuters (Professional) UK Limited
trading as Sweet & Maxwell, Friars House, 160 Blackfriars Road, London, SE1 8EZ
(Registered in England & Wales, Company No 1679046.
Registered Office and address for service:
2nd floor, 1 Mark Square, Leonard Street, London, EC2A 4EG)

For further information on our products and services, visit
www.sweetandmaxwell.co.uk

Printed and bound in Great Britain by CPI Group (UK) Ltd, Croydon CR0 4YY
Typeset by Servis Filmsetting Ltd, Stockport, Cheshire

No natural forests were destroyed to make this product;
only farmed timber was used and re-planted.

British Library Cataloguing in Publication Data

A CIP catalogue record for this book
is available from the British Library

ISBN 978-0-414-02806-7

FOREWORD

There are a number of reasons why you might have chosen a career in law. Perhaps you have a desire to speak up for the most vulnerable, or alternatively you might enjoy finding answers to difficult questions.

One of the most attractive aspects about being a solicitor is that you will have many choices and many options to decide between. Some solicitors may never have seen the inside of a court room, whereas others visit courts regularly and may have even attained Higher Audience rights and can now appear as advocates all the way to the Supreme Court.

Whatever path you choose, by becoming a solicitor you will have joined a profession which is dedicated to upholding some of the most fundamental principles of a democratic and fair society. These include a commitment to the rule of law and access to justice—shared values which define us as a single profession despite the marvellous variety of the types of work we might do.

The Law Society is committed to assisting all aspirant members of the profession to reach their potential. The Society's Junior Lawyers Division is free to join and provides support for students and for young solicitors in the early stages of their careers.

I encourage all readers to take full advantage of the information and advice available before deciding which path they wish to take.

I wish you every success as you embark on your new career.

Andrew Caplen
President of the Law Society for England and Wales 2014/15

DEDICATION

This book is dedicated with much love to my parents
Patrick and Vicki Harold-Harrison

ACKNOWLEDGEMENTS

I owe an enormous debt to the solicitors, trainee solicitors, graduate recruitment managers, students, and lecturers who contributed to this project: your voices have brought the work to life.

I must also say a big thank you to Valya Georgieva who wrote Chapter 14 for me and made some very valuable contributions to Chapter 12. The book is far richer as a result of her contributions, and it was a real pleasure to work with one of my students who is now on her own path to becoming a solicitor.

I am grateful to Juliet Brook, Kevin Chard, Cecily Holt, James Kirby, Hannah Lane, Carole McCann, Rebecca Milner, Catherine Pearce, Jenny Pelling, Nicola Potts, and Caroline Strevens for facilitating contributions, reviewing draft chapters, and providing advice on content.

Thanks must, of course, go to everyone at Sweet & Maxwell who was involved in the production of this book. In particular, I am grateful to Annabel Fritsch for all her efforts in the final editing process and to Amanda Strange for offering such sensible suggestions and advice throughout the process of writing this second edition. My son, Patrick, was born in the final weeks of writing the first edition and my daughter, Olivia, was born midway through the second. Thank you Amanda for your endless patience—I promise I will plan the timing of the third edition more carefully!

Writing a book is a very rewarding but incredibly time consuming process and I couldn't have finished this project without the endless support of my family. Thank you to my incredible mum, Vicki, my godmother, Theresa, and my mother-in-law, Margaret, for keeping everything on track and taking such exceptional care of my children when I couldn't be there. Thank you to my dad, Patrick, for proof reading chapters and to my sister, Annabelle, for many late nights reading drafts, commenting on revised structures, and giving the sort of brutal feedback that only a sister can.

I am incredibly grateful to Hugo who turned my ideas for a new website into a reality. Thank you for working so patiently and enthusiastically with me and for making it all seem so easy.

Finally, thank you to my husband, Ian, for encouraging me to take on yet another project and, as always, for supporting me through to the very end (whilst renovating our new family home in his spare time!).

CONTENTS

Foreword   iii
Dedication   v
Acknowledgements   vii
Contents   ix

Introduction   xi

PART I:
YOUR PATH TO PRACTICE: WHERE MIGHT THE JOURNEY
TAKE YOU?

   Chapter 1 – Why Become a Solicitor?   3
   Chapter 2 – The View from the Top   5
   Chapter 3 – The Routes to Qualification   13

PART II:
STUDENT YEARS: THE ACADEMIC AND VOCATIONAL
STAGES OF QUALIFICATION

   Chapter 4 – The Foundations of Legal Knowledge   25
   Chapter 5 – The Law Degree   35
   Chapter 6 – The Graduate Diploma in Law (GDL):
        Converting to Law   43
   Chapter 7 – The Legal Practice Course (LPC)   57

PART III:
THE TRAINING CONTRACT

Section 1: Preparation and Research

   Chapter 8 – Fail to Prepare; Prepare to Fail: How to Use
        Your Time Wisely   75

Chapter 9 – Researching Career Opportunities   85

Chapter 10 – What Are Firms Looking for in Prospective
    Trainees?   127

Chapter 11 – Enhancing Your CV with Work Experience
    and Other Activities   141

Chapter 12 – Developing and Demonstrating Commercial
    Awareness   171

Chapter 13 – Making Connections and Opening Doors   191

Chapter 14 – Brand Development and Social Media   203

Section 2: The Application Process

Chapter 15 – Effective CVs and Covering Letters   227

Chapter 16 – Application Forms: How to Write Winning
    Responses   237

Chapter 17 – Preparing for Interviews   253

Chapter 18 – Preparing for Assessment Centres   269

Chapter 19 – Making Use of Feedback   279

Section 3: The Training Contract and Beyond

Chapter 20 – The Training Contract & Qualification   285

Chapter 21 – A Week in the Life of a Trainee Solicitor   295

Final Thoughts   299

APPENDICES

Appendix 1: Money Matters   301

Appendix 2: Further Reading and Other Resources   307

INTRODUCTION

When I set out to write the first edition of this book towards the end of 2008, I had recently left practice and was settling into life as an academic. Then, as now, I felt very strongly about the importance of supporting students to develop their employability skills and confidence in readiness for the graduate recruitment market. I wanted to demystify the recruitment process and give students access to the knowledge and skills they would need to navigate the process successfully. As you can imagine, I jumped at the chance to write a whole book on the subject!

My own training contract was several years ago now, but I can still remember it clearly as an exciting, stimulating and challenging period. I had worked incredibly hard to secure a training contract and I was determined to soak up the whole experience and take nothing for granted. This was a time of enormous change and personal development for me: I moved to London for the first time; met some inspirational clients and senior lawyers; developed a portfolio of skills that I still draw on today; and formed some of my closest friendships. Yes, it was challenging: the hours were incredibly long; the expectations were exceptionally high; and I was daunted by the skill and experience of those around me. Yes, I felt out of my depth for large periods of time, and every time I changed seats I struggled with the inevitable feeling that I was starting from scratch with renewed anxieties about impressing my supervisor and getting to grips with a new practice area. But I drew on the support of my fellow trainees, dug deep, and ultimately thrived on it.

Of course I am not saying that everyone's experience of training and working as a solicitor will mirror mine. That is the rather wonderful thing about this profession: the breadth and diversity of opportunities that are available to aspiring solicitors (see Chs 2 and 9). As part of my research for this book, I have interviewed lawyers from a variety of practice areas and have often found myself saying "oh, I think I might have enjoyed working there" or "oh, I wish I had tried that area of law while I had the chance". I hope you feel similarly inspired as you read the case studies and listen to the different voices in the book. Use them to think about what you are looking for in a career (and what you would rather avoid), the sort of environment you would like to work in, and the clients you imagine working for. This book is essentially about supporting you to make an informed decision about whether to embark on the trainee solicitor recruitment process and, if so, to support you in making the best possible applications. It is also essential that you realise that there is plenty of hard work to be done before you start to fill in application forms (see Chs 8–14).

There is no escaping the fact that applying for training contracts is a gruelling process, which requires stamina, thick skin, iron determination, and a great deal of self-belief. When you embark on this process you have to give it your all; you have to live and breathe the goal of securing a training contract because only with this level of commitment will you have any hope of securing one. It is probably also worth saying that if you cannot cope with the rigours of the application process, you are unlikely to cope with the demands of working as a solicitor so now is the time to consider your goals carefully and engage in some honest reflection. Is this really for you?

Assuming that you have answered "yes" to the last question, hold your nerve and do not be deterred: you are already one step ahead of the rest of the pack because, by reading this book, you are thinking ahead, taking the process seriously, and putting in the groundwork. Rejection is an inevitable part of the process, but that is fine because you only need one yes vote!

Throughout the process of writing this book, I have been able to draw upon my own experience of practice and the work I do now as a university lecturer teaching employability skills and supporting students through the recruitment process. It is also the product of a great deal of research, including interviews with solicitors, trainee solicitors, graduate recruitment managers, careers advisors, lecturers, and students. During the research for the second edition, it has been particularly heartening to catch up with many contributors who were training during my earlier research and are now enjoying careers as qualified solicitors in a wide variety of practice areas. They are living proof that with hard work and determination, you can realise your goal of becoming a solicitor.

I hope you find this book useful as you plot your own course from student to solicitor. I would be very interested to hear what you think of the book so please send me feedback via my website *http://www.fromstudenttosolicitor.co.uk* or send me a Tweet **@LawTrainee**. I would also be delighted to hear from new contributors whether you are a student, a qualified or trainee solicitor, a careers advisor, or university lecturer.

Finally, it is worth noting that we have witnessed significant change in the legal services market and the regulation and training of solicitors since the first edition was published. It is likely that we will see more changes in the coming months and years, not least because the whole area of training for solicitors is under review as part of a programme called "Training For Tomorrow" (*http://www.sra.org.uk/sra/policy/training-for-tomorrow.page*). We could also expect to see changes and developments relating to legal services apprenticeships given that this is such a new and dynamic area of the market. Thus, whilst the information in this second edition is correct at the time of writing, and emerging trends have been identified, it is not possible at this stage to provide a definitive account. As such, you would be wise to keep an eye on developments in these areas and to identify new trends to ensure that you understand the impact they may have for you in your search for a training contract.

Good luck!

Charlotte Harrison
February 2015

PART I
YOUR PATH TO PRACTICE:
WHERE MIGHT THE JOURNEY TAKE YOU?

1 WHY BECOME A SOLICITOR?

Written by Jonathan Smithers

Vice President of the Law Society for England and Wales 2014/15

Many people think that solicitors only advise clients in court, but the profession and the qualification are very much more than that. The work can be difficult and personally challenging but solicitors are fundamental to the workings of a civilised society.

The bedrock of democracy is the Rule of Law. Solicitors are critical to putting legal principles into practice. Without an independent legal sector, there is a greater risk that the State would make arbitrary decisions without being challenged in the courts.

It may be part of your job as a solicitor to make it possible for people to have access to justice. As a profession, we empower individuals, businesses and other organisations to scrutinise the actions and decisions of the State, as well as upholding their rights against each other. There are many pathways in which this can be done, for example, as a lawyer specialising in human rights or working on judicial reviews or perhaps working in criminal law defending someone who has been accused of a crime.

You may take a different path, which can be just as challenging, navigating the complexities of contracts and transactions. Although we do not necessarily think of this as part of the Rule of Law, it is, and is equally important to society. Our profession is central to the facilitation of a wide range of transactions undertaken on behalf of clients. It's widely accepted that our justice system provides the necessary conditions for wealth creation by safeguarding property ownership and commercial certainty. These transactions can range from working on multi-million pound cross-border trade deals to helping a young family get themselves onto the property ladder.

If you were ever in any doubt as to the importance of the legal profession if you look in any town or city you will see that the legal profession is its beating heart. Often the legal businesses are the oldest on any high street. Our professional ethics are then, effectively imported into society. These include the Rule of Law which I mentioned above and also the proper administration of justice. The advice we give on commercial business, litigation, matrimonial, conveyancing, wills, probate and so on are often done in a quiet and unassuming way so the public is unaware of our role.

Solicitors are a trusted source of information and advice for clients. The decisions you make, whether arguing a case in court, managing their affairs or carrying out a business deal, will impact profoundly on the lives of your clients which is why you would always have to operate to the very highest ethical standards. This does not only mean avoiding unscrupulous behaviour, but also continuing to ensure that your client has the necessary advice so that they can make choices from all the paths available to them.

Being a solicitor is not a job that you necessarily leave behind you at the office. You might say that being a solicitor is not just what you do, it is who you are. This profession can give you a fulfilling and satisfying career with such a wide variety of work types that, whatever your interests, I am sure there will be a path for you. Whichever direction you choose there is much competition and no guarantee of success, but I know from speaking to many hundreds of lawyers over many years that once you get there, you will soon discover what a worthwhile profession this is to join.

2 THE VIEW FROM THE TOP

Sean Wright, Corporate Partner and Head of Private Equity, Shoosmiths LLP

It wasn't my original intention to become a lawyer—I was a year into a Business Studies degree at Sheffield University while also taking a subsidiary course in law and suddenly finding that side of things rather more fascinating. So I switched and fitted my Law degree into the remaining two years before training and qualifying with a City firm.

What tipped me towards corporate law was the year's secondment I did in-house with Shell International, working alongside both the finance and legal teams. (I also had a fabulous office on the 19th floor of the Shell building, overlooking Big Ben).

It was at Shell that I gained the invaluable foundation of learning to structure a transaction from a financial perspective. This struck a real chord with me. As a corporate lawyer, you need to understand at the outset what an individual client wants, commercially, from a transaction, and how it is to be funded.

I then moved to a national firm in Manchester, where I was a kind of hungry sponge gaining practical experience from some of the profession's best practitioners. There's no getting away from it, to do this job you need to have absolute technical proficiency and be able to draft, read and re-draft colossal and complex documents in an environment that can resemble the most extreme endurance test. Corporate transactions have their own dynamics and timescales that don't respect the "9–5". I certainly would find it that much harder without the humour of my team, which can keep you going for that extra mile—or 10!

As the years go by, the job becomes more about growing and mentoring others in your team, and getting used to having a strategic handle on eight or nine transactions at any one time, knowing what's going on in each one. Teambuilding is a key skill, and I guess you do need to be fairly driven, too.

One of the chief benefits of being in private practice is the guarantee of variety. I might be dealing with a client in the advertising business in the morning, and then going to see one in the aerospace sector. Getting to the heart of how people in these businesses make their money makes it fresh for me, every time. Maybe it's because I'm an engineer's son from Wolverhampton; I like to understand how businesses work!

Do I have any advice for someone considering being a corporate lawyer? Go into it with your eyes open—you need to expect unsocial, long hours, know your way round a balance sheet, and be genuinely interested in how a business makes its money. And if you get an opportunity to go on secondment early on in your career, take it!

Elizabeth Bradley, Corporate Tax Partner, Berwin Leighton Paisner LLP

I qualified as a corporate tax solicitor at Berwin Leighton Paisner in September 2001. I advise in all areas of corporate tax, for example, mergers and acquisitions and corporate reorganisations, and also on real estate related tax issues including capital allowances, VAT and stamp duty land tax, property development and investment for residents and non-residents, property joint ventures, and property funds.

Very few people have a burning ambition to become a tax specialist at an early age! Perhaps more people should because tax is not dry and bookish. Tax brings you into contact with every area of legal practice. Corporation tax is the driver of most corporate finance and property transactions as it is often the area of law which adds value to transactions if they are structured in a tax-efficient manner.

I chose to become a City tax solicitor due to the intellectually challenging nature of the work. I enjoy working closely with clients on a daily basis in order to deliver practical, innovative and commercial solutions to their problems. It is crucial to develop a close relationship with your clients in order to understand their business needs.

A City solicitor is, in the long term, a profession which rewards hard work, commitment, and drive. I decided to pursue a career in this field at an early age and embarked on several vacation placements at different law firms in order to experience life as a City solicitor. Securing a training contract can be difficult and very competitive. However, it is often true to say that most difficult things in life worth achieving are those things worth having!

Mark Heath, Director of Corporate Services, Southampton City Council

I was fortunate when I was at school to have outstanding career advice and made a decision while I was doing my A Levels that a career in law was the route I wished to take. I was also fortunate enough to end up at my first choice university, and they had a lunchtime slot where practising solicitors or trainee solicitors from various sectors came in and spoke about their careers to help and encourage the law undergraduates in terms of their own career choices.

I can still remember the session from the local government trainee solicitor who talked about actively being involved in court cases and presenting them on behalf of the local authority whilst still a trainee solicitor, and indicated that he was carrying a significant workload: in essence he was being trained by being thrown in at the deep end. It was this that clicked with me, and it was on this basis that I ended up applying to work in local government, starting my career at Hampshire County Council and then moving to Southampton City Council.

So what is life like in local government for a solicitor? We usually consider ourselves to have one and only one client which obviously sets us apart from our private sector colleagues, but my client spends £1 billion a year, employs many people and touches every citizen's life on a daily basis in the city. We undertake almost every sphere of standard legal work as well as the specialist areas required in local government. We also, particularly at a more senior level, have direct interface with councillors. That political interface, and all that goes with it, is a significant issue which the corporate legal advisor at a senior level in a local authority has to develop.

So when advising an aspiring law student about a career in local government, I would say don't believe everything you read about life in the public sector. It is hard work, there are major demands, and you will not get any benefits that you would not get in the private sector. What you will get is a very reward-ing job; indeed you will probably find yourself doing things that your counterparts in the private sector cannot do because of the status of local government, e.g. appearing in court in minor matters before you are admitted. If you stay in local government you will find that the career path provides you with a broad range of opportunities, for example specialising in a particular area of law to develop greater expertise, moving into management, or becoming a policy advisor.

Finally, there is still something about the public service ethos that should not be discounted. Some aspects of the work bring it out more than others. For example, I am a Returning Officer for elections. In conducting elections I am making sure that the elec-torate have the right to determine who governs them and that the democratic process is properly and effectively implemented. Undertaking roles like that provides an enormous degree of per-sonal satisfaction, and so I believe that the public service ethos remains a powerful factor in seeing the public sector as a good career choice.

Christopher Mills, Family and Child Solicitor, Deputy District Judge

I went to university to study English, but soon decided (thanks to the University of Keele's Foundation Year) that I enjoyed law. In the end my degree was a joint honours degree in Law and American Studies.

After university I had no clear idea of a career and drifted into working for a solicitors practice as a clerk dealing with liti-gation case files. I became fascinated with court work. I soon gave up crime to concentrate on civil litigation which included family cases. Eventually I obtained a training contract, attended the College of Law (as it was then) at Guildford, and qualified as a solicitor.

Although I enjoyed all aspects of civil and family law, I found the greatest satisfaction in family law. When it was first formed I applied successfully to join the Law Society's Family Law Panel. I also became a member of the Solicitors Family Law Association (now Resolution), an organisation committed to resolving family disputes in a less adversarial way. For a number of years I sat on their Hampshire committee.

I subsequently applied to join the Children's Panel, a more specialised panel. The application process involved providing case studies from my own work, solutions to scenarios set by the Panel and an interview at the Law Society's Hall in Chancery Lane. Every five years an application has to be made to renew membership. As a Panel member I can represent parents in private and public law cases and children's guardians in public law cases. I undertake as much of my own advocacy as I can both in the magistrates and county courts, now the family court.

There is great satisfaction to be derived from resolving a family case; it really is like no other form of litigation. There are no real winners or losers; it is doing the best you can for your client and achieving a resolution in the best interest of the children.

It was after a court hearing that a District Judge I regularly appeared before asked me to stay behind after a case. Wondering what I had done, I remained behind after the other parties left. He asked whether I had ever thought of applying to be a Deputy District Judge and suggested that I considered doing so. He also said that he and his colleagues would be prepared to give me references.

When the competition for Deputy District Judge opened, I applied. I was invited to an assessment day which was an intensive and exhausting experience! In 2005 I was appointed to sit in the Southeast Region. In 2012 I applied for a s.8 ticket to hear Children's Act cases and was successful.

I now sit one day a week at various courts in my region, hearing everything from small claims, fast-track trials, bankruptcies, divorce settlements and children's cases. Every day I sit presents me with a range of different cases with their own problems.

Those cases have to be read and assimilated in a very short time. The parties are entitled to a fair hearing; a reasoned decision has to be given in each case which is understandable to all parties. I do get a great sense of satisfaction at the end of my sitting days which are often busy and frustrating, but in the end rewarding.

For two days a week I now teach at the University of Portsmouth, whilst still practising as a family solicitor two days a week. Life is busy and I never seem to know what is coming next. However I do not regret the path I chose and the opportunity it gives me to meet and help a lot of different people. I also feel that I am putting something back into the community, which is worthwhile and rewarding.

Glenn Beavis, Former Senior In-House Legal Counsel and Racing Driver Manager

Law is a great profession. It can provide many things—interesting work, the opportunity to meet fascinating people, and the opportunity to travel and to make a difference by being yourself. It has everything that a soap opera has, plus a bit more—politics, power struggles and eccentrics. It is a very diverse profession indeed.

For me, being a solicitor is most rewarding when you can make a difference, particularly if you have a client who is not in a strong position and through your knowledge and the right approach and tactics you are able to improve their position.

My position in-house took me all over the world and enabled me to work on projects that really make a difference to the way people live their lives. The breadth and depth of the legal knowledge of the colleagues I worked with was very impressive.

Because of the diversity of the legal profession, as a solicitor you have many options open to you as to where to work. The common general divide is between working in private practice and working in-house. There are however many different companies and organisations that fall under the banner of "in-house"—from multinational companies, to charities and universities. Being a solicitor in-house undoubtedly brings you closer to the heart of the organisation you represent. For many solicitors in private practice who move in-house, this can be very refreshing because you are in at the beginning of a matter and integral to it, helping to shape things as they evolve.

Many solicitors that I know who have tasted the life of an in-house solicitor do not wish to return to private practice. Not because private practice is bad, but because being in-house is different in a way that cannot be replicated in a law firm. Depending where you work, it can provide more balance to your days. I would certainly recommend that you try a spell in-house and see what you think. If you are not sure about making the step away from a law firm, you could try and arrange a secondment to a company or organisation that is a client of the firm you work at, if such an arrangement is available.

It is hard work qualifying as a solicitor. It is also expensive and often there is no guarantee of a job at the end, which can be daunting. But for every 10 jobs you may apply for and not get, you only need one to say yes. If you are committed, you will succeed and you can make a difference. The key is never to give up trying, not ever.

Because qualifying as a solicitor is a hard slog at times, you will inevitably have moments when you question whether it is all worth it. It is worth it though, whatever you choose to do once you qualify. Even if you choose to step outside of the legal profession, the skills you will have learnt and taken on board will serve you very well wherever you end up.

I chose to step outside of the legal profession and set up as a manager of racing drivers. Not something that you will hear many legal career advisors talk about! The point here though is that my legal background serves me very well in my chosen profession. Work hard, qualify, get some experience under your belt and then ask yourself, "What do I really enjoy doing?"; with the skillset you have acquired, go and do it.

3 THE ROUTES TO QUALIFICATION

TRADITIONAL ROUTE TO QUALIFICATION

This book focuses on the routes to qualification as a solicitor in England and Wales. You can qualify as a solicitor with a law or non-law degree. The route is longer and more expensive if you decide to start with a non-law degree because you have to undertake a law conversion course called the GDL before you can proceed to the vocational and practical stages of training. Have a look at Ch.4 for advice on things to think about when deciding whether to take a law degree or non-law degree plus GDL. If you have already decided to commit to the GDL, you might find Ch.6 useful to help you demonstrate the advantages of your non-law background to recruiters. (See Fig.1 on p. 14)

It is worth noting that the SRA Training Regulations 2014 provide greater flexibility in terms of allowing the SRA to grant exemptions from all or part of the academic or vocational stage by reference to other assessed learning and work-based learning. See regs 2.2 and 4 for more information. You might also like to refer to *http://www.sra.org.uk/sra/policy/training-for-tomorrow/Resources/training-regulations-changes-summary.page#flexibility* for more details.

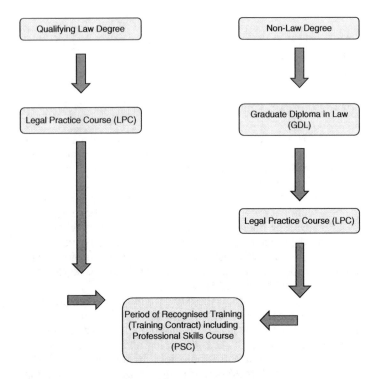

Fig.1 Graduate routes to qualification

PERIOD OF RECOGNISED TRAINING

After you have completed the LPC, you will need to complete a "period of recognised training" (traditionally known as a training contract) in order to qualify as a solicitor. The term "period of recognised training" was introduced in the SRA Training Regulations 2014 and essentially replaced the training contract with effect from 1 July 2014. There are subtle differences between the training contract and the period of recognised training. These relate largely to the degree of influence which the Solicitors Regulation

Authority (SRA) (the body that is responsible for regulating the conduct and training of solicitors in England and Wales) has over a trainee's terms and conditions of employment. Despite the official change of name, many law firms continue to use the term "training contract" in marketing and recruitment literature. Therefore, to avoid any confusion during the transition stage, the term "training contract" has been used throughout this book to refer to a period of recognised training. For a copy of the SRA Training Regulations, go to *http://sra.org.uk/solicitors/handbook/trainingregs2014*.

The training contract lasts for two years (if completed on a full-time basis) (reg.5.2 of the SRA Training Regulations 2014) and is generally divided into four "seats" of six months which are spent in different practice areas (although some firms offer a greater number of shorter seats). The training contract provides trainees with a broad training base and the opportunity to experience different practice areas before deciding where they would like to qualify. It is possible to complete the training contract on a part-time basis provided that the contract is completed within a four-year maximum period and that the trainee works at least two and a half days each week during the four-year period. Look at the SRA guidelines on part-time training contracts if this is something that is of interest to you (*http://www.sra.org.uk/trainees/period-recognised-training.page*).

The SRA states that you need to have good experience of at least three different practice areas during the course of your training. It does not specify how long you must spend in each department but suggests that the equivalent of three months would be necessary to gain appropriate experience and that opportunities should be given to develop skills in contentious and non-contentious work (reg.12.1(a) of the SRA Training Regulations 2014). If your employer cannot offer this breadth of work, it should arrange for you to be sent on secondment to another firm to gain the required experience (reg.12.1(b) of the SRA Training Regulations 2014).

The training contract can be reduced by a maximum of six months on account of previous legal experience, subject to the agreement of the training contract provider (reg.12.3 of the SRA

Training Regulations 2014). This may be something to bear in mind if you have an extended length of experience working as a paralegal in a law firm prior to beginning your training contract.

Wherever you decide to train, your training will have to meet requirements set down by the SRA. For further details of these requirements, visit the student pages of the SRA website (*http://www.sra.org.uk/trainees/period-recognised-training.page*).

Salary

As a result of changes introduced by the SRA in 2014, the regulator no longer imposes a minimum salary for trainee solicitors (reg.10.2(f) of the SRA Training Regulations 2014). Thus, law firms are allowed to pay their trainees the National Minimum Wage. Whilst this is unlikely to be an issue for trainees at City, national or regional firms, it might affect those who are thinking of training with smaller firms or organisations which (at the time of writing) have been hit hard by the recession and legal aid cuts.

Professional Skills Course

Your firm will fund this course for you and give you paid time off to attend the training sessions and assessments (reg.10.2(e) of the SRA Training Regulations 2014). The PSC consists of three core modules (Client Care and Professional Standards, Advocacy and Communication Skills, and Financial and Business Skills) and additional elective modules. Some firms choose to send their trainees on an intensive course, while others spread the modules over the course of the training contract.

Character and Suitability Issues

There is no longer an enrolment fee payable to the SRA but you must notify the SRA, and disclose any character or suitability matters, before you start training. There is also an ongoing duty to disclose any new issues which arise during the training contract and all trainees will be subject to a compulsory check before admission. There is no exhaustive list of issues which would constitute character or suitability issues, but you can find an indicative list on the SRA's website *(http://www.sra.org.uk/solicitors/handbook/suitabilitytest/content.page)*. It is worth noting that assessment offences are mentioned specifically within the category of character and suitability issues. Therefore, you should be very careful to reference your academic work correctly, and use sources appropriately, to avoid any allegations of plagiarism.

You are not eligible to start training if you do not meet the SRA's requirements for character and suitability. Disclosure before and during the training contract is voluntary so the onus is on individuals to make full disclosure of any issues before commencement of the training contract. At the time of writing, if you request a voluntary check during or after your LPC, but before you start your training contract, there is no charge. If you request a voluntary check before commencing the LPC, you will be charged £100 for the assessment.

If you have any character or suitability issues, the SRA's guidance states that you should apply at least six months before you are due to commence your training. If you fail to disclose character and/or suitability issues, your training contract may be revoked or terminated.

You can obtain further advice on this process by visiting the SRA's suitability test web page (*http://www.sra.org.uk/solicitors/handbook/suitabilitytest/content.page*). You should also refer to reg.6 of the SRA Training Regulations 2014.

CILEX ROUTE

You can also qualify as a solicitor after qualifying as a Chartered Legal Executive, though it should be noted that a career as a Chartered Legal Executive is a valuable and rewarding one in its own right (see *http://www.cilex.org.uk* and *http://www.cilex.org.uk/careers/careers_home.aspx*). Chartered Legal Executives are regulated by ILEX Professional Standards and the academic stage of qualification can be completed with or without a degree.

The Graduate Route

If you have a qualifying law degree, or a non-law degree plus a Graduate Diploma in Law (GDL), you can enrol on the CILEx Graduate Fast Track Diploma. The only condition is that you must have obtained your qualifying law degree or GDL in the seven years prior to your enrolment on the Diploma.

If you embark on the Graduate Fast Track Diploma, you will study Client Care Skills plus two units from the range of CILEx Level 6 practice modules (one of which must be linked with a substantive law subject in your qualifying law degree or GDL, e.g. land law is the substantive law subject for conveyancing).

The Non-Graduate Route

If you decide not to go to university, you can enrol on the CILEx Level 3 Professional Diploma in Law and Practice followed by the CILEx Level 6 Professional Higher Diploma in Law and Practice. If you pass both these courses, you will have achieved the academic standards which are required for qualification as a Chartered Legal Executive.

Qualifying Employment

Regardless of which route you take, if you pass the relevant CILEx exams and satisfy the work-based learning requirements during the period of three years' qualifying employment, you will be eligible for Fellowship of the Chartered Institute of Legal Executives. The definition of qualifying employment can be found on the CILEx careers website (*http://www.cilex.org.uk/careers/careers_home.aspx*). Two years must be consecutive qualifying employment immediately preceding the application (e.g. these could be during the last two years of your Level 6 studies as long as you meet the work-based learning requirements) but you cannot complete the final year of employment until *after* you have completed and passed your academic qualifications.

If you wanted to qualify as a solicitor, you would need to pass a further five Level 6 CILEx subjects after the CILEx Level 6

Professional Higher Diploma in Law and Practice, to meet the SRA's requirements.

Once you have qualified as a Fellow of the Chartered Institute of Legal Executives, you can enrol on the LPC if you still want to go on to qualify as a solicitor. If you pass this course, you can apply for admission to the Roll of Solicitors and seek exemption from the training contract, subject to the SRA's approval. See *http://www.sra.org.uk/trainees/admission/admission-criteria.page* for more details on the admissions criteria for CILEx entrants.

LEGAL APPRENTICESHIP SCHEMES

The legal apprenticeship schemes were launched in September 2013. The schemes are aimed at those who wish to enter the legal profession but do not want to go to university. The workload of an apprentice will be similar to that of a paralegal but they will combine work with a planned and nationally recognised programme of study in order to gain part of the qualification to work as a Chartered Legal Executive. This route is likely to suit those who wish to combine work and study whilst avoiding fees for undergraduate and postgraduate courses. It is, however, worth noting that (at the time of writing) the apprenticeship pathway does not offer an automatic route to qualification as a Chartered Legal Executive or solicitor.

All training costs are fully funded by the Government if the apprentice has not yet reached his/her 19th birthday on the first day of the apprenticeship or partly funded by the Government if the apprentice is between 19 and 24. Apprentices aged 24 or over will need to take out an Advanced Learning Loan (refer to the CILEx website for more details).

At the time of writing, there are two types of legal practice (rather than administration) apprenticeships: the Advanced Apprenticeship in Legal Services and the Higher Apprenticeship in Legal Services. The Advanced Apprenticeship is a Level 3 skills programme aimed at school leavers. The Higher Apprenticeship is a Level 4 skills programme aimed at those who are already working in a legal environment. There are no formal academic requirements to join an apprenticeship scheme but some firms set minimum grades and/or specific GCSE requirements for their apprenticeship programmes. See the CILEx factsheet for more information on the entry requirements *(http://www.cilex.org.uk/ careers/careers_home/school_leavers/apprenticeships/types_ of_apprenticeships.aspx)*. Apprentices are employed for at least 30 hours per week. Some are employed on a permanent contract, others on a fixed term contract.

At the time of writing there are seven pathways for the Advanced Apprenticeship (Criminal Prosecution; Civil Litigation; Employment Practice; Family Practice; Property; Private Client Practice; and Paralegal Practice) and three for the Higher Apprenticeship (Commercial Litigation; Debt, Recovery & Insolvency; and Personal Injury). It typically takes between 18 and 24 months to complete the Advanced Apprenticeship and between 24 and 30 months to complete the Higher Apprenticeship.

There are two key elements to the apprenticeship programmes:

a competency element made up of a number of units which are assessed by a portfolio and workplace visits. This element assesses workplace skills, e.g. communication skills; time management skills; ability to manage files, etc.; and

a knowledge-based technical element which includes a selection of CILEx units. Apprentices might spend time each week completing this element at college or studying in the work-place.

On successful completion of the Advanced Apprenticeship, apprentices will be awarded a CILEx Level 3 Diploma in Providing Legal Services (only studied in the context of an Advanced Apprenticeship). They will also have gained exemption from some of the units which make up the CILEx Level 3 Professional Diploma in Law and Practice (the first stage of training to become a Chartered Legal Executive). On successful completion of the Higher Apprenticeship (comprising seven units spanning sub-stantive law units, skills-based units, and practice units) apprentices will be awarded a CILEx Level 4 Diploma in Providing Legal Services (only studied in the context of a Higher Apprenticeship) and will also have gained exemptions from the CILEx Level 3 Professional Diploma in Law and Practice. In both cases, the apprentices should also have developed key transferable skills from their work experience.

At the end of the apprenticeship, apprentices may choose to finish the Level 3 qualification and perhaps continue to the Level 6 qualification. They may also decide to explore job opportunities as trainee legal executives and perhaps (much further down the line) also consider the possibility of taking the LPC and qualifying as a solicitor (they may be exempt from the training contract if they have qualified as a Fellow of the Chartered Institute of Legal Executives).

This is a dynamic and fast-moving area. The following web-sites may be useful to you in finding out more about legal apprenticeship schemes and helping you keep abreast of future developments:

http://www.cilex.org.uk/careers/careers_home/legal_ professionals/legal_apprenticeships.aspx

http://www.gov.uk/legal-services-apprenticeships

http://www.gov.uk/government/organisations/skills-funding-agency

CHANGING TIMES

It is important to recognise that the whole area of training for solicitors is under review at the time of writing. Following publication of the Legal Education and Training Review report in June 2013, the SRA launched a programme of education and training reform which is called Training for Tomorrow. You can find more details of this programme at *http://www.sra.org.uk/sra/policy/ training-for-tomorrow.page*. You would be wise to keep an eye on developments in this area to ensure that you understand the impact they may have for you in terms of the path you will need to follow in order to qualify as a solicitor, and also for the sector as a whole.

Given that the legal apprenticeship schemes are still relatively new, this is another area which you should keep under review. In particular, we have yet to see exactly how the new Trailblazer

Apprenticeship route will unfold and the impact this will have on existing legal apprenticeship routes. Indeed, we must also wait to see if legal apprenticeships continue to grow at such a fast pace, and whether subsequent governments continue to support and invest in them. If you are interested in legal apprenticeships, you would be wise to read and monitor the further reading resources listed in Appendix 2. The remainder of this book will focus on the traditional route to qualification as a solicitor.

PART II
STUDENT YEARS:
THE ACADEMIC AND VOCATIONAL STAGES OF QUALIFICATION

4 THE FOUNDATIONS OF LEGAL KNOWLEDGE

The SRA requires that, in order to complete the academic stage of training to become a solicitor, a student must cover certain core subjects. These subjects are known collectively as the "Foundations of Legal Knowledge" or the "foundation subjects". In addition, students must receive training in legal research.

THE FOUNDATIONS OF LEGAL KNOWLEDGE

Criminal Law
Law of the European Union
Obligations (including Contract Law, Tort Law, and the Law of Restitution)
Property Law
Equity and the Law of Trusts
Public Law (Constitutional, Administrative, and Human Rights Law)

See *http://www.sra.org.uk/students/academic-stage-joint-statement-bsb-law-society.page* for more details.

Law conversion courses cover the compulsory foundation subjects, as well as providing an introduction to the English legal system and the general skills required for legal study. Qualifying law degrees combine the same foundation and legal skills subjects with opportunities to explore specialist units such as intellectual property law, commercial law, health care law, or company law.

The foundation subjects lay down the basic principles upon which other specialist areas of law are built. For example, contract law is an important and interesting subject in its own right, and it also provides the basis of other specialist areas such as employment law, commercial law, and construction law. It is therefore best to avoid thinking of each subject as a separate, compartmentalised body of knowledge. It is equally important to realise that real life is rarely as straightforward as the neatly packaged scenarios that are found inside undergraduate law exam papers. Thus, a "real life" legal problem is unlikely to consist of a single issue and might well involve elements of, for example, tort, contract, and land law. The trick for the lawyer is to unravel the various strands and decide which ones hold the key to achieving the client's aims.

What Will I Study?

The key features of each of the foundation subjects are summarised below. As you will realise when you embark on your legal studies, these descriptions are somewhat oversimplified but serve their purpose in this particular context. You will learn that in most areas, our law is a mixture of statutes (Acts of Parliament, such as the Theft Act, or the Unfair Contract Terms Act), and of case law, or precedents, wherein the Higher Courts have tried to apply or interpret or clarify the words that Parliament has used in its various statutes.

Criminal Law—the study of criminal offences and related punishments. Imagine that you represent Sheila, a 26-year-old woman who has been married to Paul for six months. During that time, Paul has repeatedly beaten and mentally abused her. She is too frightened to tell anyone but dreams about having the strength to kill him to make it all stop. One evening, Paul is asleep in the chair after drinking a couple of bottles of cider and Sheila stabs him to death with a large kitchen knife. Is Sheila guilty of murder? Are any defences available to her? Does it matter that she was not actually in any immediate danger at the time she killed her husband?

Law of the European Union—the study of the formation and government of the European Union and the relationships between its Member States. Imagine that you represent the British Government. British fishermen are angry because Spanish fishermen are fishing in British waters (using UK companies to purchase the vessels) to avoid fishing quotas. The British Government has passed a piece of legislation to prevent such activity by requiring that 75 per cent of directors and shareholders of such companies must be British. Will this legislation be contrary to European Union Law? Could the Spanish Government take legal action to stop the new ownership rules?

Contract Law—the study of the law governing agreements made between two or more legal persons. Imagine that you represent Julie Jones, a well-known cat breeder. Julie's favourite cat has just given birth to a litter of kittens so Julie places a bulk order of cat food with her usual supplier. She is in a hurry and doesn't bother to read the terms and conditions when she signs the order form. If she had read them, she would have found a clause excluding any liability for loss or damage caused by the company's products. Two weeks after she starts to use the new cat food, the kittens develop a nasty sickness bug and within another week four of them are dead. Tests reveal that the cat food contained lethal quantities of a toxic substance. Can Julie sue the supplier for breach of contract? What is the effect of the exclusion clause? Does it matter whether Julie purchased the food in a domestic or business capacity?

Tort Law—the study of certain civil wrongs, including negligence, nuisance, and defamation. The injured or wronged party may be granted a remedy, usually via an award of money (damages), which will seek to compensate him for the loss sustained. Imagine that you act for Brian Smith, a keen dog walker. One Sunday afternoon, on his way back from a long walk with the dogs, Brian is forced to wait at the railway crossing while a train passes. Shortly after it passes through the station, there is a terrible crash. Brian runs to the scene to see if he can help but there is nothing he can do. Brian has been suffering from severe depression for three months as a result of the carnage and terrible injuries that he witnessed. He is unable to work and has been dismissed by his employer. An investigation has revealed that the crash was the result of defective brakes caused by poor maintenance. Can Brian bring a claim against Shuttle Trains plc, the owner of the train? Would it make any difference if Brian had been waiting at the station because he knew his wife would be on that train?

Property/Land Law—the study of the ownership, use of and rights in land and anything fixed to the land. Imagine that you represent Abigail Porter, a middle aged woman who owns a house in Surrey. For the last 15 years she has used a bit of scrubland beyond the end of her garden for growing vegetables. She doesn't know who owns the land, but no one had ever complained about her use of it. Last week she received a letter from the landowner stating that he would be taking steps to recover possession of the land. Can Abigail claim any right to continue using the land? Does it matter whether the land has been fenced off from other adjoining land? Would it make any difference if her children had simply used the land to play hide and seek? What if she had only used it for eight years?

Equity and Trusts—the study of the ownership of property on behalf of, and for the benefit of, another. Imagine that you are the judge hearing a case brought by a syndicate of businessmen who have invested in an overseas property portfolio. The businessmen appointed Mr Sly to manage the fund on their behalf. However, Mr Sly was not an honest man and used part of the fund to pay two out of five annual premiums (£10,000 each) on a £1 million life assurance policy for the benefit of his children. He died just after making the fifth payment leaving the children entitled to the £1 million payout. Should the children be entitled to keep the proceeds of the life assurance policy? If not, should they be allowed to keep part of it to reflect the premiums paid by Mr Sly from his own funds? If so, how would you divide the proceeds?

Public Law (Constitutional, Administrative, and Human Rights Law)—the study of the law governing the relationships between state bodies and between legal persons and the state. This broad category would also include criminal law and EU law (discussed above).

Constitutional Law is the study of a system of government and the limits, control, and division of government power.

Administrative Law concerns the rights of legal persons to take court action to hold the state to account for its decisions. For example, the process of judicial review allows the legality of decisions made by public bodies to be challenged. Imagine that you act for a couple living in London whose son has been rejected by the local high performing secondary school. The couple tell you that every other child in their street (comprising mainly social housing for low income Eastern European families) has been rejected even though the school is only five minutes away and other children who live further away have been awarded places. Can the families challenge the local authority's admissions policy? What powers do the courts have to investigate such decisions? What action could the families bring?

Human Rights Law concerns particular rights (arising from the European Convention on Human Rights) granted to legal persons to enforce against the state, e.g. the right to a fair trial. Imagine that you represent a client who is subject to a deportation order and is not allowed to see the reasons for this as there is a national security issue at stake. You are not allowed to see the evidence supporting the order and are therefore unable to challenge the evidence or inform your client of the case against him. Can he rely on any human rights arguments to challenge this process?

You will also be expected to engage in legal research as part of your law degree or law conversion course. You will learn how to approach legal problem questions to identify the key legal issues and to advise on the likely outcome of the problem. You will also learn how to approach legal essay questions which tend to focus on contentious areas of law or proposed legal reforms. In doing so, you will learn how to use a law library and electronic data-bases effectively in order to find sources of law, e.g. case law and legislation. You will also learn how to find, evaluate, and analyse academic commentary on particular legal issues.

THE LEGAL EDUCATION AND TRAINING REVIEW (LETR)

The LETR was a joint project of the SRA, the Bar Standards Board and ILEX Professional Standards. The project was commissioned in June 2011 with the aim of reviewing the education and training requirements across regulated and non-regulated legal services in England and Wales. The review was prompted by the significant changes in the legal practice market as a result of, for example, market liberalisation, the Legal Services Act 2007, increased use of IT, and restrictions to legal aid. This led the regulators to commit to reviewing legal services education and training to ensure that it continues to be fit for purpose in the new market place.

The findings were published in June 2013 and, as expected, the report encouraged providers to place greater emphasis on the teaching of ethics and legal values, commercial awareness and professionalism. It also prompted a detailed review by the SRA of the training and route to qualification for solicitors. For more details, please refer to the SRA's Training for Tomorrow web pages *(http://www.sra.org.uk/sra/policy/training-for-tomorrow.page)*.

If you wish to find out more about the findings and recommendations of the LETR, you can visit *http://www.letr.org.uk*.

LAW DEGREE VS LAW CONVERSION COURSE

As explained in Ch.3, the traditional route to qualification as a solicitor involves two stages of study before you can progress to the training contract. The first is known as the academic stage and consists of a qualifying law degree or a non-qualifying degree (in any subject) plus a law conversion course (the Graduate Diploma in Law (GDL)). The Legal Practice Course (LPC) constitutes the second "vocational" stage.

Some universities offer qualifying combined honours degree programmes. Such programmes satisfy the SRA's requirements in terms of the academic stage of the qualification process while also allowing students to indulge their interest in a non-law subject. Contact individual providers for more information about combined honours programmes.

> "We are very open to non-law undergraduates. The skills developed during some degrees, such as English or History, really do provide a good foundation for a legal career."
> *Lynn Ford, HR Manager, Blake Morgan LLP*

There is no hard evidence to suggest that law firms prefer either law or non-law graduates; firms are generally only interested in getting the best possible graduates. The one thing you can rely on is that you will need at least a 2:1 before the City firms (and many of the regional and national firms) will even consider your application and some look as far back as A Levels and GCSEs. While other firms might not have a policy on A Levels and degree classifications, some will weight them against other aspects of their recruitment criteria so you will have to work harder to demonstrate your competence in those areas if you have poor A Levels or a weak degree classification. Firms will also be interested in whether you have studied an academically rigorous degree course and where you studied.

The table below sets out some of the factors to take into account when deciding whether to study law at university or whether to complete a non-qualifying degree and the GDL.

Advantages of a Law Degree	Advantages of a Non-Law Degree Plus GDL
Develop a deeper knowledge of the law It goes without saying that the depth and breadth of your legal knowledge will be greater if you have studied law for three years at university, rather than one intense year on the GDL. Students on the GDL cover only the core foundation subjects so there is little time to indulge in the finer details of legal research and debate. As a law undergraduate, you will have the opportunity to study specialist options and have more time to find out what areas of law you are actually interested in and thus which practice areas might suit you. You will also have the opportunity to engage in deeper legal research on a specialist topic if you write a dissertation as part of your course.	**Intense study of the key legal subjects** The GDL is designed to cover the essential foundation subjects in one year while preparing students for the LPC and practice. The teaching therefore tends to be more commercial and practical than is the case on most qualifying law degrees. In reality, you are unlikely to engage in academic debate on the finer points of law during your career as a solicitor, which is why some might argue that the GDL is in fact better preparation for practice than a law degree. Also, since you will have studied all the foundation subjects in one year, they will be more familiar to you when you start your LPC.

Forewarned is forearmed!
Early exposure to the realities of legal practice and the study of law might convince you that a legal career is not for you after all, although you will still have a well-respected degree on which to build an alternative career. On the other hand, it could be a very expensive mistake if you only realise this once you have committed to the GDL.

Last chance to indulge your passion for a particular subject
If you have a burning desire to study a particular non-law subject at university then, provided it is an intellectually challenging, academic degree, you should seriously consider it. You are more likely to excel in a subject that you have a passion for and it will probably be your last chance for academic indulgence for a very long time. It could also be seen as a less risky approach because you are already familiar with that subject, whereas a law degree will be entirely uncharted territory—how do you really know that you will enjoy a law degree if you have not studied it before?

Preparation for interviews/ assessment centres and developing legal skills
While it is true that many firms purposely avoid legal content in their recruitment processes, law students sometimes feel more confident about embarking on assessment centres and interviews for training contracts because they are used to "thinking like a lawyer" and have some understanding of core legal principles and current legal issues.

Breadth of knowledge outside of the law
Non-law graduates can be very strong candidates for training contracts because they bring additional skills and subject knowledge to the work place. This can be especially useful if you want to go into a niche area such as Intellectual Property law where graduates with a science background can be particularly attractive to firms.

Motivation to become a solicitor
If you were to look at most firms' recruitment criteria, one of the key requirements would be for candidates to demonstrate their genuine motivation and commitment to become a solicitor. Firms spend hundreds of thousands of pounds training each trainee so you need to convince prospective employers that you are a serious candidate who is worth the investment. This is especially important in a tough economic

climate when firms are more discerning about their choice of trainee and need to differentiate between those who genuinely want to become solicitors and those who are just applying for training contracts because there are fewer jobs in other sectors.

Choosing to study law at university is one way of demonstrating an early commitment to become a solicitor but you should not be complacent; you still need to demonstrate that this was an informed choice and that you have continued to develop your skills during your studies.	Students who embark on the GDL certainly demonstrate motivation to become a solicitor. They have made a conscious decision to study a law conversion course with a view to becoming a solicitor. Firms will be well aware that this is a serious investment in terms of cost, time, and hard work.
Quicker and cheaper By studying a qualifying law degree, you can avoid an extra year of study. This means that your route to qualification will be both quicker and cheaper than your non-law counterparts.	**Greater life experience** Students who have completed a non-law degree and the GDL have another year of maturity on those who have studied law, which can be appealing to employers.
Earlier careers advice As a law undergraduate, you will probably have greater access to contacts within the legal profession than your non-law counterparts. You will probably also be exposed to tailored careers advice from the first year, which might put you in a stronger position when it comes to early preparation for vacation schemes and training contract applications. It can be more difficult for non-law students to obtain legal careers advice such as how the recruitment process works, how and when to research law firms, when to apply for training contracts, and the importance of getting early work experience, whereas this information tends to be freely available to law undergraduates.	**Very focused careers advice on the GDL** Although you will only have a year in which to build up work experience and work on your training contract applications (if you have not given this any thought while at university), you will have access to high quality, tailored careers advice on the GDL and LPC, particularly where providers specialise solely in legal training. You will also build up a strong network of friends who are focused on the same career goals, which can make for a very stimulating and motivating year of study. In doing so, you will be creating a bank of useful contacts for your long-term career.

Well respected by employers	Keep your options open
There is no denying the fact that a law degree will be well regarded by employers within the legal sector and elsewhere. A considerable number of law graduates enter alternative employment and training each year, so you would certainly not be limiting your options by choosing to study law at university.	Studying a non-law degree at university gives you more time to choose your career path and experiment with different types of work experience before you commit to a very expensive and rigorous training process.

"In some ways it can be more difficult for non-law students to find out about the legal recruitment process. You need to make an extra effort to get work experience and talk to as many people as possible so you go in with your eyes open. However, as long as you have a decent degree, come across well at interview and have obviously made an informed choice to become a lawyer, you should not be at any disadvantage."
Philippa Chatterton, Senior Associate, Nabarro LLP

5 THE LAW DEGREE

During your degree, you will gain a thorough understanding of the foundation subjects and explore additional specialist options. You will develop your skills of critical analysis, legal research, and problem solving and should also have the opportunity to participate in extra-curricular activities such as mock trials, moots (mock appeals on a point of law), and negotiation and interviewing competitions.

APPLYING TO READ LAW

Universities are ranked according to their performance in a number of different categories. Law firms do take an interest in these league tables and it is fair to say that some still recruit heavily from certain universities. It therefore makes sense to consider the league tables and to apply for the best university your grades will allow. However, you should also engage in some serious (and honest) reflection about what you are hoping to gain from your university experience and consider other factors such as culture, location, quality of teaching and facilities, quality of feedback, career destinations of graduates, whether there is a placement year, extra-curricular activities, accommodation, accessibility of lecturers, research expertise, and pastoral care/student support before making your final decision. The importance attached to each of these factors will vary between individuals and the most important thing is to make the right choice for you.

"Essentially, you need to choose a course that you are capable of doing (from academic, financial and practical perspectives), in a location where you will be happy, which will give you a degree that will facilitate your future employment. For example, if you choose a university which is miles from home, you need to make sure you can handle that emotionally. Also, consider the cost of living since this varies enormously throughout the UK. Finally, make an effort to visit the university and reflect on your impression of the campus and staff (both teaching and administrative).

You might want to compare the style of teaching (contact time, teaching hours and methods and the units offered). The facilities are equally important—how impressive is the law library; will you have access to electronic materials; what are the opening hours of the library? The efficacy of the Student Law Society is also important—do they run the events/trips/competitions that you want and need, and how much do they cost? Of course, the last factor is also one of the most important: social life—if you aren't happy at a given university, you won't achieve your full potential, and a decent social life is a key part of that."

Final Year Law Student, University of Portsmouth

To help you narrow down your choice of institution, your first port of call might be "The Guardian University Guide" or "The Times Good University Guide". You could also look at the results of the National Student Survey (available at *http://www.unistats.com*). This is an annual census of final year undergraduates based on the seven areas listed below.

Quality of Teaching
Assessment and Feedback
Academic Support
Organisation and Management
Learning Resources
Personal Development
Overall Satisfaction

Once you have narrowed down your choice to a smaller number of universities, it would make sense to visit them to speak with staff and students in person and explore the facilities on offer before making a commitment to spend three or four years at a particular institution. Check individual websites for details of open days and make every effort to attend to get a feel for the city and the culture of the university.

Applications for law degrees are made via UCAS (the University and Colleges Admissions Service). Full details of the application process can be found online at *http://www.ucas.com*. Applications for part-time degrees are generally made directly to the relevant institution so you should check individual websites if you are interested in this form of study. Some providers also offer accelerated qualifying law degrees which can be completed over two years (see *http://www.ucas.com*).

Some universities require applicants to complete the National Admissions Test for Law (LNAT). The LNAT is an online test which includes a variety of multiple choice questions in Section A and an essay question in Section B. It is designed to test your powers of critical thinking and reasoning (see *http://www.lnat.ac.uk*). You can find information and advice on writing effective personal statements and preparing for the LNAT test at *http://www.from-studenttosolicitor.co.uk*.

WHAT IS IT LIKE TO STUDY AT UNIVERSITY?

Students are often concerned about how university differs from school or sixth form. The main difference is the emphasis on "independent learning". This means that you are responsible for your own learning: the tutors will simply direct you to relevant materials and provide an outline structure for that learning.

Teaching for each unit will normally be divided into lectures and seminars. Lectures consist of large groups of students (possibly as many as 300) with one lecturer. Lectures introduce key topics by setting out the basic principles and highlighting any controversial issues or law reform proposals. They also direct students to important cases or articles for further reading. There will be little, if any, student interaction. Your role will be to listen actively to the lecturer and make effective notes to support your own independent study of the topic. The lecture is not intended to tell you everything you need to know about a particular topic (hence the focus on independent learning); you will need to build up your knowledge by preparing for, and participating in, seminars and reading around the subject.

Seminars are much smaller groups of students with a seminar

leader (a lecturer or sometimes a research student). These classes provide an opportunity to explore particular issues in more depth than is possible in a lecture. Seminars very often focus on topics that are likely to be assessed in the exam or coursework, and they offer students the opportunity to raise any concerns or answer questions relating to particular topics. Attendance is therefore crucial, but attendance alone is not enough: you must also engage fully with the preparatory reading, and contribute in class. Seminars should not turn into "mini lectures": this is frustrating for the tutor and a poor learning experience for the students.

The accreditation requirements of the Solicitors Regulation Authority mean that the foundation subjects are assessed largely by way of exam although some institutions might introduce a coursework component (perhaps 20 per cent to 30 per cent of the final grade). Exams usually consist of a mixture of essay and problem questions. A problem question is a fictional scenario (similar to those given in Ch.4) in which you are asked to identify and apply the relevant law in order to reach a conclusion as to the likely outcome of the particular situation. An essay question will focus on critical analysis of a particular area of law or topical legal issue. There is more flexibility with other non-core units, which might be assessed by way of exam, coursework, group or individual presentation, extended research project, or a moot (a mock appeal on a particular point of law).

GRADES

Whatever anyone tells you, and whatever method(s) your university uses to calculate its final degree classifications, do not make the mistake of believing that your first year grades are not important. Law undergraduates can begin applying for training contracts in their second year of study, and all students should build up their body of work experience during their first and second year at university to support future training contract applications. Think about what you are going to be putting on those application forms and/or speculative letters requesting work experience: A Level results and first year university grades. This is the only information prospective employers will have about your academic profile. Do not fall down at the first hurdle because your first year grades are poor.

WHAT MAKES A GOOD LAW STUDENT?

There is no such thing as a model student, but successful law students certainly share some common characteristics. Most of those characteristics can be developed with hard work and commitment so there is no reason why you should not become a member of this group.

Take a positive approach to your studies—one of the most important keys to success is to keep an open mind and try to be positive and enthusiastic about your studies. This might sound obvious but it is something that many students fail to do. You are bound to find some elements of the law degree dry and sometimes complicated. However, try not to dwell on those areas and instead focus on the aspects of the course that you find interesting. Students who adopt a positive attitude and maintain enthusiasm and passion for their subject will probably get better results and will certainly get more satisfaction from their studies.

Achieve deep understanding of the topics—deep understanding is achieved by really getting to grips with the detail of a particular area of law, understanding how it is applied to practical situations, and subjecting it to critical analysis. This cannot be achieved by relying solely on your lecture notes; it can only be achieved by wider reading and independent study. By all means start with your lecture notes and a basic textbook to gain an understanding of the key principles, but also dip into academic articles and judgments from key cases. Academic articles can be particularly useful in terms of identifying parallels with other areas of law; comparing the approach taken under English law with the approaches adopted in other jurisdictions; and considering how academics have responded to particular judgments or new pieces of legislation.

Think critically—you should start to understand what lecturers mean by critical thinking and writing if you spend more time reading journal articles and note how the academics analyse or challenge particular legal principles or judgments, rather than just describing them in the way that textbooks tend to. Many textbooks contain further reading lists at the end of each chapter and your lecturers will also be able to recommend additional texts and articles. You should also read the judgments of key cases so that you can see why the judges reached a particular decision and whether there were any dissenting judgments (those that disagreed with the ultimate decision). The actual decision is often less important than why and how the judges reached that decision. It is this reasoning which enables you to engage critically with the decision and to contrast it with decisions in subsequent cases or with the approach taken in other jurisdictions. You will have very little to say if you simply compare one decision or outcome with another, but you will find that you have an awful lot more material to work with if you start to engage critically with the reasoning that led to the decision.

If you get used to reading cases and academic articles from your first year, you will find it less daunting when you come to engage in research for your dissertation. This criticality is essential if you are to achieve high marks in your assessments and you are unlikely to achieve more than a 2:2 without it. You can find information and advice on developing effective critical reading and writing skills at *http://www.fromstudenttosolicitor.co.uk.*

Become an active learner—make sure that you are engaged in active, rather than passive, learning. Active learning can mean lots of things: participating in class discussions; working in a study group (as long as you choose like-minded students who share your goals and aspirations); or practising past exam questions. It does not mean sitting for hours in the library in front of the same textbook reading the same passage over again. Neither does it mean copying out reams of notes from textbooks or judgments and then filing them away until the exams. A full file of beautifully written notes might look impressive, but it will be of little comfort if you do not actually understand any of the content, let alone how to apply it to exam questions.

Make effective notes—this does not mean reading a textbook and copying out chunks of text, nor writing down every word a lecturer says (even if you could write that quickly). It means thinking about what you are reading or listening to, and being selective about what you write down and how you present it. Note-making should be an organic process, which means you should treat your notes as "work in progress" to be revisited and supplemented after each seminar and in light of your wider reading. Keep your notes organised and consolidate each topic as you work through the course.

Manage your time effectively—as a law student, you should be prepared for hard work and long hours in the library and you will need to manage your time wisely. Keep a note of key assessment deadlines and make sure you give yourself plenty of time to get the work done. You might well find that a number of deadlines fall at a similar time, but tutors will not be sympathetic if you express difficulty in meeting them. Remember that the focus is on independent learning so it is your responsibility to manage your time and achieve all that is asked of you within a particular period.

> "Organisation and self-motivation are the keys to a successful degree. You must know what you need to do, and when you need to do it, and then find the motivation to get on and do it . . . you will find that you have an immense amount of free time in some periods and an equally immense workload during others. It is effective organisation that allows you to balance this out."
>
> *Final Year Law Undergraduate University of Portsmouth*

Practice makes perfect—at the end of each topic, have a go at some past exam papers to see how well you actually understand the topic. The more practice papers you complete, the more you will develop your technique so it should become second nature by the time you reach the final exams. Do not leave everything until just before the exams: you will not obtain the best marks if you rely on revision guides and last-minute cramming.

Make use of the library services—you should find the library early on in your university studies, and make use of it. You should also get to know the law librarian in your first year since he/she will be an invaluable source of support and knowledge as you progress through the degree. You need to get to grips with the library resources and databases early on, and also become an expert in referencing sources accurately. If you focus on these things in the first year, you will have one less thing to think about as you progress through your degree when the workload gets tougher and the stakes get higher.

Work, rest and play—don't lose sight of the fact that the university experience should be far richer than just getting a degree: you should be developing your transferable skills, your social life and your real world experiences. Furthermore, a good work/life balance is essential to your health, wellbeing and personal development. Set aside some time each week to relax with friends and get involved in extra-curricular activities: remind yourself that there is a life beyond your desk and the university library. This will ensure that you do not burn yourself out and will also help to develop your CV which will be a real advantage when it comes to filling in training contract application forms.

> "It is a challenging course and it does take time to get to grips with the work but if you get too bogged down in the work and it stresses you out then you won't be able to get involved in all the extra-curricular and social activities on offer and these are important if you want to become a solicitor. You need to know that you can manage your time effectively and understand that different times of the year bring varying demands on your time."
>
> *Final Year Law Undergraduate, King's College London*

6 THE GRADUATE DIPLOMA IN LAW: CONVERTING TO LAW

INTRODUCTION

Students without a qualifying law degree must complete a law conversion course before progressing to the vocational stage of training (the LPC). The Graduate Diploma in Law (GDL) provides an introduction to the English Legal System and legal research skills, and covers the Foundations of Legal Knowledge.

The GDL is offered at approximately 40 providers throughout England and Wales (some of which have campuses or centres in a number of different cities, e.g. BPP or the University of Law) and can be completed on a full-time basis over one year or part-time over two years. For full details of the institutions which offer the GDL course, visit *http://www.lawcabs.ac.uk*. The SRA also maintains a list of GDL providers at *http://www.sra.org.uk/students/conversion-courses/cpegdl-providers.page*.

You might also like to look at the course profiles on *http://www.targetpostgrad.com* and the course search option on *http://www.lawcareers.net*. It would also be worth investigating the sources on the Chambers Student Guide. There is a comparison table of GDL providers with reference to available places, fees, methods of assessment, and electives offered, and a feature called "Law School Reviews" which offers inside information based on interviews with graduates and Course Directors from specific law schools (see *http://www.chambersstudent.co.uk*).

You might sometimes see the term CPE (Common Professional Exam) used interchangeably with the term GDL. This course was the previous incarnation of the GDL although it is effectively the same qualification. Some practitioners and the SRA continue to use this term, although course providers tend to use the term GDL or the more colloquial "law conversion course".

You really need to give serious thought as to whether or not a legal career is for you before you embark on the GDL. It is a very expensive and labour intensive course and there are arguably far better ways to spend your time and money if you do not want to be a solicitor.

> "What really strikes me when I think about the GDL is how many people were taking the course at such great cost to themselves and how many of them have still not got training contracts or who didn't even go on to complete the LPC. You have to know that you are going to want it. It's a lot of money and it might not necessarily suit you so really think hard before you embark on the course."
>
> *A GDL Graduate*

ASSESSMENT

You will need to research individual providers to find out whether their courses are assessed wholly by exam, or whether they include any coursework components. It would also be worth finding out how long the exam period lasts, and whether there is a revision week or reading week built into the course. You can expect a clear emphasis on formal exams on all GDL courses since the SRA dictates that the foundation subjects should be assessed by a minimum of 70 per cent exam. Some will make up the remaining 30 per cent with coursework or presentations but others include a larger examination component. Some providers have a multiple choice element within exams and others include a dissertation or independent research project.

Each assessment can be repeated a maximum of three times. If a student fails any exam more than three times, they must re-take the whole course or complete a law degree. The SRA guidance states that a conversion course should be completed (with all units passed) in not less than one year and not more than three years. A part-time conversion course should be completed (with all units passed) in not less than two years and not more than four years. The pass mark for the GDL is 40 per cent and your overall performance on the course will be graded as "Distinction", "Commendation", or "Pass".

For further information on the SRA's requirements you should read the Academic Stage Handbook, which can be found at *http://www.sra.org.uk/students/academic-stage.page*.

CHOOSING YOUR PROVIDER

You should research conversion course providers carefully to ensure that you make the right choice for you in terms of location, culture, cost, course structure, class sizes, opportunities for flexible study, and methods of teaching and assessment. You might like to consider the factors listed below when choosing your provider.

Course fees—at the time of writing, the GDL can cost up to £10,000 for a full-time course with a London provider starting in 2014 (although some providers charge much less than this and part-time options allow you to spread the costs over a longer period). You should ask providers about scholarship and bursary opportunities, and also look at specialist loans (see Appendix 1 for further information on managing the cost of the GDL). Do not allow this to be your only concern though; you must also make sure that you are happy with the quality of the course and the level of support provided to students. Most firms do not mind where you study as long as the foundation subjects are covered. However, it is worth bearing in mind that the GDL is a very intense course, particularly if you are also searching for a training contract during that year, so you should ensure that you will have access to good quality teaching, a good support network and facilities, and an excellent careers service.

Class sizes and study modes—class sizes can vary enormously between providers and will obviously affect the culture and atmosphere of a particular course. Where a provider offers the GDL and a law degree, you might also be interested in whether the GDL students are mixed with the undergraduates or whether they are taught separately. Most providers offer full-time and part-time study modes. The part-time options tend to be divided into evenings, weekends (usually two days per month but some providers split this over two weekends and others require a full weekend's attendance each month), and day release (a half day per week). Some providers also offer a distance learning version of the course. You might also like to consider how many start dates each provider offers. Some institutions offer a September and January start date which might offer you more flexibility in terms of saving the course fees or fitting in some travelling/work experience beforehand.

Teaching methods—find out how the course is delivered and how much face-to-face teaching you will have. Contact time varies considerably between providers as does the use of online content. Also, investigate whether additional drop-in/clinics or consolidation sessions are offered to students who are struggling. The course is intense and fast-paced, so supportive and accessible tutors are essential. Find out how IT is used in the delivery of the course. Can you access lectures online? Is this instead of, or in addition to, face-to-face lectures? Are all materials available to review online before/after classes? Are additional revision or consolidation materials posted online? Given the emphasis on exams, it would also be worth finding out whether providers offer mock exams and feedback to students before the summative exams commence. These questions are important for all students but particularly for those studying by distance or at evenings or weekends where contact time is more limited.

Facilities—find out about the standard of teaching rooms and IT facilities. Also think about the quality of the library, careers facilities and other student support services.

Extra-curricular activities—it is important to continue to build up your CV during your GDL year so consider how the provider supports students in doing so. Are there pro bono opportunities? Does the provider participate in client interviewing and negotiation competitions? What support is there for students who wish to enter such competitions? Are there student societies and sports teams?

Teaching materials—find out what materials are provided (e.g. textbooks, statute books, case books and lecture handbooks) and what you will be expected to buy. Also ask whether printing credits are included in course fees and, if so, whether they will cover all your essential printing needs or whether you are likely to have to add to them. Lastly, find out about the quality of lecture notes, revision notes, seminar packs, and other teaching materials.

Quality of careers support and pastoral care—this is especially important if you have not already secured a training contract. Does the provider have a law fair? If so, who attends? Do they organise other careers events? If so, what are they and how often do they take place? Find out about the provider's links with the legal profession. Do they operate a mentoring scheme to put students in touch with practitioners? Do they offer mock interviews? Do they have databases of interview questions and experiences? Do they offer a CV and covering letter checking service? Also think about pastoral care: is every student allocated a personal tutor; what is the expectation in terms of contact with that tutor; who writes student references?

It is probably a sensible idea to weigh up the cost of course fees against the level of pastoral and careers support that is provided to students. This is going to be a demanding and costly year whichever way you approach it so you must ensure that you have access to the level of support that you will need to maximise your chances of passing the course and securing a training contract at the end.

Location—courses vary considerably in terms of cost, and location can have a bearing on this (with London courses and the associated living costs being an expensive option). If you are a self-funding student, you might like to consider providers close to home so that you can save money. The GDL is an intense year and some students are glad to take advantage of support at home. Equally, think about where you would like to practise as many providers have close links with the local legal community. It will also make it easier to take time out for interviews and open days if you are studying in the area.

Additional qualifications—some providers give non-law graduates the opportunity to "top up" to an LLM (postgraduate degree in Law) award if they have completed both the GDL and LPC with them. Usually, this will be by studying and passing additional credits in the form of a dissertation. Contact individual providers directly if this is something that might be of interest to you.

The structure of the course—most providers run all GDL modules right across the year with all assessments held at the end, during the summer term. Some providers split the course so that students take four subjects in the first half of the academic year, which are assessed in the early spring, and the rest in the second half of the year, which are assessed in the summer. This may be a more manageable structure, given the heavy workload, and is certainly worth considering when choosing your provider.

LPC plans and/or sponsorship arrangements—some providers offer guaranteed LPC places to their GDL graduates. This might be worth bearing in mind if you have a particular provider in mind. Some firms use particular providers to deliver the LPC or GDL courses to their trainees so it might be worth checking with firms when you make an application.

As part of your research, you should visit providers' websites and make an effort to attend open days to get a feel for the culture of the institution and find out more about the surrounding area. You should also speak to representatives and current students at law fairs, and consult tutors or careers advisors for advice.

APPLYING FOR THE GDL

Applications for places on full-time GDL courses are made via the Central Applications Board (*http://www.lawcabs.ac.uk*). You can apply to up to three institutions and will be asked to list them in order of preference. You will be asked to provide contact details for an academic reference. Once you have submitted your form, your tutor will receive an email asking him/her to write and submit the reference via the online system. Your application must also be supported by a personal statement of up to 10,000 characters stating why you have applied for the course and why providers should offer you a place. There are guidance notes on the lawcabs website with some ideas of what you could include in the personal statement.

The application forms are usually made available in early autumn. Applications are considered by providers on a rolling basis so you should apply as early as you can, particularly if you have a certain institution in mind. Many GDL providers now offer two start dates each year: September and January. Visit the lawcabs website for more details of the application process and to check key deadlines. In particular, you should note that there is a registration fee of £18 (correct at the time of writing).

For part-time, or distance learning courses, applications should be made directly to the relevant provider.

Entry Requirements

In broad terms, the standard entry requirements for the GDL are:

> a first degree from UK or ROI University; or
> a first degree from an overseas university (subject to approval by individual providers by reference to UK NARIC); and
> an English Language qualification where English is a second language, e.g. IELTS.

See *http://www.sra.org.uk/sra/policy/training-for-tomorrow/re sources/training-regulations-changes-summary.page* for more in-wformation.

Accreditation of Prior Learning

If you have a non-qualifying law degree, but studied and passed subjects which would constitute a smaller part of the required curriculum in a qualifying law degree, you may be able to secure credit for them which will mean you do not have to study them again. This is known as Accreditation of Prior Learning. For full details on this, please refer to the SRA's Student Information Pack or call the SRA contact centre *(http://www.sra.org.uk/students/ resources/student-information.page)*.

Equivalent Means

Exemptions may also be available for Fellows of CILEx (Chartered Institute of Legal Executives) and Justice Clerks Assistants. For full details, you should refer to the SRA's Equivalent Means Information Pack *(http://www.sra.org.uk/students/resources/ equivalent-means-informationpack.page)*.

It may also be possible for mature applicants without a degree and applicants who have qualifications equivalent to a degree to start the GDL. This might include those who have qualifications from the Institute of Chartered Accountants or the Royal Institute of Chartered Surveyors. However, these applications will be viewed on a case-by-case basis. Further information can be obtained from the SRA Equivalent Means Information Pack (see above).

TIPS FOR SUCCESS ON THE GDL

The GDL is an intense year and should be taken seriously from the outset. In reality, you will be cramming the best part of a three year law degree into a one year course. There is a lot of ground to cover, an astonishing amount of reading, and new skills of analysis and problem solving to be developed. You should expect to feel overwhelmed at some point during the course, but you will not be alone and must try to remember that it is just a year and a vital stepping stone to your future career.

> "The GDL full-time course runs for 36 weeks. In those nine months students will get under their belts the same seven Foundation Subjects as students who study for three years as law undergraduates. It is, therefore, an intensive course. The key is to work consistently and steadily throughout those nine months. Good work management skills are vital.
>
> It is certainly good advice to GDL students to: (1) prepare thoroughly for each session; (2) attend all sessions, even if there is a coursework submission date looming; (3) consolidate notes immediately after a session; and (4) make sure that their revision covers not only learning the legal principles

underpinning a subject but also how to *apply* those principles to a problem question. The first three steps will help GDL students to avoid a stressful sprint for the line before the final examinations. The fourth step should give them confidence in an exam that they not only know the law relevant to the question but can answer the question as well."

Sarah Pooley, Centre Director, University of Law, Guildford

Keep on top of the work from the very first day—the course moves at an incredibly fast pace so you cannot afford to get behind. Treat the course like a professional job and make time each day to consolidate what you have learnt and prepare for your next class.

"Treat the GDL like a treadmill—you just have to keep going. It's only a year so just immerse yourself in it and keep on top of the work. I worked a 9–5 day (maybe not even that) and that worked. That way, all your tutorial notes are up to date, you've studied every case, and when it comes to revision it's not actually that hard. If you try to cram it all in at the end, there's just too much information to cope with. We had to learn something like 700 cases and you just can't get that into last minute revision sessions."

A Trainee Solicitor

Keep your notes in order as you go along—do not leave it all until the revision period, there simply will not be enough time. In particular, create a case list for each subject and update it at the end of each topic. This will save you time when it comes to revision and should encourage you to learn the cases as you go along.

Attend every lecture and seminar—do not be tempted to skip a class and catch up on the reading later. The classes are an essential part of the course and will direct you to the most important aspects of a particular topic for the purposes of the assessment. A good GDL course will distil the mass of information arising from each foundation subject into manageable chunks, and the teaching materials and seminars will be closely focused towards the assessment. If you do not take advantage of this guidance, you will probably find the volume of work unmanageable and there is a real risk that you could fail your assessments.

> "The difficulty with the GDL is that it moves incredibly fast so, if you get behind, it is very easy to come unstuck – there just aren't enough hours in the day to catch up if you fall behind because the topics are so tightly packed."
>
> *Thomas Moore, Solicitor*

Consider forming a study group—you could divide up the reading for each seminar and share your knowledge with the rest of the group, or perhaps you could share lecture notes or swap essay plans for practice exam papers. The students on a GDL course tend to be focused and professional in the way they approach their studies because they are making a serious investment in their chosen career path. You will find therefore that most people are motivated to do well and happy to pull their weight in group work.

Read selectively—yes, you are covering the same foundation subjects, but this is not a law degree and therefore you cannot be expected to cover everything in the same level of detail as a law undergraduate. By all means read the judgments of key cases in full, but for other cases it is fine to rely on a case book or even a good textbook.

Find out about the format of the exams as early as possible— given the limited time available, your learning must be targeted and practice exam papers will help you to get the focus right. They also reduce the risk of a nasty shock when it comes to the assessment period. Many providers offer students mock exams. Take advantage of them if you can: they are a great way to test your knowledge of key principles and your technique, which is crucial to exam success.

Make a note of key deadlines and manage your time—you should be putting in a full working week and working consistently throughout the whole year, rather than leaving it all until the last minute. Stick to a strict study plan but also make time for extra-curricular activities and socialising. This is a very tough year but you do need some light relief to avoid burning yourself out.

Use vacations for work experience and careers based activities—you cannot afford to lose sight of the ultimate goal: securing a training contract. If you find it difficult to fit things in during term-time, you will have to make effective use of your holidays. The year will pass quickly: before you know it you will be embarking on the LPC and time will be running out to secure a training contract.

Use the Easter holidays to get a head start on revision—although some providers incorporate a revision period into the course programme, this is unlikely to give you sufficient time to prepare fully for the exams.

Do not forget about your long term career goal—one of the main challenges of the GDL is the combination of intense academic study with the search for a training contract. Competition is fierce and, having invested considerable time and money in the conversion course, you cannot afford to lose your focus when it comes to building up your CV and making applications for training contracts. Even if you do not apply for training contracts during your GDL year, you should continue to develop your experience so that you have plenty to draw on when it comes to making applications during your LPC.

HOW CAN NON-LAW/GDL APPLICANTS SET THEMSELVES APART FROM LAW GRADUATES?

Chapter 4 explores the advantages and disadvantages of taking a non-law degree plus GDL rather than a qualifying law degree. If you have already decided to pursue the non-law degree route, you now need to think about how to sell your degree to recruiters.

First of all, you need to have faith in yourself and recognise the benefits that you offer, rather than making the assumption that firms will prefer a law graduate over you. To that end, read ahead to Ch.10 (What firms are looking for in prospective trainees). You will see that there is no mention of legal knowledge or degree discipline. This is because firms assume that by the time you finish your law degree/GDL and LPC, you will have the requisite legal knowledge. That is not what will set you apart from others. Firms are looking for motivation to become a solicitor, key transferable skills, commercial awareness, resilience, and all the other skills and qualities listed in Ch.10. So, now is the time to think about how your status as a non-law graduate has enabled you to develop those key skills and to ensure that you have sufficient work experience to demonstrate your motivation to become a solicitor.

Get some work experience—this is covered fully in Ch.11, but suffice it to say that work experience is essential to all aspiring lawyers, but particularly so if you are a non-law graduate. You need to demonstrate that you have a clear understanding of what it is to be a solicitor and have made an informed decision to pursue that career path. You cannot rely on the knowledge and contacts that you have gained during your degree so you will need to be proactive in developing this area of your CV. Take advantage of any existing contacts and try to arrange as much work experience as possible during the holidays.

Contact the law faculty and/or the student law society at your university—this will be a good way to meet like-minded students and to find out about guest lectures or other law related careers events. The law faculty might distribute careers newsletters or information about law placement opportunities so ask whether you can be added to the relevant distribution lists. You could also find out whether there are any useful Facebook or Twitter feeds and join them. Some universities have a "law for non-law students" society. Find out whether there is one at your university and, if not, consider starting one yourself.

Contact your careers service—they will have spent considerable time working with students in your position so they will be well placed to advise you on how to focus your CV to a legal career, and how to secure work experience. They will also be able to direct you to law careers events which you might otherwise miss out on if they are predominantly aimed at the students in the law faculty. However busy you are, make a concerted effort to attend any careers events such as law fairs, guest lectures or workshops.

Engage in some pro bono work—this is covered fully in Ch.11. For now, it is enough to note that this is an excellent way to demonstrate key transferable skills, understanding of the realities of legal practice, and motivation to become a solicitor. As a non-law student, you will need to seek out such opportunities either by using contacts at your university or law school or volunteering independently to help a local charity/organisation. If you can manage it alongside your studies, try to build in some time to join pro bono projects or participate in negotiation or interviewing competitions.

Think about the key skills that you have developed in your degree—for example, if you have a science or maths background, you might find that you adapt easily to the intellectual demands of legal study and practice. You are also likely to have developed excellent skills of analysis in degrees such as History, Politics or International Relations, and these will be invaluable to the study and practice of law.

Think about how your degree subject could be a benefit to a firm—some firms welcome students with a non-law background. For example, a firm specialising in construction law might welcome a student with a surveying background; a firm specialising in intellectual property law might welcome someone with a science or medical background; a firm with a significant presence in banking, finance and tax law might welcome someone with an accounting or finance background; a firm with clients in the retail sector might welcome someone with a business degree and an industrial placement year at the Head Office of a large retailer; and an international commercial firm might welcome someone who is a fluent mandarin speaker with knowledge of the culture and history of China following an overseas placement.

Finally, take heart in the fact that you can show recruiters that you have made a conscious decision to get legal work experience and apply for training contracts. This is a clear indicator of your motivation to become a solicitor and your ability to take the initiative so shout that from the rooftops. You will find that some law students start applying for work experience and training contracts simply because everyone else on their course is doing the same thing. Your degree did not lead you naturally to qualify as a solicitor: you are here because you have made a clear and determined choice to follow this particular career path out of all the others that would have been available to you, and which might in fact have been cheaper, quicker and more straightforward. The door is open so go through and take your place at the table: you have as much right to be there as anyone else.

"The GDL is an excellent preparation for a legal career. There are many highly respected solicitors and barristers who completed the GDL rather than study for a law degree. Looking at the employability rates amongst GDL students, it is clear that a GDL is no disadvantage in a student's search for a training contract.

The GDL will give a student a firm grounding across all seven Foundation Subjects as well as giving an opportunity to research an area outside the course (which the Solicitors' Regulation Authority call the 'eighth subject'). A GDL student will often find that all seven Foundation Subjects are fresh in their minds as they start their LPC whilst for some law graduates some subjects, like Contract or Tort, can be a distant memory as they studied them in their first year. The GDL course will also tend to focus on what you need to know to be a practising solicitor, and therefore problem solving is a skill which is developed, not just essay writing. As a result, former GDL students can often get off to a flying start in their chosen vocational course."

Sarah Pooley, Centre Director, University of Law, Guildford

7 THE LEGAL PRACTICE COURSE (LPC)

WHAT IS THE LPC?

Completion of the LPC is a compulsory requirement in order to qualify as a solicitor; it is known as the vocational stage of training. Students must have completed the academic stage of training before enrolling on the LPC although some courses, known as "exempting law degrees", combine both the academic stage and the LPC. The SRA maintains a list of exempting law degree providers at *http://www.sra.org.uk*.

The LPC provides the transition between the academic stage of the qualification process and your training contract. During the LPC you learn how to apply legal principles in a practical setting. For example, on the law degree or GDL you learn the principles of land law as an academic subject, but on the LPC you learn about the process involved in selling or leasing a property. You will need to understand the underlying land law principles which are involved in the sale or lease of the property, but the LPC is much more focused on the practical aspects of the transaction: risk factors for the client; ethical considerations; paperwork to be completed; taxes due; registrations required, etc.

The tasks you carry out during the LPC look very much like the tasks that would be asked of a trainee solicitor. There is a significant emphasis on learning the skills you need for practice, so that you "learn by doing". You will role play client interviews, make applications to court, draft letters of advice and formal legal documents, and research practical problems using practitioner resources. Because of this practical emphasis, much of the LPC is not as difficult conceptually as the degree or the GDL, but the workload is very heavy and some students find it difficult to switch into a true understanding of what is needed from a client's perspective.

> "The LPC was quite a relief because I had found my law degree
> difficult. It was really refreshing to do the LPC where suddenly
> the focus is so much more practical and based on what you will
> actually do as a trainee. It was a good preparation for practice."
>   *A Trainee Solicitor*

THE STRUCTURE OF THE LPC

While certain core units must be covered, the SRA has given considerable autonomy to LPC providers in terms of the design and
focus of their courses. This has enabled providers to tailor courses
to particular types of firms or practice areas and to place greater
emphasis on particular units or skills. It has also provided greater
flexibility for students.

Traditionally, the LPC was completed either as a one-year full-
time course or a two-year part-time course. However, relatively
recent changes have given students more flexibility in terms of
the time taken to complete their studies and the choice of institution for each of the two stages of the course.

Stage 1 covers the core practice areas (Business Law and Practice,
Property Law and Practice, and Litigation), Course Skills (Practical
Legal Research, Writing, Drafting, Interviewing & Advising, and
Advocacy), plus the following additional areas: Professional
Conduct and Regulation, Taxation, and Wills & Administration of
Estates. Stage 2 consists of three vocational electives.

As long as an LPC course gives students an awareness or
understanding of the core areas of practice, providers have the
freedom to develop one or more practice areas on their courses
and to tailor their course to particular areas of practice. So, for
example, one provider might choose to teach the Business Law
and Practice unit in the context of large international commercial enterprises whilst others might focus on small domestic businesses. The SRA states that providers should highlight their focus
in marketing materials and this is certainly something that you
should consider when choosing your provider.

Providers can be authorised to provide either of Stages 1 or 2,
or both of them. Students must complete Stage 1 with a single

provider, but Stage 2 may be completed with three separate providers if the student chooses to do so. Both Stages 1 and 2 must
be completed and passed within a five year period (running from
the date on which the student attempts the first assessment)
regardless of whether they are full- or part-time students. If there
is an outstanding Stage 2 subject after the expiry of this period,
the student must repeat both Stage 1 and Stage 2 in their entirety
and pass all assessments.

The window of five years within which to complete the LPC
course is likely to be particularly attractive to those who wish to
spread the cost of their studies over a longer period, or those who
choose to combine their studies with work. Indeed, it is now possible for students to start their training contract while studying
for the LPC provided that Stage 1 is completed and passed before
the Professional Skills Course (PSC) is taken (see Ch.3 for further
details on the PSC). The fact that students can complete Stage 2
at three different providers also means that they can tailor their
vocational electives to the work of a particular firm or type of firm
if one provider does not offer all the specialist options that they are
interested in. That said, it is probably fair to say that the majority
of students will choose to take both stages with the same provider.

> "The LPC is a challenging course in terms of the volume of
> work. Do not underestimate how much time you will have
> to devote to your studies during this year. It also felt quite
> unbalanced because so much of the work is front loaded: it
> was a struggle to keep on top of everything during the first
> part of the course, but it did settle down once we reached the
> electives."
>
> *A Trainee Solicitor*

STAGE 1

Core Practice Areas

Business Law and Practice – in this module, you will learn
about the different vehicles available to individuals who wish

to start their own businesses; the legal issues arising from various business relationships; what happens when businesses get into financial difficulties; and the methods of taxation that affect companies and individuals.

Property Law and Practice – in this module, you will learn about the procedural, practical, legal and regulatory issues surrounding the disposal, acquisition, and lease of property in a commercial and residential context.

Litigation – in this module, you will learn about how civil cases are conducted, and the procedures that must be followed, and documents that must be drafted, when preparing for a trial. You will also learn about how criminal cases are conducted, including powers of arrest and the procedures to be followed at the police station.

Other Areas

Professional Conduct and Regulation – in this module, you will learn about professional ethics and the importance of client care. This will include understanding the relevance of financial services and money laundering regulation to solicitors and their work. It will also cover the distinction between office and client money and the rules and procedures governing the collection, investment, accounting, and use of each one.

Wills and Administration of Estates – in this module, you will learn about the administration of an estate when someone dies testate (leaving a will) and intestate (without a will).

Taxation – in this module, you will learn about different methods of taxation and tax planning.

You are likely to have some stand-alone modules for each of these areas at the beginning of your course. You will then revisit the topics during your study of the core practice areas so you can see how they work in practice.

Course Skills

Practical Legal Research – in this module, you will learn how to approach legal problem questions to identify the key legal issue and how to report your findings to your client(s). You will also develop research skills to enable you to engage effectively and efficiently in legal research using a law library and electronic databases.

Writing and Drafting – in this module, you will prepare professional correspondence such as letters, reports and memoranda and learn how to draft legal documentation.

Interviewing and Advising – in this module, you will learn how to conduct a client interview in order to find out more about the client's situation and desired outcome. You will also learn how to gather the relevant facts and identify irrelevant information, and how to present advice in a manner that is appropriate to the particular client. This will often require you to explain complex legal issues in an accessible and meaningful manner.

Advocacy – in this module, you will learn how to present your client's case effectively in court and how to argue points of law from a particular perspective.

Note that the Course Skills are often incorporated and tested with the Core Practice Areas, rather than by completing a standalone module or assessment on each skill.

STAGE 2

Vocational Electives

Students must complete three distinct electives from at least two different elective groups. The elective groups are listed in the SRA's LPC Information Pack (*http://www.sra.org.uk/students/ resources/legal-practice-course-information-pack.page*) and they cover a broad range of public, private, commercial and private client practice areas. This enables you to choose whether to maintain a very broad knowledge base, or to specialise in a particular area. Providers offer different electives so it is important to do your research to choose the course that best suits your areas of interest and aspirations for practice. At the time of writing, the current elective groups are:

Acquisitions and mergers
Advanced civil litigation and advocacy
Advanced criminal litigation and advocacy
Banking and debt finance
Charity law
Children (public law)
Civil litigation
Clinical legal education practice
Commercial dispute resolution
Corporate finance
Criminal litigation
Employment
Family and children (private law)
Housing
Immigration and asylum
Insolvency
Insurance law
Intellectual property
IT law
Media and entertainment
Personal litigation
Planning and environmental law
Property (commercial and domestic)
Public sector organisations
Social welfare law
Vulnerable client law
Will, probate and tax planning

"If you have a funded training contract then you need to speak to your firm to see if they have any preferences or requirements in terms of your electives. If not, make sure you choose the electives that interest you as you are likely to do better in those subjects. Having said that, you do also need to tailor your choices to some extent to the firms you are likely to target—there is little point taking a social welfare law elective if you are planning to apply to national commercial law firms."

A Trainee Solicitor at a National Firm

METHODS OF ASSESSMENT

The SRA states that assessment of the core practice units and the vocational elective units must be by way of a three-hour (minimum) exam or other supervised assessment. The Litigation assessment must be divided into two parts: one Criminal and one Civil. Each elective assessment should have one assessment lasting a minimum of two hours in the form of an exam or other supervised assessment.

Professional Conduct and Regulation must be assessed partly by way of a discrete two-hour (minimum) assessment and partly by allocating five per cent of the marks in each Core Practice assessment to professional conduct/regulatory issues. There will also be a separate two-hour (minimum) supervised assessment of the Solicitors Accounts Rules.

Like the GDL, each assessment can be repeated a maximum of three times. If a student fails any Stage 1 assessment on the third attempt, they will fail the whole of Stage 1 and all assessments must be taken again. If a student fails any vocational elective unit on the third attempt, they will have to re-enrol on that elective course, or enrol on a different elective course. However, you should remember that Stages 1 and 2 must be completed and passed within a five-year period (running from the date on which the student attempts the first assessment) regardless of whether they are full- or part-time students. If there is an outstanding Stage 2 subject after the expiry of this period, the student must repeat both Stage 1 and Stage 2 in their entirety and pass all assessments.

The pass mark for all core and elective assessments is 50 per cent. The skills assessments are graded as either competent or not yet competent.

For further information on the SRA's requirements, you should refer to the Legal Practice Course Information Pack. You can download a copy from *http://www.sra.org.uk/students/resources/legal-practice-course-information-pack.page*.

CHOOSING A PROVIDER

The LPC is offered by around 30 providers throughout England and Wales (some of which have centres in a number of different cities). Some firms specify particular LPC providers for their train-ees and some even commission tailor-made courses where their solicitors are involved in the preparation and delivery of some of the teaching materials.

It is worth looking at different LPC providers as they vary in terms of course content, culture, teaching methods, and the level of course fees. Unless firms specify particular providers, they are more likely to be concerned about what electives you chose to study rather than where you completed the course. For example, a student who has studied public sector organisations, social welfare law and advanced criminal litigation and advocacy is likely to be less appealing to a national commercial firm or a City firm than someone who studied banking and capital markets, commercial law, and commercial property.

> "Choose the provider that will work best for you and suit your learning preferences. The way my provider structured the LPC probably wouldn't be right for everyone—I was only in college for about two and a half hours four days a week to begin with so I had to do everything else myself. That's not going to work for everyone: some people might prefer a provider with more structure and classroom time."
>
> *A Trainee Solicitor*

You might like to consider some of the factors set out below when choosing your provider.

Course fees—at the time of writing, the LPC can cost around £14,700 for a one-year full-time course with a London provider. The fees are lower for regional providers, and part-time options allow students to spread the cost of their tuition over a longer period. If you decide to study electives at different institutions, you will pay somewhere in the region of £7,000–£10,000 (depending on location and pro-vider) for the Stage 1 modules, and approximately £1,100–£1,500 per elective for Stage 2. Thus, the overall cost remains the same but you have more flexibility in terms of location and content.

The LPC is an enormous financial commitment and you need to think carefully before you commit to it. Some of the larger commercial firms will sponsor their trainees through the LPC by paying course fees and perhaps also providing a maintenance grant. However, if you are self-funding, the level of fees is likely to be an important factor in your choice of provider. Do not allow this to be your only concern though: you must also make sure that you are happy with the quality of the course and the level of support provided to students. On a positive note, many providers allow the cost to be spread over instalments, and the five-year window and flexible study modes give students greater opportunity to combine paid work and study. You should also ask providers about scholarship and bursary opportunities, and also look at specialist loans (see Appendix 1 for further information on managing the cost of the LPC).

Flexible study modes—most LPC providers offer a host of flexible study modes and these are well worth considering, particularly if you are self-funding. Options include full-time accelerated courses over seven months and blended learning options which combine online learning and/or self-study with part-time courses either in the evening, at weekends, or on certain days of the week. You will need to do your research carefully to find a mode of study which suits your finances, lifestyle, work commitments and other responsibilities.

Student numbers and class sizes—these can vary considerably between providers and will obviously affect the culture and atmosphere of a particular course.

Choice of vocational electives—this is likely to be particularly important to you if you wish to specialise in a niche area of legal practice, or if you intend to target particular firms when you apply for training contracts. However, beware of limiting your options too much if you have not secured a training contract by the time you start the course.

Teaching methods and facilities—find out how the course is delivered and how much face-to-face teaching you will have. You might wish to find out about part-time study opportunities and, if you are planning to commute from home, how often you will actually need to be on campus. Find out about the level of pastoral care and the standard of teaching and IT facilities. You should also look at the quality of the library, careers facilities and other student support services—these are likely to be very important to you when you start the course.

Teaching materials—find out what materials are provided (e.g. textbooks, statute books, case books and lecture handbooks) and what you will be expected to buy. Also ask whether printing credits are included in course fees and, if so, whether they will cover all your essential printing needs or whether you are likely to have to add to them. Lastly, find out about the quality of lecture notes, revision notes, seminar packs, and other teaching materials.

Extra-curricular activities—it is important to continue to build up your CV during your LPC year so it makes sense to consider how the provider supports students in doing so. Are there pro bono opportunities? Does the provider participate in client interviewing and negotiation competitions? What support is there for students who wish to enter such competitions? Are there student societies and sports teams?

Quality of careers support and pastoral care—this is especially important if you have not secured a training contract by the time you leave university or complete the GDL. By committing to the LPC without a training contract, you are making a serious financial investment and you should be looking for reassurance that your provider will provide targeted support for those still searching for a training contract. Does the provider have a law fair? If so, who attends? Do they organise other careers events? If so, what are they, and how often do they take place? Find out about the provider's links with the legal profession. Do they operate a mentoring scheme to put students in touch with practitioners? Do they offer mock interviews? Do they have databases of interview questions and experiences? Do they offer a CV and covering letter checking service? Also think about pastoral care: is every student allocated a personal tutor; what is the expectation in terms of contact with that tutor; who writes student references?

> "It is a myth that all students who start the LPC have a training contract. It is certainly not necessary to have a training contract in place before you start. In some practice areas, firms do not recruit more than one year ahead of a trainee's start date, so starting with a training contract is not possible in any event. In the case of larger firms, they do under recruit on occasion and may therefore be seeking trainees long after the usual recruitment process has ended.
>
> In considering which provider to choose, a student who has yet to secure a training contract should look for an institution with a strong employability service whose staff specialise in helping students to secure a training contract. Students should check the providers' employability statistics and the service they offer. Services such as one-to-one advice on vacation scheme applications, training contract applications, drafting a legal C.V. and writing a covering letter, together with mock interviews, will all help to ensure that a student has the best possible chance of securing a training contract whilst studying on the LPC. Other areas employers will be interested in include 'hands on' experience such as pro bono work. If a student has the opportunity to demonstrate involvement in such activities whilst studying on the LPC, they will be able to introduce a 'value added' aspect to their C.V."
>
> *Sarah Pooley, Centre Director, University of Law, Guildford*

Location—there will be time for enjoying yourself in between your studies so take this into account when choosing your provider. What is the cost of living? What is the nightlife and culture like? How far is it from home? How strong are the transport links? Where would you live in relation to the college? Could you imagine yourself living there? If you are a self-funded LPC student, you might like to consider providers close to home so that you can save money. Also think about where you would like to practise. Providers generally have close links with the local legal profession, which provides a good opportunity to make contacts in the area in which you wish to practise.

Additional qualifications—many providers offer LPC graduates the opportunity to extend their LPC into an LLM (Masters in Law) by completing some additional units and writing a dissertation. Contact individual providers for more information if this is of interest to you.

As part of your research, you should visit providers' websites and make an effort to attend open days to get a feel for the culture of the institution and find out more about the surrounding area. Also speak to representatives from LPC providers at law fairs and students who have already completed, or are currently enrolled on, the course. If you manage to secure work experience or vacation schemes, take the opportunity to speak to current trainees about their experiences of the LPC and any advice they would give you when choosing a provider.

For full details of the institutions which offer the LPC course, visit *http://www.lawcabs.ac.uk*. The SRA also offers detailed information on the structure and assessment of the LPC and maintains a list of LPC providers at *http://www.sra.org.uk/students/courses/lpc-course-providers.page*.

The course profiles on *http://www.targetpostgrad.com* are useful as is the course search option on *http://www.lawcareers.net*. It would also be worth investigating the sources on the Chambers Student Guide. There is a comparison table of LPC providers with reference to available places, fees, methods of assessment and electives offered and a feature called "Law School Reviews" which offers inside information based on interviews with graduates and Course Directors from specific law schools (see *http://www.chambersstudent.co.uk*).

APPLYING FOR THE LPC

"Think very carefully before embarking on the LPC. Getting a training contract is a very competitive process and there is no guarantee of getting one just because you complete the LPC."
A Trainee Solicitor

Some universities have entered into agreements with particular LPC providers to give their students a guaranteed place on the LPC programme and some LPC providers offer discounted fees for students who complete both the GDL and LPC with them. It is worth checking with your university and LPC provider to find out about such schemes.

Regardless of where you intend to study, it is worth noting from the outset that there is no longer a time limit within which you must complete the LPC after graduating from your LLB or GDL. It is also worth noting that applications for all full-time LPCs must be made via the Central Applications Board. Visit its website (*http://www.lawcabs.ac.uk*) for more details of the application process.

Many providers offer two start dates for the LPC in January and September. There are no longer any application deadlines for the LPC but candidates are advised to apply at their earliest possible convenience. The application form is available via the Central Applications Board from early autumn and applications are sent weekly to providers. They are processed by providers on a rolling basis.

You can apply to up to three providers and will be asked to list them in order of preference. The form must be supported by a personal statement of up to 10,000 characters as well as details of your employment history and details of your degree, including your actual or predicted result. If you obtained your degree outside of the UK, or completed it more than four years before your LPC application, you will need to submit a copy of your degree transcript as part of your LPC application.

Lastly, you will need to arrange for a tutor to provide an academic reference to support your application. Make sure you ask your tutor's permission before giving their name as a referee and make sure that they will be available to complete the reference when the request comes through. On that note, it would be worth submitting your application well before the summer vacation when tutors' availability may be more limited than during term time as a result of annual leave and research commitments.

As part of your LPC application, you will be asked to disclose any criminal convictions which are not spent. If you have any character or suitability issues, you should submit your application at least six months before you intend to start the LPC (see Ch.3 for more details on disclosure of character and suitability issues).

Applications for part-time or distance learning courses should be made directly to the individual institution.

Accreditation of Prior Learning for BVC and BPTC Graduates

The SRA has introduced a policy on the accreditation of prior learning (APL) in relation to the LPC. You can find details of that policy at *http://www.sra.org.uk/lpc/accreditation-prior-learning. page.* At the time of writing, the SRA's APL policy only applies to Bar Vocational Course (BVC) or Bar Professional Training Course (BPTC) graduates (i.e. those who have completed the vocational course for barristers). However, the exemptions can only be awarded where students have completed the BVC or BPTC no earlier than five years prior to the date of his/her enrolment on the LPC Course.

Successful BVC graduates may (if permitted by the LPC provider) be granted exemption from the Stage 1 Litigation, Advocacy, Drafting, Practical Legal Research modules and two vocational electives at Stage 2. Successful BTPC graduates may (if permitted by the LPC provider) be granted exemption from the Stage 1 Litigation, Advocacy and Drafting modules and two vocational electives at Stage 2.

TIPS FOR SUCCESS ON THE LPC

Keep on top of the work from the very beginning and do not be tempted to miss classes—whilst you may not find the work conceptually challenging, the volume is fairly high, particularly when coursework is due. Therefore, you must manage your time effectively and not allow work to mount up.

> "The LPC felt quite evenly paced compared to the GDL. Certainly it is conceptually less challenging, although the volume of work remains high."
>
> *Thomas Moore, Solicitor*

Do not ignore the preparation for workshops—this is a key part of the learning process and you will not be able to catch up by cramming at the end of the course.

Adopt a practice of working between 9am and 5pm every day—this is good preparation for the world of work, which is now not too far away, although you can expect much longer hours in real life! Of course, you will have to be prepared to work extra hours during exam periods or in the run up to coursework submission dates but, on the whole, it should be possible to balance a full working day with plenty of time for socialising.

"The best advice is to treat the LPC as if it were a job. The LPC moves swiftly and it is important to keep pace with the course and avoid falling behind. The Solicitors' Regulation Authority expect LPC students to attend all sessions so it is vital to do just that. However, it is also important to attend having prepared thoroughly for the session as without preparation a student will gain a lot less from the face-to-face contact time.

As the course is a vocational course, learning the law and legal processes is only half the story. The LPC is also about developing a range of skills for legal practice. To get the best out of the course, it is worth remembering that the LPC classroom is a safe haven where a student can make mistakes without any impact on a real client. Therefore, every session represents a perfect opportunity to practise one or more of the skills which pervade the LPC, such as advocacy, interviewing, negotiation, problem-solving and presentation skills. The more a student participates in the classroom, the better these skills will become."

Sarah Pooley, Centre Director, University of Law, Guildford

Do not ignore your future career—if you have not yet secured a training contract, use the year to make contacts and network. Attend all careers events and law fairs and take advantage of any application workshops or mock interview services offered by your provider.

Take advantage of any Pro Bono opportunities and/or other extra-curricular activities—it is important to continue to develop your CV and make contacts within the profession, particularly if you have not yet secured a training contract.

Do not be fooled by open book exams and multiple choice questions—as with all good multiple choice questions, you still need to know the topic in depth if you are to have any chance of success and each possible answer will be very similar to the next. You will not have time to search for an answer in the materials; they are there as a quick reference tool and you need to have sufficient knowledge to use them effectively.

Adopt a professional attitude at all times—this is the beginning of your future career, and you never know who might prove to be a useful contact in the future.

> "In some respects, the LPC is quite good preparation for life as a trainee. It's not like university; you can't just turn up to a seminar and not say anything. You are expected to contribute and to have read the preparatory materials and thought about your answers, which is similar to what it is like when you are asked to present something to a partner or an associate during the training contract. It forces you to work on your organisational skills, be prepared, and think about what sort of issues are likely to come up."
>
> *A Trainee Solicitor at a City Firm*

PART III
THE TRAINING CONTRACT

Section 1
Preparation and Research

8 FAIL TO PREPARE; PREPARE TO FAIL: HOW TO USE YOUR TIME WISELY FROM THE BEGINNING

INTRODUCTION

This part of the book will examine the trainee recruitment process in detail. Section 1 will provide you with an overview of the recruitment process, identify the key recruitment periods, and encourage you to develop your personal brand. It will also show you how to support your applications with evidence of research, and how to identify and address any gaps in your knowledge or experience in good time. Section 2 will provide practical advice on the application process: how to prepare winning responses to application forms; how to write an effective CV and covering letter; and how to prepare for, and succeed at, interviews and assessment centres. Section 3 will provide you with a clearer idea of what to expect from the training contract and how to get the most out of it.

TIME MANAGEMENT

I have lost track of the number of times that students have postponed their training contract applications, or made a poor attempt at them, or given up half way through several forms, simply because they have not managed their time carefully. This is such a shame as the field is not going to get any easier as you get further through your studies, your academic workload is certainly not going to diminish, and the pressure to secure a training contract is building all the time. Also, the earlier you start to submit applications, and hopefully attend some assessment centres and interviews, the more time you have to make mistakes and learn from them.

> "Students must not underestimate how challenging it is to secure a training contract and I think it's only going to become more challenging. One of the things that they will need to demonstrate is that they are absolutely committed to a career as a solicitor. There is a sense in the industry that we are likely to see more applications from people who would not naturally have chosen law so recruiters are going to be very aware of the need to weed out those who genuinely want a career in law and will be committed and enthusiastic trainees and lawyers."
>
> *Sam Lee, Head of Recruitment, Bond Dickinson LLP*

Many students fail to realise that there is a lengthy preparatory stage before they can even think about filling in an application form for a training contract. This means that they waste a lot of time and it often leads to false starts as they sit down to fill in their first form only to discover that they are woefully under prepared and have nowhere near enough experience or material to support answers to the questions asked. Don't let that happen to you. Read the advice given in this chapter and get ahead of the game. How effectively you use this preparatory stage could mean the difference between success and failure during the application process.

There are three key aspects to the preparatory stage of applying for training contracts. First, you need to ensure that you understand how the process works and make a note of key deadlines (this is covered in this chapter). Secondly, you need to research the different types of firms/organisations and practice areas and identify your target employers (see Ch.9). Finally, you need to find out what law firms are looking for in prospective trainees and critically appraise your qualities and experience against those criteria to identify areas which need work before you embark on the application process (see Ch.10).

AN OVERVIEW OF THE RECRUITMENT PROCESS

The first hurdle for most training contract applications is an online application form, although some firms do still ask for CVs and covering letters. The forms will be reviewed and a shortlist of candidates will be drawn up. If you are on this list, you will usually be asked to attend an assessment centre with a group of other applicants. At some firms, there is a telephone interview before you get to the assessment centre stage. The assessment centres are followed, or sometimes combined with, final interviews. You will find detailed guidance on the application process, including how to prepare for interviews and assessment centres in Chs 15–19.

Most large firms offer vacation schemes to enable students to gain an insight into the culture of that firm and to help them decide whether to apply for a training contract there. For some firms vacation schemes are an intrinsic part of the training contract selection process so it is worth checking with individual firms to find out what approach they take.

"Students need to be aware of the recruitment process at a very early stage because it will alert them to the importance of work experience. They really need to be trying to get as much legal experience or exposure to the legal world (which can include court visits, etc.) as early as possible and at the same time learn about what's ahead of them in terms of the route to becoming a solicitor."

A Law Careers Consultant

THE RECRUITMENT TIMETABLE

You should be aware of the fact that International, Magic Circle, City, and large national and regional firms recruit their trainees two years in advance. This means that, if you want to qualify as soon as possible after graduation, you should be applying for training contracts in your second year of university if you are a law undergraduate and your final year if you are a non-law undergraduate. This would enable you to be in a position to secure your training contract offer at the beginning of the GDL or your final year of the Law degree, and to start the training contract two years later. Figure 2 summarises this goal. It is based on the assumption that applicants are taking a three-year degree with

Year	Law Graduates (Qualifying Law Degree)	Non-Law Graduates Plus GDL
2016	First year of university	First year of university
2017	Second year of university Apply for training contracts—offers made in September 2018 to start in September 2020	Second year of university
2018	Third year of university	Third year of university Apply for training contracts—offers made in September 2019 to start in September 2021
2019	Legal Practice Course (LPC)	Graduate Diploma in Law (GDL)
2020	Training Contract – Year 1	Legal Practice Course (LPC)
2021	Training Contract – Year 2	Training Contract – Year 1
2022	Qualification	Training Contract – Year 2
2023		Qualification

Fig.2 Qualification timeline

no study breaks and no placement year. It also assumes that the applicants are taking a full-time GDL and LPC. There is a fuller explanation of the routes to qualification, including work-based training opportunities and qualification via the CILEx route, in Ch.3.

Note how important it is to have strong first and second year grades, rather than being lulled into the popular, but entirely unfounded, belief that first year grades "don't count". It is true that they will not count towards the ultimate degree classification at most institutions, but they will be important when it comes to supporting your training contract applications. The same is true of A Level and GCSE grades.

Most summer vacation scheme applications close sometime between December and March each year, with the majority closing at the end of January. As you would imagine, winter and spring schemes have even earlier closing dates. This means that you will be working on these applications during the academic year alongside coursework deadlines and exam preparation so you will need to manage your time carefully. You should also be aware that some firms fill their places on a rolling basis so it is worth checking and, if this applies to your target firms, submit your application as early as possible.

Training contract applications close between May and August each year with the majority of firms having a 31 July closing date, and only a handful running into August. However, you should not be lulled into a false sense of security by thinking that you can leave these applications until the exams finish. First, you should check with individual firms how they review applications. As with vacation schemes, some firms review forms as they come through the door (in which case you are at a disadvantage if yours arrives at the end of the cycle) whilst others review them all after the closing date has passed. The other thing to consider is that if you sit down to start filling in forms in June once your exams are finished and you discover that you do not have the right experience or evidence to do so, you will have wasted another academic year which could have been spent gaining experience and filling gaps in your CV.

Even if you decide not to apply straight away, it would be worth spending a couple of hours at the beginning of the academic year reviewing a selection of forms for firms that you might consider applying to. Think about what key skills they focus on and what experience they are looking for. Then think about whether you would have appropriate examples or experience on your CV to address the questions asked of you. Do not take a superficial approach to this analysis: actually try to write a response to one of the questions; it is more difficult than it looks.

From there, you need to identify some development points which you can work on throughout the year. For example, if you are struggling to answer the questions about communication skills without falling back onto the standard university coursework presentation example, perhaps you need to think about how you could develop and demonstrate those skills. Perhaps you could take part in a mooting or negotiation competition through your student law society; or perhaps you could volunteer to work at a local law centre or take up a position as a student guide at your university's open days. It doesn't matter where or how you develop these skills; the important part is that you have the skills and can demonstrate that. Do not feel that all examples have to be given in a legal practice context; recruiters are looking for well-rounded individuals so it is perfectly acceptable to draw on examples from your hobbies, part-time work, or volunteering roles.

> "The competition for graduate jobs in the legal profession is increasing rapidly. It is therefore important to ensure that you stand out from the crowd. This can be achieved by developing your CV as soon as you start university: don't wait until you've graduated (it might be too late!). Getting involved in university competitions, pro bono activities and, most importantly of all, gaining a wide variety of work experience are things that recruiters will expect to see in your applications. By being organised and starting your research early, this can be achieved whilst getting good marks in your assessments. You don't have to get involved in every single activity that comes your way, perhaps try and do one every term or semester."
>
> *A Solicitor*

PREPARATORY WORK: WHAT TO DO AND WHEN TO DO IT

The timetable below provides suggestions for activities that will enhance your CV and ensure that you make effective use of your time at university. To avoid missing important deadlines in the application process, it should be read in conjunction with the specific timetables provided by law careers websites such as *http://www.lawcareers.net* or the Chambers Student Guide *http://www.chambersstudent.co.uk*. Some students find it helpful to put a year planner on their wall to mark out key coursework or revision periods and specific application deadlines. This might help you to manage your time more effectively and avoid a situation where you fail to submit a training contract application simply because you get overwhelmed by university work. You will need to become an expert at time management if you are to succeed in practice, so you may as well start to perfect that skill now.

First Year Law and Second Year Non-Law Undergraduates

Get as much legal work experience as you can and make the most of any contacts within the legal profession.

Participate in as many client interviewing competitions, negotiating competitions, court visits, mock trials and moots as you can without compromising your studies (if your university does not have these initiatives in place, speak to your student law society or tutors, or consider establishing one yourself).

Attend careers fairs and any guest lectures or careers workshops to find out as much as possible about the recruitment process, the different areas of legal practice, and the breadth of training opportunities that are available to you. It is important to get this preparation out of the way this year to put yourself in the best possible position when the recruitment process starts in earnest next year. Never miss an opportunity to make a new contact and always invest time in following them up.

Consider volunteering at your local Citizens Advice Bureaux or Trading Standards office. Your university might run a clinical legal education programme offering such training schemes. If not, get in touch with your local office to find out about volunteering opportunities.

Find out about, and get involved in, any other pro bono initiatives at your university (see Ch.11 for more information on pro bono initiatives).

Use your long summer holiday wisely to gain as much experience as possible to enhance your CV. This is particularly important this summer as you might be applying for training contracts next year and will need all the ammunition you can find when it comes to tackling the tricky questions on application forms.

Consider getting involved in charity work or fundraising events. This is a great way to develop key skills such as teamwork, negotiation and communication, and it will give you something interesting to talk about at interviews. This experience is likely to be particularly useful if you are interested in public legal work as employers will be looking for candidates who have shown a genuine interest in helping people and can demonstrate a commitment to their community or a particular cause.

Make a serious commitment to researching the legal recruitment process, and the breadth of opportunities available within the profession, so that you can start making informed decisions about which career path you would like to follow (see Ch.9).

Visit your university careers centre and get to know the careers advisors. They are an invaluable source of help so it is worth getting in touch with them as early as possible, rather than waiting until the busy periods when everyone else is also desperate for advice.

> "I got most of my information about the recruitment process during the first year of my degree from the vocational events that my Student Law Society put on. I even went along to a lot of the second year events so I had an idea of what I had to work up to. The vocational events included guest lectures, application workshops, commercial awareness training, networking drinks receptions, and law fairs."
>
> *Joanna Pennick, Solicitor*

Second Year Law and Third Year Non-Law Undergraduates

Continue to follow last year's advice (as appropriate) although by now you should have made some decisions about your chosen career path and therefore your research and networking should become more targeted.

At the beginning of the year, list the key deadlines in the recruitment calendar and the dates of any important careers related events (these are usually available from legal careers websites and/or your university careers centre).

Continue to participate in pro bono initiatives.

Apply for vacation schemes and training contracts (check deadlines for each firm at the beginning of the year).

Talk to students who have already secured a training contract and ask them to review and provide feedback on your CV and application forms.

Attend mock interviews and assessment centre workshops at your university careers centre.

Some law schools and university careers centres maintain databases where you can review feedback forms from students who have attended interviews at particular firms. This is an excellent form of preparation and should give you a clearer idea of what to expect from the interview and a better understanding of what that firm is looking for in prospective trainees.

Collect prospectuses and attend law school open days to find out more about the LPC/GDL.

Non-law undergraduates should apply for a place on the GDL.

Third Year Law Undergraduates and GDL Students Who Have Not Already Secured a Training Contract

Continue to follow last year's advice (as appropriate).

Attend law school open days to find out more about the LPC. Apply for a place on the LPC. If you are concerned about embarking on the course without a training contract, get in touch with someone from your chosen provider and ask about the percentage of students who join without a training contract and how many secure one before completing the course. Also investigate what careers support is available at each provider.

Continue to apply for vacation schemes and training contracts. Seek feedback if you are unsuccessful and take full advantage of the support available from your careers service. Find out whether your university or law school operates a formal or informal mentoring programme to enable you to learn from other people's experiences and make some useful contacts within the profession.

LPC Students Who Have Not Already Secured a Training Contract

Continue to follow last year's advice (as appropriate).
Critically review your CV, application forms and interview performance. Seek advice from careers advisors, friends, or tutors as they might pick up on weaknesses that you have missed.

9 RESEARCHING CAREER OPPORTUNITIES

WHAT ARE YOU LOOKING FOR FROM YOUR CAREER?

Perhaps one of the most appealing aspects of the solicitors' profession is that it is a very broad church offering a wide variety of opportunities. It probably goes without saying that the life of a market town property lawyer is a world away from the life of a City banking lawyer or a criminal defence lawyer and, while each has its own unique rewards and challenges, what is most important is that you follow the right path for you, not the one that offers the greatest financial incentives or will most impress your family and friends.

At the most basic level, solicitors' practice areas can be broadly divided into three categories: commercial work; private client work; and public work. As you would imagine, solicitors involved in commercial practice tend to deal with corporate clients who need business-related advice (e.g. commercial contracts, mergers and acquisitions, intellectual property, corporate tax, and commercial property transactions) while private client solicitors deal with individual clients helping them with legal issues relating to their private affairs (e.g. personal taxation, residential property transactions, divorce, or personal injury claims). Public work includes criminal defence or prosecution work, judicial review cases, and immigration matters.

It is also important to realise that you do not have to work for a firm of solicitors in private practice. Solicitors can also work as "in-house" lawyers within companies, not-for-profit organisations, local authorities, Central Government, or the Crown Prosecution Service.

Given the breadth of practice areas and training opportunities available, you must engage in thorough and timely research, and honest self-reflection, before you even consider applying for training contracts. This is important on two counts: first, it will help you make an informed decision about whether this is really the career for you; and, secondly, it will help you decide which of the many and varied practice areas you would be most suited to. Ultimately, your goal is to find a training environment that will best suit your work aspirations, academic profile, personality, and lifestyle choices. It is important to be honest with yourself. There is no point applying for a City firm when, in reality, you want to be able to leave the office at 18.00 every evening, can't imagine surviving on less than eight hours sleep each night, and have no interest in commercial affairs. Unless you are honest with yourself, you are simply wasting time and setting yourself up for disappointment. However, if you get this part right, you will greatly improve your chances of securing a training contract and, crucially, of enjoying a long and satisfying career.

Consider All Avenues

Forget about what your friends are doing and ensure that you make the right decision for you. You will be at work for a very long time and, after all the hours of study and financial investment, you should give yourself the best possible opportunity to enjoy your work and have a fulfilling career in the long term. It is so easy to follow the crowd into the traditional private sector law firm training ground but have you considered a career in the public sector working for the Crown Prosecution Service, Government Legal Service, or a local authority? Or have you thought about a career in the third sector working for a not-for-profit organisation? While these career paths will not suit everyone, there are others for whom they are absolutely the right choice and if they miss the opportunity, they might find that they never achieve the job satisfaction they are searching for.

> "Any prospective trainee should spend time working out which type of firm they want to apply to before submitting applications and not just blindly applying for big name firms. I have encountered so many miserable trainees and even associates that were good at being a lawyer, but the culture of the firm

> and the type of people they were working with just didn't suit them and they were so miserable that some quit the law altogether as a result."
>
> *A Solicitor*

Even if you think you know exactly where you want to train, make an effort to find out about other options and complete a variety of work experience placements. You do not have to mention them all on your CV but it will at least reassure you that you have considered all possible avenues and made the right decision for you. It will also make it easier to convince a prospective employer that you have explored alternative options and that your application is based on informed decision-making and thorough research. You will have more to talk about at interviews and, when asked why you are interested in a particular practice area or why you wish to work for a particular type of firm, you will be able to support your answers with evidence.

Factors to consider when deciding what type of training and working environment would most suit you.

What are you looking for in the type of work that you do (and what do you want to avoid)?

Would you like to work on transactions for commercial clients, or do you see yourself working with individuals helping them to resolve issues arising from their personal life?

Would you like your training contract to cover both commercial and private client work, or are you already sure which type of practice would suit you best?

Do you see yourself working for a large law firm with hundreds or thousands of employees, or in an organisation where you are more likely to know most people who work there?

What has motivated you to become a solicitor? Try to find an organisation which matches those aspirations and ideals.

What are your expectations in terms of working culture and lifestyle?

What hours do you see yourself working? Would you be prepared to work late nights and weekends on a regular basis, or to cancel personal plans at short notice? Do you really have the stamina to sustain the working hours that will be required by the larger firms?

Which area of the country would you like to practise in? Would you like to work in a busy city or a smaller town? Is commuting time likely to be an issue for you?

What sort of office culture and environment would suit your personality?

Are you keen to take responsibility for your own small client files from day one, or would you prefer to be working on major transactions as part of a large team with little (if any) direct client contact?

Would you prefer to work for a firm which employs a small number of trainees each year or a firm with a large trainee intake?

Think about the structure of training contracts at different firms. Most firms offer four seats of six months each, but others offer a greater number of shorter seats and some offer an entirely flexible training structure where you are exposed to work from a broad range of practice areas at the same time. Which would you prefer?

Where do you see yourself in five and then ten years' time? What type of training and working environment is likely to help you achieve those goals?

Are you looking for a career with an element of public service and the opportunity to make a difference to your community?

Would you like to have the opportunity to participate in secondments to commercial clients?

Are you looking for a job involving international travel and/or which offers the opportunity to work overseas for a period of time?

Will your A Level grades and degree result limit the type of firm you can apply to?

A Word of Warning

It is fair to say that lawyers have significant earning potential, but this should not be your primary consideration when deciding whether you want to qualify as a solicitor and where you would like to train. It is very easy to think that financial reward is the most important aspect of any career and that money will compensate for anything, but this is certainly not the case for everyone. There are some very unhappy solicitors out there and, for some people, a significant salary, and the lifestyle that is built upon it, can become a barrier to job satisfaction rather than a gateway to happiness.

> "Money was not a factor that I thought about when I chose law as a career. Obviously it's nice to have that security there and I'm probably earning more than my friends are but that's not why I do it. You have to enjoy the work first and foremost."
>
> *A Trainee Solicitor at a City Firm*

> "Ignore the salaries. Do not be attracted to the bright lights of London just because the firms will pay you so much more than they will in the regions. Ignore that part of the information that the firm produces. There are easier ways to make money! A lot of people are blinded by the big salaries and don't appreciate the kind of work and hours you will have to put in to achieve that. It needs to be about what you want to do and the areas of law that you think you might enjoy. It's so important to get your research right."
>
> *A Trainee Solicitor*

PRIVATE PRACTICE

Many law graduates think they must head for a career with a large City law firm, but smaller firms can offer very good training and will suit some people better. You should choose a firm where you are likely to fit into the culture and which carries out the type of work that you are interested in. The client base and work on offer at a particular firm will determine the experience you gain during your training, your future marketability as a solicitor, and whether or not you are likely to be happy there. Therefore, choosing the right firm *for you* is a crucial decision. The profiles below outline the key features of each type of law firm.

> "I was quite realistic about my applications. I was conscious that there was no point wasting my time applying to large City firms. First of all, I wasn't sure I would actually be very well suited to them and, secondly, I knew that my A Level grades would not let me past the first round of selection. Given the amount of time that you haemorrhage on these applications while trying to get a degree, it seemed pointless to me to apply to those firms. So I used the Training Contract & Pupillage Handbook and drew a line under firms of a particular type and narrowed down the remaining firms according to size and location. Also my work experience allowed me to get a better handle on the kind of firms where I thought I might be a good fit."
>
> *A Trainee Solicitor*

Large City Firms

As you would expect, these firms are based in the City of London (although many are global firms with a vast network of international offices). They include the top five "Magic Circle" firms (Clifford Chance, Allen & Overy, Freshfields Bruckhaus Deringer, Slaughter & May and Linklaters) and other large City firms.

These firms will have over 100 trainees and focus on high value corporate finance and banking transactions, often with an international element, and complex commercial work. With a large network of international offices, international seats and secondments are widely available, and the perks are impressive. They offer incredible facilities, superb benefits packages, and pay very high salaries. However, these rewards reflect the work invested by the fee earners: lawyers and trainees at these firms work incredibly long hours and you will need to be exceptionally resilient to keep up with the pace. You will also need to be genuinely interested in corporate work, and demonstrate high levels of commercial awareness. In short, if you decide to join a City firm, you must be realistic about how hard you are going to work and the sacrifices that you will be expected to make.

> "People say that they could easily do an 'all-nighter' but they don't actually know what it means to do three all-nighters in a row, or whatever. That has been quite an eye opener in my first seat."
>
> *A Trainee Solicitor at a City Firm*

> "Really think about the kind of pressures that are involved in working for a City firm, as well as all the benefits that you will receive. It takes someone with a real drive and an individual desire to pursue success, perhaps at the cost of other things."
>
> *A Trainee Solicitor at a City Firm*

> "Passion is a key factor because if you have no incentive to work the hours that are expected of you, then you are going to fall down very quickly. You have to genuinely want to be here. You have to understand that you will sometimes be stuck in the office late at night doing less glamorous tasks, but keep an eye on the bigger picture—you are playing an important role as part of a wider team and you must be prepared to get involved. You can't just be drawn by the thought of the money and the glamour or what your friends are doing."
>
> *A Trainee Solicitor at a City Firm*

US Firms

Historically, US firms were considered to be a sub-section of City firms but many now prefer to be referred to as International firms. It would be sensible to check the website for each firm to ensure that you mirror the language it uses to describe itself.

The US firms in London divide broadly into two types: US firms which have established a UK office; and US firms which have merged with a UK firm. These firms tend to offer a much smaller number of training contracts compared to other City firms and some do not recruit trainees at all (preferring to recruit solicitors post-qualification).The salaries paid by these firms are exceptionally high (even by City standards) but, if you join a US firm, you should be prepared for a tough working culture and extremely long hours. Like the City firms, they specialise in complex, high value corporate and commercial work, often with an international element.

Mid-tier London Firms

These firms are based in London and specialise in corporate and commercial work, but they tend to be a bit smaller with less focus on international work. They also tend to take a smaller number of trainees each year (perhaps between 20 and 40).

Small London Firms

These firms tend to take a very small number of trainees each year and the work can vary from purely commercial and corporate work to private work for high net worth individuals. The salaries are not as high as the larger firms but the hours are more reasonable so it's all a question of balance.

Niche Firms

These are firms that have become well known for their work in a particular area of law, for example, intellectual property, shipping, media, family, or employment law. They will probably recruit around 5 to 10 trainees each year.

National Firms

These are large firms with a strong nationwide presence. They tend to specialise in commercial work (although this is not always the case). They will recruit between 30 and 130 trainees each year depending on the size and number of offices nationwide. If you decide to train with a national firm, it would be worth checking the firm's policy on location of seats. Some will expect you to accept seats in different geographic locations depending on the business needs of the firm, which might come as an unwelcome surprise if you are not prepared for this.

Regional Firms

These are large firms with several offices within one region. They often provide a range of legal services covering both private client and commercial work. They will probably recruit between 10 and 40 trainees each year depending on the size and number of offices.

High Street Firms

These are much smaller practices in high street locations, which tend to specialise in private client work such as family law, residential conveyancing, criminal defence, and employment law. You will be dealing with members of your local community in relation to issues that affect them personally, e.g. the sale or purchase of a house; the drafting of a will; a divorce or relationship breakdown; immigration advice; a personal injury claim; or a dispute with a neighbour. These firms recruit a small number of trainees depending on the needs of their business and, since the minimum trainee salary set by the SRA was abolished in 2014, the only applicable minimum salary threshold is the national minimum wage.

High street firms have been through a challenging time in recent years, and some have joined large national franchises (e.g. Quality Solicitors) or Alternative Business Structures (see below). It has been particularly challenging for those who advise publicly funded clients given the significant cuts in legal aid (see the Legal Aid, Sentencing and Punishment of Offenders Act 2012 and related press coverage).

Alternative Business Structures

Since the implementation of the Legal Services Act 2007, which took effect in autumn 2011, non-lawyers have been allowed to manage, control or invest in law firms. These firms are known as Alternative Business Structures (ABS) and their entrance to the legal services market has been one of the most significant changes in the landscape for many years. The new structure allows greater flexibility in terms of partnership with non-legal organisations, appointment of non-legal management staff and stakeholders, and access to external funding. It has also meant that well-established commercial organisations have been able to bring their consumer focus and competitive pricing structures to the legal market place. We have seen ABSs used in a number of different ways in the last two years: some established law firms have converted to ABSs perhaps to facilitate their growth plans and secure external investment or to retain non-legal directors; others have been newly established to take advantage of the more flexible regulatory framework; and the final tranche of ABSs are those established by an existing commercial brand (such as the Co-operative or BT) usually to offer a distinct range of legal services (often family law, production of wills, employment advice, and residential conveyancing).

See *http://www.lawsociety.org.uk.support-services/advice/practice-notes/alternative-business-structures* for more information.

Drawing Up a List of Target Firms

If you have decided that you wish to train in private practice, your next task is to narrow down your choice of target firms. In doing so, your first step should be to review law careers websites to find out more about specific firms. These publications provide general guidance on the recruitment process and set out profiles of hundreds of law firms and other legal employers. You can use them to find out about the size, client base, practice areas, and culture of individual firms, and to narrow down the list of those you wish to apply to.

> "Completing training contract applications takes a very long time so you cannot apply indiscriminately. Know the type of firm you want to train with (but be realistic) and really think about the practice areas you are interested in and what particular skills you could bring to them."
>
> *Lorna Sansom, Associate, B P Collins LLP*

The Chambers Student Guide (*http://www.chambersstudent. co.uk*) is an excellent source of information when it comes to researching individual firms. You can use the A–Z list of law firms to identify specific firms and gain access to a wealth of information about each one. Or, you can compare firms by size, location, salaries and benefits using the various tables on the website. There is also a "Firm Facts" feature which identifies key facts such as location, number of partners, number of trainees, and details about seat choices, etc, and the Chambers "True Picture" feature which provides an insider's view to the firm based on interviews with trainees and recruitment managers. Another useful source is *http://www.lawcareers.net* which has a directory of nearly 1,000 organisations that offer training contracts. You can use the database to search for specific firms, or to create a shortlist of firms which meet certain criteria, e.g. region, city, total staff, etc.

As well as finding out about the size and location of a firm and the work they carry out, you should research its reputation and the retention rate for trainees at the end of their training contract (i.e. how many are offered permanent contracts at the end of their training), and how much choice you will have in terms of the seats that you will cover during your training contract. You will also probably be interested in whether or not they will offer funding for course fees and maintenance during your LPC year.

Once you have completed this research, you should be able to compile a shortlist of firms that you are interested in. You can then review individual websites to get a clearer feel for the culture and philosophy of each firm. Of course, you need to remember that websites are marketing tools aimed at impressing clients and prospective employees. Nonetheless, they are a very useful source of information and the way that a firm has chosen to present itself can often give a good insight into its culture and aspirations.

You might find it helpful to keep in mind the questions below when reviewing websites for your target firms.

> What stands out from the way each firm presents itself on the website and in other marketing material?
>
> What impression is created by any messages from the Managing Partner or CEO, or the Head of Recruitment?
>
> Does it have a clearly identifiable mission statement?
>
> What sort of people does the firm seem to attract?
>
> How is the firm structured?
>
> Does it have a key area of expertise in terms of practice areas or clients from particular sectors?
>
> What are the career development opportunities and how supportive does the culture seem to be?
>
> How much emphasis is put on training and development?
>
> Does the firm display any information about its pro bono programme?

In short, can you imagine yourself working there and why? You will need to prepare a persuasive and well-researched answer to this question if you manage to get to the interview stage, so you may as well start thinking about it now. If you don't know why you are targeting that firm, how will you ever convince the recruitment partner to employ you over and above hundreds or even thousands of other applicants? The website will also help you to identify the key decision makers (e.g. the Training Partner and Graduate Recruitment Manager) so you can try to make contact with them at law fairs or guest lectures.

After this initial research, you should be left with a manageable list from which to start applying for vacation schemes and training contracts. At this stage, you might also find it helpful to look at some of the other Chambers publications, including Chambers UK and Chambers USA (if appropriate) to read the firm's profile and find out more about specific practice areas, key clients, and recognised experts at the firm.

As part of your on-going research into your target firms, you should also keep an eye on the legal press in *http://www.thel-*

awyer.com and *http://www.legalweek.com* and *http://www.law-gazette.co.uk*. Look out for any deals or key cases involving your target law firms and any changes or key developments in the following areas:

the firms' training or recruitment processes, e.g. any changes in LPC provider if they use a "tailor-made" LPC;

a change in retention rates or the recruitment of legal apprentices for the first time;

a change in management or ownership;

a move into new markets;

a merger with another firm;

the creation of a key international alliance;

a group of lateral hires (where a law firm recruits lawyers from other firms to establish or boost a particular practice area); or

the launch of a new office or the closure of an existing office.

You will need to keep updating this research as the application process unfolds because employers will expect to see evidence of your current awareness and research in your application form and particularly during the interview.

"Think carefully about the types of firms you are applying to; choose a selective few that appeal to you and research each firm thoroughly. It is far more effective to send off a small number of well-targeted applications than to send off lots of applications with generic answers. Your application will have a much stronger impact on the employer thereby increasing your chances of being selected for the next recruitment stage."

Cecily Holt, LPC Graduate

"Trainees can be a really good source of information about a firm, which can help you when it comes to filling in the application forms. Ask them what they think sets their firm apart from other firms and what they enjoy most about training at that firm or why they chose it over others. You can even mention them in application forms to show that you've made an effort to find out about the firm and that you can network effectively."

Joanna Pennick, Solicitor

COMMERCIAL ORGANISATIONS

Opportunities to train in the legal departments of large companies or banks are relatively scarce but there are plenty of opportunities to move "in-house" post qualification if you train with a reputable law firm and have relevant commercial law experience. For in-house training contract vacancies keep an eye on The Lawyer (*http://www.thelawyer.com*), Legal Week Jobs (*http://www.legalweekjobs.com*) the Law Society Gazette (*http://www.jobs.lawgazette.co.uk*), and the jobs pages of LawCareers.Net (*http://www.lawcareers.net*). You should also look at individual companies' websites.

"Are you personable and have strong communication skills? Can you adapt quickly to changing circumstances? Would you enjoy developing close and long-lasting relationships with a small yet valuable number of clients? If your answer is yes, then an in-house training contract might be the best route to qualification for you.

I began my legal career as a paralegal in the Legal Services Department of a large financial institution after responding to a role advertised via my LPC provider. After working as a litigation paralegal for a year, I was offered a training contract. The availability of in-house training contracts will often be dependent on the demands of the organisation in question, and do not always mirror the recruitment practices of large commercial firms. It is therefore important to research the legal press and contact organisations directly with regard to in-house vacancies.

Working as an in-house trainee solicitor varies dramatically from organisation to organisation. In my case I undertook seats in Commercial/IT, Corporate, Real Estate and Commercial

Litigation (which included a secondment at a large commercial firm). Having said this, not all of my work fitted neatly into these headings as I was often called upon to help other teams depending on the needs of the business. One common misconception of working in-house is that the quality of work is not as good as in private-practice. This was certainly not my experience as I often found that I was given more responsibility than my friends working in private practice.

The types of work I was involved in varied a great deal. I negotiated contracts with external suppliers, gave advice regarding problems with Land Registry titles, and defended customer claims against the bank. I was also fortunate to be involved in some highly publicised matters such as press injunctions and corporate deals.

One substantial difference between my training contract and what might be experienced in private practice is that my internal clients were also my colleagues. This meant that clients would often turn up at my desk at a moment's notice expecting me to advise them at the drop of a hat! Although this was quite testing at times, it also meant that I developed strong relationships with my clients, which is a vital part of working as a solicitor.

I eventually qualified into the commercial litigation team and have since worked in banking litigation for both in-house departments and private firms."

Rebecca Milner, Solicitor

In-house legal teams generally have very high volumes of work to get through and often have far less administrative support than solicitors in private practice. You may therefore find that opportunities arise to fulfil temporary administrative or paralegal contracts with in-house legal teams while you are at university or law school. This is a good opportunity to make contacts and get a clearer idea of whether this type of work is likely to suit you.

"I work for a US company as part of a small in-house legal team who provide support throughout EMEA to all aspects of the business including licensing, procurement, compliance, employment, property and dispute resolution issues. Given the geographical area which we cover there are regular challenges to be overcome with language, time-zones and approaches to working practice.

The much talked about perks of not having billing targets, time sheets and having to set aside dedicated time for business development are welcome; however, these must be weighed up against being taken out of the familiarity of a solicitors firm and the reassurance that comes from being surrounded by a plentiful research tools and legal minds.

In our business we work in financial quarters so busy periods are cyclical and inevitably, especially around quarter-end, co-workers invariably want to progress their matters quickly. For legal counsel this means being both proactive in task-management and being flexible enough to react appropriately as and when priorities change.

It's important that legal is not perceived as an obstacle, and the challenge is on one hand to maintain momentum but on the other to ensure that the necessary checks and balances are carried out. Ultimately you will have ownership of the deal documents and you must be prepared for the immediacy of dealing with issues and people, there's no 'hiding' behind emails, voicemail and secretaries when senior management sit in the same office—if they want to know something they'll walk in and ask you for it.

One myth which seems to endure about working in-house is that you can expect to start at 9am and leave at 5pm every day. This may be the case in some heavily resourced organisations but for smaller in-house teams it is not and you will be expected to work the hours required for the business to meet its targets since ultimately legal's contribution to getting transactions concluded promptly has a direct effect on the success and therefore profitability of the organisation.

I was keen to move in-house since I wanted to have the opportunity to understand more about what it was to be genuinely commercial which whilst important in practice, as I quickly discovered is fundamental in industry. In-house you are not simply there just to red-line contracts you're a facilitator and an important part of the business. What this means day-to-day can take a bit of getting used to but once achieved it manifests itself as a quality which is a valuable one."

An In-House Lawyer

THE PUBLIC SECTOR

Crown Prosecution Service (CPS)

The CPS employs around 2,200 prosecutors and is respon-sible for prosecuting people who have been charged by the police. It also advises the police service on prosecutions. The CPS recruits trainee solicitors and pupils (trainee barristers) under its CPS Legal Trainee Scheme. The CPS tends to recruit trainees after completing the vocational stage of training and generally advertises vacancies four to six months in advance of the start date. The CPS does not necessarily recruit train-ees every year so you will need to keep an eye on the CPS careers website for the latest position (*http://www.cps.gov.uk/ careers*).

"A typical day for a trainee solicitor with the CPS would begin by checking whether your supervisor has specific work for you. In addition, you can expect to attend court to observe, review cases, carry out research and draft applications and skeleton arguments. You will tend to work from 9.00 am to 5.00 pm—although if something urgent comes up you might need to stay later. To be a good prosecutor, you need to be able to deal with a significant volume of work, remain calm under pressure, and not be afraid to stand your ground if you have to—you will sometimes be arguing with very experienced lawyers and must not be intimidated by that. You must be an excellent communicator because you will need to explain the law in simple terms to victims, witnesses and judges, and, of course, you must be able to construct a persuasive argument. You also need a positive attitude and can't let the work get you down. It takes a while to realise that you can't save the world and that sometimes you won't get the result you hoped for despite your best efforts.

The best thing about working for the CPS is the diversity of work and opportunity. For example, once you have qualified, you could undertake more training to allow you to conduct advocacy in the higher courts, or you could take on a more managerial role, move into the policy department or consider joining the training unit. I also enjoy the fact that I am making a real difference to my community through the work I do."

Sibylle Cheruvier, Senior Crown Prosecutor
Crown Prosecution Service

Government Legal Services (GLS)

GLS lawyers advise the Government on a range of legal issues including charity law, constitutional matters, education, agriculture, human rights, and health and safety. The GLS recruits approximately 30 graduates a year who want to train as solicitors or barristers. They tend to recruit two years in advance and will pay LPC course fees and sometimes also a maintenance grant (although payments will not be made retrospectively, i.e. if the course has already been paid for). See *http://www.gov.uk/government/organisations/civil-service-government-legal-service* for more information on careers with GLS and the GLS open days and work experience scheme.

Local Government

Solicitors in local government advise on the relationship between the local authority and the surrounding community and legal issues arising out of the services provided by the authority. This could include, for example, planning law, property law, or education law. Opportunities to train in local government are relatively scarce. They tend to recruit trainees after completing the LPC and advertise vacancies a couple of months, rather than years, in advance. For local government vacancies, keep an eye on the Law Society Gazette and individual authorities' websites. You could also visit the Local Government Lawyer website (*http://www.localgovernmentlawyer.co.uk*).

> "I work in litigation, so much of my time is spent in case preparation and advocacy. As a local government solicitor, I have a wider brief than the private sector seem to follow, with a wide range of departments using my time. I spend most time at work with clients helping them to achieve solutions to the problems facing our local area—these rarely fit into departmental or organisational boundaries so my breadth of knowledge is pushed at all times. To give you an idea of the breadth of my work, I am currently working on files from personnel, planning enforcement, the ASBO team, information law officers, environmental health, council tax debt recovery, bankruptcy, charity law workers, and street trading! What makes it all worthwhile is the knowledge that I am contributing to making this a better place to live by enabling people to live happier, safer and cleaner lives.
>
> To be a good local government lawyer, you must remember the place you serve and that your role is not to find excuses to say no—your challenge and fulfilment comes from finding ways to achieve positive things. Each victory makes the others working with you more hopeful that they can achieve improvements and slowly we make an area which everyone deserves."
>
> *A Local Government Lawyer*

PRACTICE AREAS FOR SOLICITORS

The remainder of this chapter explores a variety of practice areas within which solicitors operate. The aim is not to provide an exhaustive account of every conceivable practice area, but rather to illustrate the breadth of opportunities that are available to aspiring solicitors. It also illustrates the significant differences between the various practice areas and thus reinforces the importance of thorough research before you embark on the recruitment process, to ensure that you choose a practice area that suits your skills, interests, career aspirations, and personality. Although it is sometimes possible to change direction after qualification, you will find it difficult to move to a firm with an entirely different focus if you have not completed any relevant seats during your training contract.

Aviation

Aviation Law often involves advising on the leasing and financing of aircraft whether for a bank which is financing the purchase of a jet, or a company which is leasing an aircraft. However, aviation lawyers also advise on commercial, regulatory (e.g. competition or emissions trading rules), and insurance matters.

> "Whilst primarily being an aviation lawyer is about transactional work and simply stated is about ensuring deals close successfully and that aircraft are being utilised. The role of a solicitor working in aviation can be a varied and challenging one and will inevitably at some stage involve international work. The international aspects may arise because an aircraft is registered in a foreign jurisdiction or that the parties to a transaction are themselves incorporated outside of England. As a consequence you will have to understand and apply both English law and international conventions and treaties in order to best serve your clients' interests.
>
> Aviation is also a highly competitive market and in order to advise in this industry you must be commercially astute and constantly mindful of how a transaction affects your clients and their business.
>
> On a day to day basis you could find yourself advising on a wide range of issues which could involve the sale and purchase of aircraft, the leasing of aircraft, the financing of aircraft or the taking security over aircraft to name but a few. Depending on this you could find yourself drafting and negotiating documentation and at the same time having to instruct and liaising with foreign counsel or deal with Government bodies; no two transactions are ever the same.
>
> Whilst the variety and cross-border nature of aviation is

what attracted me to become an aviation lawyer, being one will on occasion involve long hours and pressurised situations where deadlines have to be met—otherwise operational requirements cannot be met and aircraft cannot be operated all of which means that your client's business will suffer—but if met will mean that the aircraft can keep flying!"

Gareth Hawes, Solicitor, Blake Morgan LLP

Banking and Private Equity

Banking and finance lawyers work on the legal aspects of financial transactions on behalf of banks, investment funds, or large corporations. They are usually involved from the early stages, when they advise on the structure of the deal, through to completion. They are also involved in drafting, negotiating and executing the loan agreement and ancillary documents and monitoring compliance with the conditions of the loan to ensure they are fulfilled. Specialist advice might be required on certain aspects of the transactions, for example tax, so finance lawyers must be good team players and able to take responsibility for managing a large team of internal and external advisors. Since deals will often have to be completed at very short notice, you should expect to work very long hours and must be able to work effectively under pressure.

Charities

Solicitors specialising in Charity Law advise non-profit organisations on all aspects of their activities. You might find yourself dealing with a disputed legacy (where someone has bequeathed money to a charity in his/her will but it is contested by a family member), or negotiating a commercial agreement with a charity's commercial partner, or establishing a new charity, or advising on governance issues, or advising on the protection of intellectual property rights, or advising on the formation of a trust for a particular programme. Some larger charities have their own in-house lawyers, whilst others use specialist external lawyers.

"As a solicitor specialising in charity law the work is extremely varied and diverse. I advise charities, schools, academies and other not-for-profit organisations on a wide range of issues. Some examples of my workload include advising on governance, corporate structures, charity formation, registering with the Charity Commission, incorporations, mergers and acquisitions, partnering ventures, trading, trustee issues, contracts and academies, and academy conversions. Like the work itself, the timescales and urgencies are also varied, sometimes there is a very long timescale within which the clients wish a charity to be formed, or incorporated, and other times, for example on a merger, we are often tasked with working to very tight demanding deadlines.

The team I work within is a nationally recognised charity law team providing a fully comprehensive service on every aspect of our client's legal requirements, and we work with some of the largest and prominent names within the charity sector.

We deal with a wide variety of matters relating to charities, and co-ordinate other sector experience where required, for example, employment, property and litigation.

There are often urgent situations involving our charity clients, which can range from disaster appeals, reputational issues, defamation etc, and the role requires you to work well under pressure and in stressful situations. It is also important to be organised, able to prioritise, able to come up with practical solutions, and be commercial and at all times having our client's aims and goals in mind.

It is also a very rewarding role, I work on a large number of new charity formations, and we work with all types and sizes of charities from small community charities to large international leading charities, and have the privilege of being involved in their projects and seeing those charities grow and develop.

I am also tasked with co-ordinating the charity law e-bulletin and writing articles on issues affecting charities and not-for profit organisations, as well as delivering training for charity trustees."

Kirsteen Hook, Solicitor, Blake Morgan LLP

Commercial Contracts

Commercial law involves the negotiation of commercial contracts including, for example, outsourcing arrangements, contracts arising from PFI initiatives, sale and purchase terms and conditions, agency or distribution arrangements, and franchising agreements. The role of a commercial lawyer is to negotiate on behalf of their client and to draft documentation that reflects the terms of the commercial arrangement. They usually act for a wide variety of clients which could include local authorities, universities, family owned businesses, banks, and other large corporations.

Lawyers in this field need to work closely with clients to understand their businesses and commercial focus, to identify the client's objectives, and to manage any potential risks arising from the arrangement. Therefore, commercial lawyers need to be good communicators who are able to build and manage relationships effectively. The nature of the work also requires excellent drafting skills, an eye for detail, and an ability to think creatively—you will often find yourself putting a client's ideas onto paper without the security of a precedent document to work from.

"The practice area of commercial law is extremely wide ranging. Essentially, the role of a commercial lawyer is to provide clients with a service that enables them to navigate through complex legal issues to achieve their goals and enhance the value of opportunities.

Daily work can involve anything from drafting or advising on terms and conditions, to the completion of large scale outsourcing or IT projects, so strong drafting and negotiation skills, as well as an excellent attention to detail, are required. A client's main concern is furthering their business so it is important for a commercial lawyer to also have a good understanding of the client's industry to advise effectively. As the practice area is so broad, it is often the case in larger firms that a commercial lawyer will specialise in a certain industry, such as Retail, Energy or IT.

Furthermore, as the use of technology continues to increase

and develop, clients require more and more advice on their legal obligations and/or opportunities when it comes to using and exploiting technology in their business.

I chose to specialise in this area because of the variety of work involved and also because I enjoy the forensic nature of trawling through a document to check that it works and that it includes appropriate protection for my client. To be a good commercial lawyer you also need to enjoy drafting as although there are precedent documents and clauses which you can use, no two commercial transactions are the same and you are often called upon to prepare bespoke wording from scratch to cover particular situations.

Commercial law covers many different areas—advertising and marketing, distribution and agency arrangements, franchising, the supply of goods and services, outsourcing and IT and e-commerce and so life is rarely dull. However, you tend to work more independently than corporate transactional lawyers and the work is perhaps more cerebral and so although working on a large commercial transaction can involve high pressure, if you enjoy the intense highs and lows and excitement of a transactional environment then commercial law is probably not for you."

Chidem Aliss, Senior Associate, Clarke Willmott LLP

Commercial Litigation

As a commercial litigator, you will be dealing with a varied caseload of matters. This could include, for example, a breach of contract dispute between two businesses, a dispute between company directors, or a professional negligence claim between a professional and their client. The day-to-day work of a commercial litigator could include: meeting with clients to consider a particular aspect of their case and to advise on a next step; meeting with the client's opponents and their solicitors to try and reach a settlement in a dispute; answering correspondence and making telephone calls to opponent solicitors; drafting court documents; reviewing evidence; attending court hearings; and instructing a barrister to provide more specialist advice.

"Litigation is a controversial practice area and rarely glamorous! You will meet a lot of hostility at times and your client will expect you to put forward their case in the strongest possible terms, whether or not their case is strong in merit. In those instances, you will need to be able to advance your client's case as coherently and convincingly as possible whilst managing your own client's expectations about their likelihood of success—it is never easy to tell a client that they are likely to lose! You also need to be prepared to act on your feet at a moment's notice and maintain a level head and calm approach when unexpected issues arrive. A successful litigator must therefore fulfil a number of roles—you must be a negotiator, an advocate, an advisor and a mediator.

Being a litigator will inevitably require you to work well in stressful situations. You will often have days where every telephone call involves either a stressed client who needs to be appeased or difficult opponent who wants to make life tricky for your client. Opponent solicitors can make what seems like an easy dispute become entangled and long winded, which makes for a frustrating time.

Never underestimate the number of mundane tasks that also need to be done. For every adrenalin-filled day of Court hearings and urgent work, you will have five days of administration, billing and other necessary, but often unexciting, paperwork. You will also be required to network with other lawyers and business professionals and do plenty of business development work to win new clients. You will need to keep up with training requirements for lawyers as well as reading law journals to maintain your knowledge of changes in the law and procedures. Finally, be prepared for the long hours that you may need to put in where there is a deadline that needs to be met.

To be a good litigator, you must be organised so that you can keep ahead of deadlines and prioritise daily tasks; be able to keep calm in a stressful or hostile situation; be able to think on your feet and sometimes outside the box; be flexible and

> adaptable to changing situations; be a keen problem solver; a team player and, above all, always maintain a good sense of humour."
>
> *A Civil Litigation Solicitor*

Some litigators specialise in particular fields such as property litigation, insolvency litigation or social housing litigation.

> "I work in the litigation department dealing with contentious aspects of housing management and my work includes high profile anti-social behaviour cases; advising on the housing association's policies and procedures; drafting Tenancy agreements; and litigating on all aspects of housing management from contractual disputes to rent review hearings.
>
> I enjoy the fact that social housing is never far from the forefront of the political radar and the anti-social behaviour work has grown tremendously over the last few years. The nature of the work means that you often partner agencies such as the Police, local authorities and social services. In certain cases you also get to see that the court proceedings can make a real difference to the quality of life of people who are suffering as a result of anti-social behaviour.
>
> As with any type of litigation, the essential skills are an eye for detail, the ability to draft concise and relevant pleadings that bring a case to life, a technical knowledge of housing law, and commercial acumen when advising large housing associations on how to spend their legal budget."
>
> *Christopher Skinner, Associate, Capsticks Solicitors LLP*

Commercial Property or Real Estate

This area of practice involves the sale and purchase of commercial properties, legal issues arising from the redevelopment of land, and issues arising from the management of commercial properties. This could include the disposal of a chain of hotels, the redevelopment of a city centre, leases of units in a shopping centre, or the acquisition of a warehouse.

"My day-to-day work includes drafting and negotiating leases and licences for shopping centres and industrial estates; buying and selling commercial properties such as office buildings, industrial estates and warehouses and shopping centres; assisting the finance department in reviewing properties which will provide security for loans; assisting the corporate department in checking properties owned by companies which are being bought or sold (this includes drafting and negotiating parts of the corporate documentation); and reviewing properties owned by insolvent companies and selling them either as part of a sale of the insolvent company's assets or as a sale of the various properties themselves.

I chose to qualify into real estate because of the wide variety of work. The trainees and junior solicitors in the team have their own files and have immediate direct contact with clients when running those files. The ability to take a file from start to finish appealed to me and I really enjoyed this when I was training. I had also enjoyed my finance and corporate seats and liked the fact that, in real estate, I would still work closely with these departments and their clients.

To be a good property lawyer, you will need to be able to work alone and to be organised in order to manage your time efficiently. In other departments you might have one or two large transactions which you will work through from start to finish, in real estate you will probably work on one or two large transactions and anything from 10 to 50 smaller files which you need to keep moving forward while dealing with the larger transactions."

Kelly Myles, Supervising Associate, Berwin Leighton Paisner LLP

Competition

This is a challenging area of law which involves advising on UK and EU competition law. Competition lawyers advise on the competition implications arising from the structure of commercial agreements, and how the deal might be re-structured to minimise the impact of them. They also negotiate clearance for corporate deals and bring or defend claims in the UK Competition

Appeal Tribunal. Lawyers may work in private practice or they may join a regulator.

Construction

Construction law divides into contentious and non-contentious work. Contentious work involves disputes arising from construction contracts, whereas non-contentious work involves advising clients on the procurement, preparation and negotiation of construction contracts.

Corporate

A corporate lawyer may be called upon to advise on a broad range of corporate deals, including joint ventures, private equity and venture capital transactions, mergers and acquisitions, or listing companies on stock exchanges. They might also be asked to provide general advice on, for example, directors' duties or the formation of new companies. Their work will include advising on the structure of a particular deal and drafting and negotiating the main agreements and ancillary documentation.

Specialist advice might be required on certain aspects of the deal (for example tax, property, employment, or competition law) so corporate lawyers, like banking lawyers, need to be effective team players and able to take responsibility for managing a large team of internal and external advisors. Since deals will often have to be completed at very short notice, you should expect to work very long hours in pressurised conditions.

> "I specialise in corporate transaction work which involves advising clients on buying, selling and investing in companies and businesses, setting up businesses, and restructuring them. I work for small to medium sized businesses, family owned businesses, banks and other investors. I chose to qualify into this area because of the wide variety of work involved. I enjoy the mixture of the high pressure environment as a transaction heads for completion and the resulting sense of achievement and relief when the transaction finishes.

A corporate lawyer needs to be very organised, able to process large amounts of information coming in from a variety of sources and be able to pick out key commercial and legal issues from that information. He/she must also have an eye for detail, be able to draft and understand large complex contracts and ensure that such documents do what the client requires them to do. Negotiation is another key skill and linked to that is the importance of understanding what your client's parameters are. It's also essential to be able to work effectively under pressure and accept demanding deadlines.

If you choose to work in a corporate team as a trainee/junior lawyer you are likely to start on a mixture of research, reviewing documents and simple drafting but with experience should progress onto drafting and negotiating more complex agreements, advising clients and even running smaller transactions. Although the work will be enjoyable and challenging it can also require a large number of hours and working nights or weekends, often with very little notice."

Kelvin Balmont, Partner, Clarke Willmott LLP

"I work in the corporate department for a wide variety of clients, including FTSE 100 companies, international companies, and some smaller clients. On a day-to-day basis, my work involves a large number of conference calls and meetings as well as drafting new documentation and reviewing and commenting on documents that are already in place. On any particular deal there will always be a team involved so there is also a lot of interaction and discussion with other people on the deal. The job is intellectually challenging and it is very satisfying when a deal is done and the client is happy with the result."

Philippa Chatterton, Senior Associate, Nabarro

"There are times when you work for 48 hours straight, get in a car to come home, have a shower and get straight back to the office. You can't really prepare yourself for that, but it's a reality of life in a big corporate department. It's not all the time but it does happen. Having said that, I spent three months in tax and three months in dispute resolution which were much more cerebral, involved more research, and the hours were less intense, but I didn't really like it. I much preferred the team atmosphere of a transactional seat. I suppose the thing is that different things work for different people."

A Newly Qualified Corporate Solicitor

Corporate Tax

Corporate tax lawyers advise on the most tax-efficient way for companies to re-structure their business or to sell or acquire a business. Tax law is incredibly complex and intellectually challenging. You will need to have a keen eye for detail and be comfortable working with black letter legal principles and complex legislation.

Criminal Law

As a criminal solicitor, you will spend your time either defending those who have been accused of a crime or prosecuting them. It is worth noting that the on-going cuts to criminal legal aid have had a serious impact on criminal defence practices and access to justice for individuals. This is something that you need to research further if you are serious about a career in this field.

Employment, Pensions and Incentives

As an employment lawyer, you will advise companies or individuals on legal issues arising from the employer/employee relationship and the workplace. You might be asked to draft and negotiate new employment contracts or employee handbooks, to provide advice on issues arising out of existing contracts, to advise on how to bring an employment contract to an end and to manage any resulting liabilities, or to provide representation at Employment

Tribunals or mediations. Employment lawyers also deal with discrimination claims, staff restructuring and whistleblowing claims. You might also be asked to work as part of a wider team to advise on employment issues arising from corporate deals.

As a pension lawyer, you will advise on the creation of pension funds, and the way they are structured, managed, funded, and taxed. You may also be involved in resolving any disputes arising from these matters or working as part of a corporate deal advising on the implications of a particular transaction on a company's pension scheme.

"Employment is an extremely diverse practice area providing a mix between contentious and non-contentious work; enabling the development of a wide range of skills that are not always possible to develop in other practice areas. The type of work you do is ultimately determined by whether your practice focuses on advising individuals or commercial employer clients. I work in a commercial practice and really enjoy the breadth and diversity of the work for a variety of clients; including internationals and household names as well as senior individuals.

Commercial clients can be demanding due to the reactive nature of employment law—a client may call needing to understand how they can dismiss an employee with the least risk at 4.00pm on a Friday, so it can be pressurised. You need to be able to react to clients' needs promptly and to present commercial and practical solutions in a concise form, interpreting and cutting through the black letter law.

Equally employment law allows you to work on longer term projects with clients such as contract and policy reviews and large scale consultations; so you can build up great client relationships.

Tribunal litigation work in particular can be very rewarding (whether the client is successful in Tribunal or you succeed in negotiating a commercial settlement) but requires a high level of both communication and negotiation skill. It is important to appreciate that Tribunals have particular ways of working that you need to conform to whilst putting the client tactically in the best position; you need to be organised, proactive and mindful of deadlines. In addition managing clients' expectations is key—the outcome they seek may not be reasonable. Negotiating a settlement with a claimant in person can be frustrating so you need to be able to adapt your style to varying levels of understanding.

Client training, whether for senior HR personnel or shop floor managers, is a key part of employment practice and it is essential that you can present clearly and are confident speaking to range of audiences. Public speaking is therefore a key skill along with advocacy. Don't be concerned by this—the more you do, the easier it gets.

Employment law is a consistently changing area meaning time needs to be taken to keep up to date with legislative amendments and case law—particularly as these often hit the press quickly; so clients will be on the telephone wanting your advice, especially if they are well known and need to protect their reputation.

Corporate support is another challenging aspect of employment work; this requires the ability to work as part of a cross department/office team and in larger deals with other firms. You will need to be able to assimilate vast amounts of information and distil it down into the required format—usually highlighting employment risks, action points and calculating potential quantum. A working knowledge of corporate law and deal process is an asset. You also need to be ready to work corporate hours too when needed!"

Pamela Morris, Solicitor, Shoosmiths LLP

Environment

Environment lawyers advise on the potential environmental consequences of transactions and help their clients to operate within the requirements of the regulatory regime. They may also be called upon to defend clients who have been accused of failure to comply with the regulatory regime. There are limited opportunities to work with local authorities or the Environment Agency or a central government department, e.g. the Department for Environment, Food and Rural Affairs.

Family & Child Law

This is an increasingly broad area of practice ranging from legal issues arising out of the breakdown of relationships (e.g. divorce proceedings and the negotiation of financial settlements or living arrangements for children after divorce or break ups), to advising clients on cohabitation agreements or pre-nuptial agreements, and applying for injunctions in cases of domestic violence. Family law also involves situations where children could be taken into care (known as public family law). It is worth noting that family law has been another victim of the significant cuts in legal aid (though not all firms rely on publicly funded matters) and it would be worth investigating these cuts and the impact they have had on family lawyers and individuals who would previously have been eligible for legal aid but are no longer eligible.

"I decided to become a family lawyer because it is challenging and no two situations are ever the same. My work includes divorce proceedings and financial settlements, cohabitation disputes, dissolution of civil partnerships, separation agreements, pre and post nuptial agreements and residence and contact arrangements. To be a good family solicitor you need to have sound judgement, be committed, supportive and willing to listen as well as advise, and be able to create a professional balance. You must also have good communication and negotiation skills, be sensitive and trustworthy, and able to advise clearly and detach yourself from the emotional details of the case."

A Family Law Solicitor

Immigration

Corporate immigration lawyers advise companies and their employees/prospective employees on work permits, visas, and schemes for highly skilled migrants. They might also advise on visa issues for large sporting events or help business men and women secure visas and bring their families here from overseas. Other immigration lawyers advise individuals on their status and rights to remain in the UK and deal with asylum cases. This might include advising clients who have fled from persecution in their home country or individuals who have lived here for many years and are now being threatened with deportation. The work is challenging not least because of the restrictions in public funding and the vulnerability of the clients.

Insolvency

Insolvency lawyers advise on individual bankruptcies, corporate insolvencies, and restructuring of businesses. This work could include buying and selling assets belonging to insolvents, advising on corporate reorganisations, recovering assets through litigation, and bringing actions against directors of insolvent companies. Insolvency lawyers need to be flexible and commercial in order to achieve maximum value for creditors often within a very tight timeframe.

"I am a partner in a regional law firm specialising in restructuring and insolvency law. I am also a licensed insolvency practitioner. I have been specialising in re-structuring and insolvency for about 15 years, since qualifying as a solicitor.

My practice is focussed on acting for accountant insolvency practitioners, corporates and lenders. As a policy, we do not act for individual bankrupts or their families in disputes with IPs or lenders. I advise on all aspects of personal, corporate and partnership insolvency and re-structuring, primarily in relation to distressed businesses. I deal with all of the usual insolvency regimes, particularly administrations. The practice is a mixture of contentious and non-contentious advice and action, which ranges from solvent re-structuring through to High Court litigation.

The skills required to be an effective insolvency lawyer are quite disparate. A very sound working knowledge of the insolvency legislation is vital. Some of the law is fairly logical but a considerable amount is quite hard to distil into coherent advice and some of the new legislation is badly drafted. Also, a good working knowledge is needed of trust law, employment law (around TUPE), landlord & tenant, intellectual property and real property. As important is a practical approach to the work. Frequently, clients require advice or transactions documented in very short timescales and a good lawyer has to be able to assess what issues are commercially important in a deal. I have, on occasion, been instructed to handle a disposal in the afternoon, and closed the sale that night. As my clients are professional and sophisticated, I have to be on top of my game to win and maintain their confidence. Insolvency law develops quickly with several groundbreaking pieces of primary legislation in the last few years, ever changing case law and constantly changing best practice directives from professional bodies and the courts. This means that an effective insolvency lawyer needs to be technically adept and has to take the time to keep up to date on all legal developments. I probably spend on average four hours a week just keeping up to date.

What is great about being an insolvency lawyer is that I have a small number of key clients, where I have developed close working relationships. The ideal is to end up doing a portfolio of cases with the same clients, so you truly get to understand their commercial objectives. The work is intellectually very stimulating both from a technical legal perspective and in terms of understanding commercial issues surrounding business. I wouldn't want to do any other kind of law. I would get bored."
An Insolvency Lawyer

Intellectual Property

Intellectual Property lawyers advise clients on most effective ways to protect and exploit their intellectual property rights. You might find yourself advising on disputes arising from alleged infringement of intellectual property rights or carrying out searches at the beginning of a marketing campaign or product development process to ensure that your client does not infringe someone else's intellectual property rights. You might also advise clients on the registration of new intellectual property rights, the preparation and negotiation of commercial agreements to licence other parties to use the client's intellectual property rights, and the intellectual property implications of corporate transactions.

Media, Entertainment & Sports

The key areas of law underpinning these areas are contract law and intellectual property law. You might be dealing with reputation management issues, copyright claims, sponsorship deals, merchandising agreements, or claims arising from allegations of foul play, football transfers, and exploitation of intellectual property rights nationally and internationally. If you are working for a large corporation in the sports or entertainment world, you are also likely to get involved in advising on, structuring, and negotiating finance arrangements, corporate transactions and other commercial work.

Personal Injury/Clinical Negligence

Personal injury lawyers pursue or defend claims involving injuries and fatalities caused by accidents at work, on the road, or elsewhere. Lawyers tend to specialise in either claimant work (i.e. pursuing a claim) or defendant work (i.e. defending a claim). They often specialise further in particular areas of personal injury such as clinical negligence, employer's liability cases, or road traffic accidents.

> "My clients are all victims of negligence and will inevitably have been significantly injured through the fault of a third party, whether it is another road user or a skilled surgeon. They are vulnerable and in need of sound, solid legal advice. It is the role of the personal injury lawyer to understand the client's needs and goals and to ensure that they are met with speed and efficiency.
>
> My clients can be angry, upset and confused with what has happened to them and so it is important to have sympathy

and empathy in equal quantity. The personal injury lawyer would not be at all surprised to be acting for any given client for up to five years and sometimes even more. Personal injury and clinical negligence cases are rarely straightforward and require skills in each of the areas taught throughout the LPC and training contract, not least, advocacy, drafting and negotiation skills.

What makes my job worthwhile is to know that, at the end of a case, my clients are confident that they have received a quality service and knowing that those who are most severely injured are being cared for without hindrance of financial constraints.

For those hoping to specialise in personal injury or clinical negligence, firstly, you will need to leave any fears of blood and gore that you may harbour at the door. Secondly, you will need to be fastidious and confident in your advice and when discussing a case with your opponent or in Court. Thirdly, and very importantly, you must be able to explain things clearly and to talk to people who, quite often, are incredibly apprehensive about seeing a solicitor. After all, you're the one who has to make the "No Win—No Fee Agreement" sound simple for the client!"

James King, Partner, GoodLaw Solicitors

Private Client

Private client lawyers provide specialist advice on the legal aspects of their clients' personal affairs. This could include drafting and administering wills, setting up or reorganising trust funds, and advising on tax liabilities.

"My work involves advising clients about their personal affairs within a legal framework, including making wills, appointing people to act on their behalf in dealing with finances and personal welfare, administering estates, setting up trusts and providing advice about different types of taxes and general advice about elderly client issues, for example nursing home fees and welfare benefits. The elderly are often forgotten and I enjoy the time spent with elderly clients and the fact that for them a visit from their solicitor can be fun, rather than daunting. A good private client solicitor is someone who is intelligent with a friendly and approachable nature, a sense of humour, good communication skills, and a commercial mind."

Jennifer Walker, Solicitor

"I work in the private client team of a leading regional firm. I already knew that I would be interested in private client work because I previously worked in financial services and there are a number of parallels between the two. I really enjoyed the equity and trusts modules of my degree course and found that I loved everything to do with tax on my LPC. I realise that puts me in a minority! What I really love about private client work is the enormous variety. Private client solicitors advise on wills and lifetime tax planning, protecting family wealth, powers of attorney and mental capacity issues, probate and the administration of estates and the creation and administration of trusts. You need to have excellent inter-personal skills, be really proficient at drafting, good at maths and be prepared to get to grips with complex tax rules. You also get to meet all sorts of fascinating people.

Private client practice is an area where you can expect to carry on studying after you qualify. As soon as I qualified, I embarked upon attaining the Society of Trust and Estate Practitioners' Diploma in trusts and estates. This consists of four three-hour exam papers and is a must if you want to get on as a private client solicitor. I have recently also taken an accountancy exam in inheritance tax, trusts and estates. Over the past three years I have started to specialise in trusts, which is a really complex area of law. As well as advising clients on creating of trusts, I also manage around 100 family trusts, which requires me to build good working relationships with the families, accountants and investment managers. Another aspect of my work is advising clients on how to put things right when a trust has been incorrectly managed; sadly this sometimes means being the bearer of bad news in the form of a large tax bill.

> I love the complexity of the work, the intellectual challenge and the fact that there is always so much more to learn."
> *Lorna Sansom, Associate, B P Collins LLP*

Professional Discipline

All professionals must comply with the professional and ethical standards which are set out by the relevant regulator. If an individual breaks the code of conduct set down by their professional regulator, they will face investigation and, if a finding is made against them, they might be suspended, disciplined or struck off. Lawyers in this field represent either the individual or the regulatory body in the investigations and the preparation and conduct of such disciplinary hearings.

> "Regulatory (or Professional Disciplinary) law is a niche but thriving legal sector. As a Regulatory solicitor at one of the UK's leading Regulatory law firms, I deal with a range of healthcare and non-healthcare cases, some of which are high profile matters. Examples of regulated individuals include: doctors, dentists and nurses in the healthcare sector; and architects, accountants and solicitors in the non-healthcare sector.
>
> A large part of my role involves completing a fitness to practise investigation on behalf of regulatory bodies. This comprises of: conducting witness interviews; drafting statements; seeking disclosure of documents; liaising with experts and reporting the investigative findings; as well as providing advice to the client.
>
> A fitness to practise investigation will often proceed to a hearing. When preparing for a hearing, I will be involved in instructing counsel, drafting charges and disclosing evidence to the defence.
>
> My work as a Regulatory solicitor is not always prosecution based. Where no conflict arises, I act on behalf of individual registrants and defend their case against their regulatory body.
>
> Many Regulatory solicitors will also be involved in High Court and Court of Appeal cases. Therefore a working knowledge of

the Civil Procedure Rules is always helpful. I have had to prepare both Applicant and Respondent cases for the High Court.

To succeed as a Regulatory solicitor you must be capable of managing a large and complex case load which will undoubtedly have competing deadlines. On the technical side, it is helpful to have a reasonable knowledge of the Civil Procedure Rules and the Data Protection Act. Regulatory law also has a strong human element and many of the cases that you deal with will have had a serious impact on a person's life; whether that person is the registrant themselves, a patient, client or a witness. Due to this, good interpersonal skills are a must."

Keziah Pearson, Solicitor, Blake Morgan LLP

Public Law

Public law is wide-ranging and could involve anything from judicial review of a decision taken by an education authority to challenging the level of care provided to an elderly resident of a local authority care home. It might also involve proceedings to determine whether a child should be taken into care, planning enforcement, or environmental health issues.

"I enjoy solving problems and quite often the people who succeed in local government are those who like to get their teeth into a problem and find a solution to it. Quite often this involves lots of legal research and going back to the statutes to make sure there is a legal power for the council's actions. I also enjoy the breadth of experience and diversity of work, and the fact that you never know what you will be doing from one day to the next. But, for me, one of the best things about working for a public authority is that we are delivering services to the local community and if you make something happen in local government, quite often it has a wider benefit for the community."

Sarita Riley, Legal Services Manager (Corporate & Environment) Southampton City Council

Residential Property

Residential property work involves buying and selling domestic properties for individuals. The lawyer's role is to draft the legal documentation, investigate the title to the property and address any defects, ensure that the transfer of funds at completion goes smoothly, and deal with post-completion formalities.

> "I specialise in both residential and commercial property transactions. My residential property work involves drafting contracts for the sale of land and property, approval of contracts, preparation of transfers, investigation of legal title, raising pre-contract enquiries, carrying out conveyancing searches and reporting to clients, completing stamp duty land tax returns, and dealing with commercial lending institutions. My role is to ensure that the process of transferring the legal title to the property is dealt with correctly. If there are any defects in the legal title to a property, my role is to ensure that these are properly rectified or addressed before completion. The most enjoyable aspects of my work are the direct contact with clients and the positive feedback I receive from them. It is also very satisfying to be able to manage and take responsibility for your own workload and take charge from the beginning right through to a successful conclusion of the transaction.
>
> To be a good property lawyer, you must have a clear understanding of the principles of land law, be able to communicate with individuals from all walks of life, be honest, hardworking and extremely organised as you will have a significant caseload at any one time."
>
> *A Real Estate Lawyer*

Shipping

Shipping law divides into two areas: dry shipping and wet shipping. Dry work involves contractual issues concerning carriage of goods and ship building. You might also get involved in sale and purchase agreements and insurance. Wet shipping involves disputes over ships and accidents at sea causing the loss of, or damage to, goods or ships. Some lawyers specialise in ship finance which involves structuring the finance for a new construction or the re-financing of an existing ship.

10 WHAT ARE FIRMS LOOKING FOR IN PROSPECTIVE TRAINEES?

DO YOU FIT THE PROFILE?

It is essential to find out what law firms are looking for in prospective trainees so you can tailor your applications accordingly. This requires more than a general appraisal of the key qualities that make a good solicitor; you need to find out about the culture of the firms you are applying to and what they look for in their recruitment processes. Inevitably, there will be some overlap between firms, but each one might place emphasis on certain skills or experience over others so you must do your research and target your applications carefully. Regional firms will expect you to justify why you wish to work for that firm in that particular area, and all firms will expect you to have a clear understanding of their profile, key practice areas and clients. Thus, a significant part of your preparations should be spent researching individual firms, building your network of contacts within the profession, critically reviewing your CV and addressing any gaps in your experience or key skills so that you are well placed to meet the expectations of your target firms.

It would not be unreasonable of you to think that this is a very time consuming exercise with little immediate gain. However, rest assured it will pay dividends in the end because success in this process requires you to play the long game. If you get this part right, and make 10 carefully targeted applications, your success rate should be higher than if you had made 40 applications to random firms using recycled standard form responses.

ACADEMIC QUALIFICATIONS & UNIVERSITIES

It would be worth investigating whether your target firms attract and/or recruit trainees from particular universities. You will find that some firms draw heavily from Oxbridge (University of Oxford and University of Cambridge) or Russell Group (24 Leading UK Universities—see *http://www.russellgroup.ac.uk* for more information) institutions, whilst others take trainees from a more diverse range of institutions. This is worth investigating to help you to make realistic applications and to make sure that you find a firm which will offer you a good cultural fit. You will get a sense of the profile of trainees by reading testimonials on websites, speaking to recruitment officers and trainees at networking events, and by reading firm profiles in publications such as *http://www.lawcareers.net* and the Chambers & Partners Student Guide (*http://www.chambersstudent.co.uk*). Your university or law school careers advisors will also have a good feel for the profile of trainees at particular law firms so it would be well worth speaking to them before you make your applications. None of this is to say that there is no point applying to a firm if you are not attending one of its preferred universities but it is probably as well to be aware of any connections which other applicants may have over you.

It is also important to research the threshold academic qualifications. Most firms require a 2:1 degree and many will take A Level grades and sometimes GCSEs into account at some stage during the recruitment process (some even set specific minimum requirements, particularly International, Magic Circle and other City firms). It is fair to say that, unless you have compelling extenuating circumstances, it is pointless applying to a firm which requires a minimum of BBB at A Level, if you have only achieved BBC because your application will be rejected automatically.

If you desperately want to train with a particular firm but have missed their threshold grades by a small margin, you could consider getting in touch with the graduate recruitment manager if you have evidence of compelling extenuating circumstances to explain the lower grade. Some firms might be willing to make an exception if they are persuaded that you had a bad experience and if you can play your strengths in other areas (work experience, exceptional skills development in a particular area, pro bono activities, etc.). For some firms, however, exceptions will not be made where grades are concerned and, for yet others, they will only be prepared to lower their grade requirements to a certain point no matter how unfortunate your circumstances.

Notwithstanding all of that, do not lose heart if your grades are weak, you may still be able to secure a training contract but you must be aware that you will have to be more flexible and creative when deciding which firms to apply to. You might also need to boost your CV with some relevant work experience or paralegal experience to compensate for the weaker grades. Be ambitious, but be realistically ambitious.

TARGETED APPLICATIONS AND REGIONAL LINKS

London firms expect to attract candidates from a wide geographic area, and therefore it is less important to demonstrate links to the city. However, firms based in other parts of the country will want to know that you are likely to stay with them after qualification. If you are from Manchester and apply for training contracts in Bristol, the firms will want to know why you want to train with them. They do not want to spend a considerable amount of time and money training you, only for you to return to Manchester on qualification. You will need to be able to justify your choice of location at interview.

MOTIVATION TO BECOME A SOLICITOR

All legal recruiters look for evidence of motivation to become a solicitor and a motivation to join that particular firm (or at the very least an equivalent firm in terms of size, culture, practice areas, and location). The training contract is a significant investment for firms so they want to be sure that you are worth investing in. They certainly do not want to spend money training you only for you to leave at the end of your contract because you do not want to be a lawyer anymore or have decided to move to a different type of firm.

You can demonstrate your motivation through evidence of work experience or because you have been involved in particular voluntary work or projects at university, e.g. pro bono work. You need to show that you understand what it is to be a lawyer and how law firms work. If you have researched your options thoroughly, you will be able to speak knowledgeably and confidently at interviews and show that you have given serious consideration to alternative options to reach an informed decision to pursue this career and train at that type of firm.

KEY COMPETENCIES

Whilst it is important to research individual firms, there are certain skills and characteristics which all law firms are looking for and which are commonly tested in application forms and during interviews. I have listed these key competencies below with a brief explanation of each one. Keep these in mind as you draft CVs, covering letters and application forms and think about how you can demonstrate them through your own experiences. I have included some examples of how you might demonstrate each competency and I hope you will find it reassuring to see how many of your day-to-day experiences can be used to support your responses.

> "It's not just about advising on the law; you have to be able to go out there and develop the business. We will expect you to have excellent academics, impressive critical reasoning skills, and you must also have something about you in the personality stakes (although that is difficult to define). It's all about building relationships at the end of the day and that is not necessarily related to having a brilliant academic brain."
>
> *Lynn Ford, HR Manager, Blake Morgan LLP*

Attention To Detail

The nature of their work means that lawyers are expected to demonstrate attention to detail. Recruiters will be looking for evidence of this in your application form and during interviews. You may have had a job which required close attention to detail, e.g. as an assistant in a pharmacy or as a secretary. Have you participated in any stock taking activities at work where attention to detail is a key part of the process? Have you participated in a negotiating competition which required close analysis of the facts and careful planning to ensure success?

Paralegal at Law Firm X: *During this period of employment, one of my responsibilities was to cover the phones at lunchtime to take new enquiries on our personal injury helpdesk. This involved several key skills: the ability to listen carefully to ensure that I recorded the key details from the client; the ability to ask pertinent questions to make sure I clarified important details and obtained a clear understanding of the potential claim; and the ability to create a full and accurate record of the call so the case manager could allocate the work to the most appropriate fee earner.*

Communication Skills

Solicitors have to explain complex areas of law in simple terms to clients and they also need to ensure that clients' goals are achieved through the legal documentation which they prepare. Thus, excellent oral and written communication skills are essential. Good listening skills are also an important part of this; you must be aware of your client's key concerns and priorities and able to sift out irrelevant details from all the information they mention. You may be able to demonstrate these skills through your extra-curricular activities. Have you had a job where you have had to communicate with customers or clients? Have you taken part in mooting or debating or client interviewing competitions? Have you acted as a course representative? Are you a member of a drama club? Do you maintain a blog or have you ever contributed to a magazine or newsletter? Have you had a role in a society where you have had to communicate with members or advertise events? Are you a member of a sports team where communication with other players is essential? Do you coach or teach others?

Industrial Placement: *I spent a year working as a Business Development Assistant at a company which supplied make up and beauty products to trade and retail customers. My key* *responsibilities in this role were to write articles to email to customers and post on the website; to update the company blog; and to manage the corporate Twitter feed. Excellent written communication skills were intrinsic to these tasks since I had to be able to communicate information clearly and effectively. I also needed to adjust the style and content depending on who the communications were aimed at (trade or retail customers) and how they were being distributed.*

Organisational Skills

In legal practice you will have to balance a varied caseload and meet the needs of several clients at the same time. Effective time management and organisational skills are therefore essential and recruiters will be looking for evidence of these skills from your application form or CV. Have you had to balance paid work and study? Have you had any positions of responsibility that required excellent organisational skills? Have you organised any charity events? Do you have a part-time job which requires good organisational and time management skills?

Hockey Team: I am a member of the university hockey first team. I train twice a week and have two matches a week. This is a heavy schedule to balance alongside my studies and means that I have to be organised and manage my time effectively, especially during the exam period or the run up to coursework deadlines. I have developed good working practices to ensure that I use my time efficiently, e.g. writing up notes immediately after seminars and lectures, dedicating a set time every weekend for consolidation, making use of my electronic diary to note key deadlines, and starting coursework early to avoid last minute panics.

Ability To Use Your Initiative

Often as a solicitor you find yourself in a situation where there may not be a senior fee earner available to help you so you need to be prepared to have confidence in your ability and be able to take the initiative in certain circumstances. How can you demonstrate this to employers? Have you worked as a student representative where you have had to take the initiative to achieve change for others? Have you taken action on behalf of your housemates in response to problems with your student housing? Have you had to use your initiative during a crisis at work? Have you had to take the lead during a trip with friends? Have you held a management role on a committee or in a shop or restaurant? Have you set up your own small business or a university society?

Volunteer at After School Club: *Whilst at university, I volunteered at a local after school club. It became clear to me that parents wanted to know what their child had done during the session and whether they had had anything to eat and drink. Therefore, I suggested to the Club Leader that we could give out a simple form when each child left the club which would highlight two activities that the child had been involved in, whether they had eaten or drunk anything, and whether there were any other issues to highlight to the parent. The Club Leader liked the form and obtained permission from the Head Teacher to start using it straight away. The form was approved and proved to be very popular with parents.*

It is also important to note that there is a balance to be struck here: you need to demonstrate sound judgement in deciding whether to act on your own initiative or whether to wait and seek advice from a senior colleague. You will be working in a highly regulated professional environment and negligence claims can result all too easily so you need to take care in deciding when to act and when to seek advice.

Resilience and Stamina

Working as a solicitor requires resilience whether you are intending to specialise in commercial or private client work. You will often find yourself working to tight deadlines and/or late into the night so you must be able to develop strategies to enable you to work effectively under pressure. You will also need to accept that you will be on a steep learning curve which will continue throughout your career and you will need to learn how to take constructive criticism in order to develop into a competent and well-rounded solicitor. You will sometimes need to deliver unwelcome news to clients about their case or transaction, which will require thick skin as you may end up bearing the brunt of their anger or frustration. Lastly, you may well encounter some very demanding clients and colleagues and you will need to find a way to work with them.

Can you draw on any examples to demonstrate these skills? Do you work in a pressurised environment, perhaps a busy pub or restaurant? Have you ever worked in a highly competitive sales environment? Do you have experience of any endurance sports or experiences which have required considerable stamina? Have you survived in challenging environments during a period of independent travel? Have you achieved a high level of achievement in a particular hobby, e.g. a black belt in martial arts or Grade 8 with a musical instrument?

Kitchen Assistant: My work as a kitchen assistant at Green Gables Pub requires me to work effectively in a challenging, high pressure environment. There are 15 tables in the restaurant and we have 2 sittings at the weekends so it gets very busy and hot in the kitchen. I have to get the orders out on time and to a good standard despite the time pressures. I have been working in the kitchen for 18 months during which time I have proved that I can work effectively under pressure and still maintain a good level of service and a safe working environment.

Leadership and Teamwork

The ability to build relationships and work as part of a team is a key skill in the armoury of any good lawyer. For example, as a corporate lawyer acting for a client on the disposal of a business, you will be working on the deal with lawyers from other departments in your firm (e.g. those advising on tax, property, employment, and pension issues), lawyers acting for the buyer, and other professional advisors working on both sides, e.g. accountants and bankers. Your client will rely on you to develop effective working relationships in order to get the deal done. You may be able to demonstrate these skills through your extra-curricular activities. Are you a member of any clubs or societies? Do you play any team sports? Have you worked with other students on assessed presentations? Have you participated in any group challenges, e.g. Duke of Edinburgh Awards? Do you work with other students as part of a pro-bono initiative? Do you work as part of a team in your part-time job in a bar or shop?

Captain of Football Team: I am a keen footballer and enjoy the opportunity to exercise and socialise with a great group of people. Success depends on everyone investing time in training and during matches to avoid letting the team down. It also requires players to encourage each other and to put the needs of the team first. Taking on the role of captain has provided me with a fantastic leadership opportunity. It can be difficult when we have had a run of poor results but I have learnt the importance of encouraging and motivating the team by identifying and praising positive aspects of a game even if the end result was disappointing. Of course, we also have to discuss and address weak areas, but it is usually possible to find something positive to end the team talk with!

Commercial Awareness

This is something that all law firms are looking for. Essentially, it means that you understand how businesses operate and the effects of current affairs/business trends on your clients' businesses. It also means that you appreciate the importance of "fee earning" and the commercial challenges facing the legal sector. Chapter 12 covers commercial awareness in more detail and provides guidance on how you can develop it.

OTHER ATTRIBUTES

Evidence of Vocational Skills and the Potential To Be a Good Lawyer

How can you show that you have the key skills that are required to be an excellent lawyer, e.g. negotiation skills, problem solving skills, advocacy skills, research skills? You do not necessarily have to have worked in a legal environment to demonstrate these skills, but participating in pro bono work is a great place to start. Can you demonstrate any experience of applying the law to real life practical problems (perhaps through Citizens Advice Bureau experience or other pro bono work)? Can you demonstrate that you have developed your interviewing, negotiating or legal research skills to an impressive level through work experience or extra-curricular competitions? Have you ever drafted legal documents and/or business correspondence?

Research Skills: I took a gap year between university and law school. I spent the first six months working at Sainsbury's and planning my four month trip. This required very careful planning and lots of research because I was on a tight budget but I had certain sights I really wanted to see whilst the opportunity was available to me. I researched each part of the trip in detail to find the most cost-effective flights, internal transfers, and accommodation. I also kept an eye on exchange rates so I converted my money at the best possible moment.

Problem Solving: I work in a café on a part-time basis. At the start of a busy Saturday morning shift, the coffee machine broke down. Customers were not happy and we were worried that we might lose some of them to the other café in the village. I suggested that we could buy some instant coffee from the local supermarket and offer all customers a free instant coffee and refill as a temporary measure until the machine was fixed. I realised that the instant coffee would cost us next to nothing to make, and hoped that this idea would stop us from losing profitable food orders and the goodwill of regular customers. We implemented the idea and it worked well.

Negotiating Skills: My housemates and I found a house we liked but the fridge freezer was too small. The landlord refused to install a larger one, stating that the old tenants had been happy with it and it was only recently purchased. I negotiated with him and *managed to convince him to buy and install a larger model. I was able to take advantage of the fact that the market was slowing down because most students had found accommodation and I was confident that he would not want to lose our tenancy over a fridge freezer. I presented him with a pack of particulars for other student houses in the area which all had larger appliances, and I said that we would pay our deposits that day if he promised in writing to install a larger fridge freezer by the time we moved into the house. He agreed and we ended up staying in the property for two years!*

Outside Interests

Recruitment partners are looking for evidence of achievement other than academic success. This shows that you are a well-rounded individual and can also demonstrate focus and motivation. Your extra-curricular achievements and outside interests can provide an excellent bank of evidence to show that you have what it takes to be a first rate lawyer.

DEMONSTRATING YOUR SKILLS TO EMPLOYERS

"Whenever you make an application, it is not enough to just say that you are good at something. You must have evidence to support every claim."

Lorna Sansom, Associate, B P Collins LLP

When preparing responses to questions in application forms, you must support your application with examples to demonstrate how and when you have developed or used a particular skill. You will be used to drawing on sources or other evidence to support your statements in academic essays and now you must develop the same skill for your training contract applications. Many students fail to make effective applications because they do not stop and think about how to sell their experiences to prospective employers, or perhaps they fail to recognise the value of those experiences themselves. You may have had a rich and varied range of amazing life and work experiences but that is of no use to you if you do not know how to capitalise on them in application forms and at interviews to show how and why they demonstrate potential to be a successful solicitor.

To help you with this process, make a list of your hobbies and other interests, your work experience history (paid and unpaid), any competitions you have been involved in at school, college, university or law school, voluntary work you have undertaken and any other experiences you have had in the last five years (e.g. travelling, fundraising events, sports tournaments, etc.). Then use that list to complete the "Map of Experiences" at the end of this chapter. The aim is to have one or two experiences to evidence your competence in the areas listed in the left hand column. Ideally, you should draw on a different example for each competency. You can add additional criteria for the particular role you are applying for (you should be able to identify these by reading the firm's website and recruitment information).

Examples could include experiences arising from a part-time job, pro bono work, sporting activities, academic work, positions of responsibility at university, or participation in curricular or extra-curricular competitions such as mooting, negotiating, debating or client interviewing. Think about why you got involved in each activity, what role you played, what you learnt, and how and why it shows that you have the potential to be a good solicitor. Try to draw on specific examples, rather than general experiences (e.g. your involvement in organising the Student Law Society fundraising ball, rather than the fact that you were the social secretary of the Student Law Society in a particular year).

Once you have finished the Map of Experiences, review it with a critical eye and try to identify areas where you need a bit more experience or where you have no experience at all. Try to rate each skill between one and three where one would indicate that you have no experience in that area and three would indicate that you are very confident in that area. You can then set some specific goals and take a strategic approach to enhancing your CV in the future.

This process involves a good deal of work at the outset, but many students report that it becomes a really useful tool and saves a lot of time when it comes to actually filling in competency based application forms (i.e. those that ask you to draw on past experience to demonstrate your skill in a particular area). There is no point sitting down to write application forms later this year, or in a year's time, only to find that you have no material to work from: it would be far better to make that discovery now so that you can start addressing the problem straight away.

If you wish, you can download this document at *http://www. fromstudenttosolicitor.co.uk*. I have included a sample map of experience at the end of Ch.16 to show how this process makes your life easier when it comes to completing application forms.

Competency	Situation	Task	Demonstrate the Competency
Attention to detail			
Excellent oral and written communication skills			
Excellent organisational skills and ability to prioritise/manage time effectively			
Ability to act on your own initiative			
Resilience and ability to work under pressure			
Ability to work effectively within a team			
Excellent research skills			
Excellent problem solving skills			
Ability to negotiate effectively			

Fig.3 Map of Experiences

11 ENHANCING YOUR CV WITH WORK EXPERIENCE AND OTHER ACTIVITIES

WHY IS LEGAL WORK EXPERIENCE SO IMPORTANT?

In today's competitive legal market, you are unlikely to secure a training contract, and possibly even a vacation scheme, without some evidence of legal work experience on your CV. Although the prospect of applying for work experience might seem daunting and time consuming, the rewards are more than worth the effort. Read the list below to get a sense of the benefits of work experience for students.

Gain an insight into the profession/develop commercial awareness—even a short period of work experience in a law firm provides a valuable insight into the day-to-day working life of individuals within the profession. Spending some time in law firms or other commercial organisations will also allow you to understand how organisations are structured, how offices are run, and how line management chains operate. You will also find that you pick up on key business language/terminology and will hopefully be able to use it in context during interviews or subsequent placements.

You should refer to Ch.12 for more advice on what commercial awareness means and how you can develop it. In fact, it would be a good idea to read that chapter in detail before you embark on a work placement to make sure you maximise the benefits of your exposure to a commercial environment.

Find networking opportunities—if you have completed some work experience with a particular firm, you will not be an anonymous application when you apply; the recruitment partners or managers will have had first-hand experience of your abilities. They will have seen how you perform in a work environment and therefore will be able to make an informed decision about whether or not to employ you. Many firms ultimately offer training contracts to students who attended vacation schemes with them. Furthermore, one work experience opportunity might lead to others if you make a good impression and the fee earners are prepared to recommend you to other contacts within the profession.

Demonstrate commitment and informed decision making—law firms will expect to see evidence of legal work placements. It reassures them of your commitment, demonstrates an appreciation of the realities of a career in law, and shows that you have made an informed decision to pursue this career path. When you apply for training contracts, you will be asked "Why do you want to be a solicitor?" and "Why do you want to work for a firm like this one?". Work experience will help you formulate and support answers to those questions and will demonstrate that you are a motivated individual who has been willing to invest time and effort to further your career.

Test your decision making—this is not just about proving your commitment to prospective employers. Securing work experience opportunities is in your own interest so you can be sure that you have considered all avenues and made the right choice of career, practice area and firm before you embark on a rigorous application process and career path. It will also help you determine whether or not you have the skills and motivation to get through the training and survive as a qualified solicitor. You might find that you do not actually enjoy your work experience, or you discover that you lack the key skills and motivation to survive the recruitment process. This is an equally valuable outcome: it is much better to make this decision before you invest considerable time and money in the GDL or LPC. You will also have a good idea of what you want to avoid in other career options, which should make your research easier.

> "Work experience is the only way you can find out what will suit you. If you can get work experience before your vacation schemes then that will help but, if not, try to use your vacation

schemes to work out whether that type of career or firm will suit you because studying the law is so different to actually working in it. Even if you love the law degree, you might hate legal practice and vice versa. Also don't forget that it's a really broad profession and there will be areas of law and legal practice that you haven't even studied at university."

Joanna Pennick, Solicitor

Bolster answers on application forms and at interview—work experience (in every sense, not just legal work experience) is also a useful way to demonstrate key competencies in application forms and at interview. For example, you might like to draw on part of your work experience to demonstrate that you can work effectively under pressure or that you can take the initiative to complete a task on time. You will also find that you will develop some key transferable skills through work experience, e.g. communication skills, team working, time management, customer service skills, etc. and these can be used to support answers to questions at interviews.

Show that you are an attractive candidate—evidence of work experience placements on CVs and application forms suggests to prospective employers that you are worth considering because you have obviously impressed other employers enough to convince them to take an interest in you. Work experience also demonstrates to employers that you were sufficiently motivated to find experience and commit to it alongside your studies and other interests.

Boost confidence—it can be daunting to find yourself in a professional working environment when you are straight out of university. Spending time in a law firm or other commercial organisation will teach you how to navigate social interaction with people at different levels within the organisation. Hopefully, you will also gain some experience of basic office administration such as preparing reports or presentations, photocopying, taking telephone messages and drafting basic correspondence. You will also understand the importance of respecting a professional dress code and will have an understanding of general office etiquette. These experiences will prove invaluable in boosting your confidence when you embark on a vacation scheme or training contract, and they will also help you to project a more professional impression at interview.

WHEN SHOULD I SECURE WORK EXPERIENCE?

The short answer is that it is never too early to get some work experience and many students have already completed one or two placements before they start university. However, do not be deterred if you are in your first or second year of university and have never set foot in a law firm. It is never too late to start, and you will be amazed at how quickly you can make up lost ground if you are committed and motivated. If you don't have any work experience at all, you are probably going to have to accept that your training contract applications will have to be delayed while you focus on securing work experience opportunities but a year's delay will be well worth it if you end up making better quality, carefully targeted applications as a result of the work experience.

HOW MUCH WORK EXPERIENCE DO I NEED?

There is no definitive answer to this question. The bottom line is that you need to complete enough placements to suggest to an employer that you have made an informed decision to pursue a training contract, and to reassure yourself that you have made the right decision in terms of your future career choice. You will also need to show some consistency in terms of gaining work experience by completing at least one placement a year. An employer might question your commitment if you have a small cluster of placements in your first year and then nothing else on your CV until after your LPC.

DIFFERENT TYPES OF LEGAL WORK EXPERIENCE

Legal work experience can be divided into a number of different categories. Each type of work experience is dealt with separately below, followed by some general tips for success during extended work placements or work experience.

Open Days

Some firms run open days as a way of getting a large number of prospective trainees to visit the firm on one day, rather than running weeks of work experience programmes. The open days are usually offered in addition to formal vacation schemes, although sometimes they are part of the application process leading to a place on such schemes. You will need to visit individual firms' websites to find out if they run open days, and when they will be taking place. You will also need to make sure you apply in good time as competition for places can be fierce.

Open days provide an opportunity to visit a firm and speak to members of its staff (generally trainee solicitors, the graduate recruitment manager and perhaps also one or two of the recruitment partners). An open day provides an excellent opportunity to get a feel for the culture of a firm, to find out more about the structure and quality of its training contract, and to make a positive impression on the key decision makers. Generally speaking, candidates will be given a tour of the offices, a talk by the recruitment partner or graduate recruitment manager, an opportunity to meet and ask questions of members of staff (often over lunch or coffee), and perhaps also a group exercise which will be good practice for assessment centres and vacation schemes. You will need to look at firms' websites to find exact details of what to expect from their open days and how to apply. You should also find out whether they will reimburse your travel expenses.

Why Should You Attend an Open Day?

You can mention attendance at open days in the work experience section of your CV. It shows that you have used your initiative and are motivated to find out more about the legal recruitment process and career opportunities. It is also a very effective and efficient way of gathering information about the culture and working environment of individual firms: you are able to spend time in their offices and meet key members of staff but the whole visit is over in one day. Finally, open days are a great way to make contacts and they provide an opportunity to create a positive impression on those involved in the recruitment process.

Tips for Open Days

Make sure that you arrive on time (if not a bit early).

Think carefully about your appearance. You should wear a suit and make sure that your shoes are polished and your hair, nails, and any accessories are neat and appropriate for a business environment.

First impressions are crucial. Never underestimate the power of a firm handshake, a warm smile, and a confident (but not arrogant) demeanour.

Take open days seriously and treat them as part of the recruitment process. Maintain a professional attitude throughout the day and be polite to everyone you meet, regardless of their status within the firm. Feedback will be given at the end of each event and you do not want to be remembered as the one who over indulged in the wine or was rude to the receptionist on arrival.

Mix with the other candidates as well as the firm's employees. Recruiters will be interested to see how you respond to your peers and how confidently you can navigate a networking event.

Research the firm before the event and, if possible, find out about the background of any important individuals who will be attending, e.g. the graduate recruitment manager and any partners.

Speak to trainees as well as the HR Manager and Partners. The trainees are closest to where you are now and their insights are likely to be particularly useful in deciding whether this is the firm for you. Read the guidance in Chs 13 and 18 on networking skills and assessment centre activities. Read a quality newspaper regularly and make sure that you are well informed about current affairs to avoid being caught out. For open days at City firms and other commercial firms, make sure that you read the financial pages regularly and are well informed about economic issues, recent deals, and financial news stories.

Think of questions to ask but remember that your question will reveal a lot about you. Do not ask something that you could find out easily by reviewing the firm's website or that shows you to be poorly informed about the legal recruitment process. Do ask something which shows a genuine engagement with the firm and/or its key practice areas, or which reveals a genuine understanding of the challenges/ opportunities facing the legal sector in the current market. Send a thank you email after the event to acknowledge the effort that was invested in the day, and to remind the graduate recruitment manager of your name.

Work Shadowing and Informal Work Experience

Students used to be able to write directly to firms and arrange ad hoc periods of work experience during the holidays. While this is still the case with some of the smaller high street firms and public sector employers, larger firms have formalised their work experience programmes so that they have become almost as difficult to secure as vacation schemes and training contracts. So, how can you maximise your chances of securing work experience?

Enter competitions—sometimes universities and LPC providers run internal competitions where the first prize is a period of work experience with a local firm of solicitors. You should seriously consider entering such competitions: you will have a new skill to add to your CV and there is the prospect of work experience if you win.

Keep your eyes open—some adverts for work experience will be distributed via your Law Faculty or university/law school careers centre. Make sure you are on the circulation list for such emails and pay a visit to the careers centre early in the academic year to make sure you know how to access information about forthcoming vacancies.

Follow up on contacts—make use of each and every contact in your professional and personal networks. If your friend's mum is a solicitor, why not ask for work experience with her firm? If your dad's business uses a particular firm of solicitors, perhaps you could ask to spend a couple of days with them. If you meet a solicitor at a networking event, why not follow up with an email to ask if you could shadow him/her for a day. Don't be afraid to make new contacts either. Perhaps you could sit in on some court hearings and approach one of the solicitors at the end. This is quite daunting, but perfectly acceptable as long as you are professional and courteous, respectful of the other demands on their time, and accept that there is no guarantee that they will say yes.

> "I know a couple of people who rang up the graduate recruitment people at a particular firm and asked if they could go in and speak to them. I'm sure not every firm will do that but it might be worth picking up the phone to see if you can get in and speak to somebody."
>
> *A Trainee Solicitor*

Do not be too fussy about the level of contact that is offered to you—if someone offers to meet with you for an informal chat about your career, accept their offer and see where it leads. A short meeting after work or a series of email exchanges might eventually lead to a work experience opportunity or an introduction to another useful contact. Neither should you make the mistake of thinking that the only worthwhile opportunities are those with senior partners or graduate recruitment managers at law firms. Quite often junior members of staff will be just as helpful and they are likely to have more time available to spend with you. Finally, do not be too fussy about the content of the work experience. The most important factor is often not what you did, but how effectively you "sell" the experience to prospective employers.

> "Don't underestimate any contact or period of work experience, however insignificant it might seem. I didn't have any contacts in the profession but my friend's mum was a personal injury lawyer so I did some work experience with her and put together a database of recent claims and percentage success rates. Even that gave me something to talk about at interviews although the work wasn't actually relevant to a City firm."
>
> *A Trainee Solicitor at a City Firm*

Make a speculative application—it is still possible to arrange work experience by writing to a firm directly. These are known as speculative applications and can be made by letter or via email. Try to direct your application to a named individual, rather than writing an impersonal "Dear Sirs" letter. Once you have targeted specific firms, you need to look at their websites or call them to find out who the graduate recruitment officer is. This will enable you to direct your letter to someone specific, and you can follow it up with a telephone call if you haven't heard anything within a couple of weeks.

If you decide to write to firms to arrange work experience, you should be flexible in terms of the length of the placement and who you will be working with. You might like to start by asking to shadow a solicitor for a day. Essentially, this means that you will follow the solicitor for the day sitting in on meetings, accompanying him/her to court (if applicable) and generally watching what goes on in the day-to-day working life of that solicitor. In a busy law firm, a day's shadowing is often much easier to arrange than a full week's experience because you will not necessarily be given any work of your own and it is a much shorter time commitment for the solicitor. It is also less of a risk for the law firm because they can get to know you and your abilities before they commit to a longer period of work experience.

Your letter should be no more than one side of A4 and will need to be targeted towards each individual firm. You should explain what you hope to gain from the experience, your background and future career plans, and why you are particularly interested in working for that firm. If you have an interest in a particular area of practice, you should state that in the letter and explain how and why you have developed that interest. Perhaps you have been studying the area in one of your units or perhaps you have decided to focus on that area of law in your dissertation. Perhaps you have had personal experience of the area of law, which has fostered an interest in it and a desire to help others in a similar situation. It doesn't really matter what the reason is as long as you can establish a genuine interest and some evidence of research in that field.

The letter should enclose a copy of your CV which, ideally, should not span more than two sides of A4. Chapter 15 provides more detailed guidance on how to write an effective CV and covering letter.

Try to be creative in your quest to secure work experience—for example, if you are interested in property law, consider writing to the planning department of your local council to see if you could spend a few days or weeks shadowing someone in their team. You might be able to carry out research, accompany officers on inspections or attend planning meetings, which will give you exposure to the wider context within which property transactions are completed. Public sector organisations are very often under-resourced so they might be grateful for longer term support if you express an interest in their work.

If you are interested in family law, you could consider becoming a student member of Resolution (*http://www.resolution. org.uk*). This is a voluntary organisation which campaigns for improvements in family law and the family justice system. Its focus is on a constructive, non-confrontational approach to the resolution of family problems. It also supports students who are interested in qualifying as family lawyers. LPC students who are taking the family law elective are eligible for one year's free membership. This means that you will be entitled to discounts on training courses, a regular family law news-letter, and access to the members' website. Membership of the organisation could lead to some useful contacts and will ensure that you are up to speed on current issues in the sector when it comes to preparing for interviews or work experience placements.

If you are interested in intellectual property law, you could consider spending time working for a trade mark or patent attorney. Alternatively, you might be able to secure work experience with the brand protection or marketing team of a company to learn about key intellectual property concerns from a commercial client's perspective.

Vacation Schemes

Formal vacation schemes have replaced ad hoc work experience opportunities within most City, national and regional law firms. These firms run a series of work placements during the summer vacation (and sometimes also during the Christmas and Easter breaks) to give students the opportunity to find out more about their firms and what it is like to train and work there.

Many firms recruit heavily from students who have participated in their vacation schemes. Even if the schemes are not treated as a formal part of the recruitment process, they are an excellent way to find out more about a firm's culture, and to establish a relationship with the key decision makers. They provide an invaluable opportunity to see inside individual firms so you can get a good idea of what it would really be like to train and work there. By applying for, and participating in, vacation schemes you also demonstrate a genuine motivation to become a solicitor and show that you have made a concerted effort to find out more about the profession.

> "Vacation schemes are very good for gaining an insight into how different firms work and their individual cultures. They also give you a sense of what life as a trainee solicitor is actually like. You might find some aspects of the work

surprisingly mundane; equally, you might find some things more interesting than you had expected. Once you know what lawyers do on a day-to-day basis, you have more of an idea of what firms are looking for and why. Most importantly, vacation schemes enable you to decide whether law is for you and which type of firm is likely to suit you before you sign up to your training contract. Given that the training contract plus LPC will take three years to complete, it's worth knowing what you actually want before you invest all this time in qualifying as a solicitor."

A Law Undergraduate

The Application Process

Competition for places on vacation schemes is fierce, especially amongst the larger law firms. Therefore, be prepared to apply for placements during the Christmas and Easter vacations, as well as the more popular summer schemes.

Since City firms and most national and regional firms recruit two years in advance, if you want to start your training contract straight after the LPC, you should apply for vacation schemes during your second year at university if you are a law undergraduate and during your third year for all other undergraduates. The deadlines for submitting applications for summer placements usually fall in January or February each year (although some remain open until April) and the deadlines for Christmas and Easter schemes are even earlier. Some firms use a single application form for vacation schemes and training contracts, while others run two separate application processes. You will need to research individual firms for exact details of their application processes and submission deadlines. The Chambers & Partners Student Guide (*http://www.chambersstudent.co.uk*) has some useful information on applying for vacation schemes, including a table setting out the key deadlines and a table which compares the pay, number of vacancies and timing of vacation schemes at different firms. There is also a useful diary feature on *http://www.lawcareers.net*, which highlights key dates in the recruitment calendar, and has a useful feature called "MyLC.N" which enables you to save key dates into your own personalised career planner.

What to Expect From Vacation Schemes

Schemes usually last for between one and three weeks but the content of the placement varies from firm to firm. They generally involve a selection of the activities listed below.

Talks from partners or members of the graduate recruitment team
Shadowing a trainee or junior solicitor and getting involved in fee earning work
Research tasks
Court visits
Assessment centre activities
Social events

Remuneration varies: some firms pay their vacation scheme students (up to £400 per week at some US firms); others will reimburse reasonable travel expenses; and some do not offer any financial support at all.

Paralegal Experience

A paralegal is a non-lawyer who carries out legal work. They can work in a variety of organisations, including law firms, local authorities, in-house legal teams within large corporations, HM Court Service, and the voluntary sector. The work of paralegals varies according to the type of organisation they are working for. Duties could include carrying out legal research, preparing legal documents and correspondence, instructing barristers, preparing court documents, interviewing clients or witnesses, taking notes of meetings or court hearings, and assisting with general administrative duties.

As a general rule, employers will look for a law graduate or someone who has completed the GDL. However, bear in mind that many students apply for paralegal positions after the LPC if they have not managed to secure a training contract so those who have only completed the academic stage of training will be competing with candidates who have a greater understanding of the practical application of law and legal transactions. You do not need any formal qualifications to become a paralegal, although the National Association of Licensed Paralegals offers some qualifications and the Institute of Paralegals offers a Certified Paralegal qualification. For more information visit the Institute of Paralegals site (*http://www.instituteofparalegals.org*) and the National Association of Licensed Paralegals site (*http://www. nationalparalegals.co.uk*).

> "Paralegals provide legal support to solicitors. It is usually administrative work that can be distinguished from secretarial work. Paralegals are involved in a diverse range of tasks. In litigation departments, you can expect to prepare bundles, summarise disclosure, interview witnesses and carry out research. Many legal recruitment agencies find work for paralegals and most law schools keep a list of agencies and specialist recruiters in their career department. Some firms advertise vacancies on their website but some place adverts on legal careers websites or in the career departments of law schools. Sometimes it is also worth making speculative enquiries to firms that employ a large number of paralegals. If you have a very specific interest, but no relevant experience, it might be a good idea to offer to do work experience to begin with and see where it leads."
>
> *Moira Campbell, Solicitor, Kingsley Napley LLP*

Pro Bono Work

"Pro bono" comes from the latin "pro bono public", meaning "for the public good". It is generally understood to involve legal work that is being carried out free of charge as a public service. Some universities run formal pro bono schemes, which are often sponsored by local law firms. Such schemes are becoming increasingly important in local communities as a result of the continuing cuts to legal aid and the resulting loss of access to legal advice. Not only does pro bono work provide a great way to enhance your CV and develop key transferable skills, it also offers you an opportunity to use your legal knowledge to the benefit of people in your local community. What could be more rewarding than that?

If your university does not operate any pro bono initiatives, you could consider getting involved in one of the activities listed below. Or you could speak to your lecturers or student law society and think about setting something up with a group of friends. That would be a fantastic way to demonstrate your ability to take the initiative! It would give you some interesting material to support responses to application forms questions and some great things to talk about at interviews. Details of other pro bono organisations are listed in Appendix 2 (Further Reading).

Innocence Network UK

Innocence Network UK is the umbrella organisation for a body of projects co-ordinated by various UK universities. Each project is run by a group of students under the supervision of a practising lawyer. These groups investigate the cases of convicted prisoners who maintain their innocence but have exhausted the initial appeals process. The student groups review prisoners' cases looking for evidence that might form the basis of an application to the Criminal Cases Review Commission or the Scottish Criminal Cases Review Commission. They evaluate the evidence, carry out research, and prepare a report of their findings.

"The Innocence Project provides a terrific opportunity to show that you have practical experience of working as a lawyer and that you have learnt how to apply your academic knowledge of the law to help clients in the 'real world'. The key to obtaining a training contract is being able to demonstrate to potential employers that you have the essential transferable skills needed to be a good lawyer. Anyone can put on their CV

> 'I have excellent team working skills', but how do you prove it?
> The Innocence Project is the perfect way to demonstrate those
> transferable skills."
>
> *LLB Law Graduate, University of Portsmouth*

You can obtain more information about Innocence Network UK by visiting its website at *http://www.innocencenetwork.org.uk*.

Streetlaw

Streetlaw is a programme which encourages students to provide legal education to particular groups of people within their local community. They visit places such as schools, prisons, youth centres, day centres for the elderly, or young mothers groups and speak about legal issues that affect people's everyday lives. This could include, for example, speaking to elderly people about age discrimination legislation or speaking to youth groups about their consumer rights or the use of CCTV systems in public places. Through these activities, you will have the opportunity to show that you can work effectively as part of a team, research legal issues, apply them to everyday situations, and explain them in a way that is accessible to a particular audience.

Law in the Community

Some law schools run their own legal advice clinics, which provide students with the opportunity to advise clients and help them find solutions to their legal problems. If your university does not operate its own legal clinic, you could consider volunteering at your local Citizens Advice Bureau or Trading Standards office. You will work alongside trained advisors and lawyers and have the opportunity to interview clients, research particular areas of law, update the case management system, and see how the law works in practice. This experience will also give you a good understanding of some of the social problems that are prevalent in your local community.

For more information on the Citizens Advice Bureau, visit the website *http://www.citizensadvice.org.uk.*

For more information about your local Trading Standards office, contact your local council.

You could also consider volunteering to help at a Law Centre. They are not-for-profit centres that provide free legal advice and representation to those most in need. They advise on a variety of matters such as employment law, housing law, discrimination law, welfare benefits, education and immigration. For more information on Law Centres, visit the website *http://www.lawcentres. org.uk.*

For more information about other pro bono projects, you could also visit *http://www.lawworks.org.uk.* This charity provides a range of volunteering opportunities to lawyers and law students through its projects which provide free legal help to those who cannot afford to pay for it and do not qualify for legal aid.

Why Get Involved in Pro Bono Work?

As well as the obvious social benefits and the satisfaction that you have made a meaningful contribution to your local community, pro bono work can really enhance your CV. It shows that you have used your spare time constructively and that you have some understanding of the practical application of legal principles. Some of the other benefits of pro bono work are listed below.

You will have direct contact with real clients and will need to explain complex legal principles to them in simple terms. This will be an essential skill if you are to become a successful solicitor.

You will develop your critical thinking and problem solving skills as you try to find the best solution for your client.

You will often collaborate with others as part of the project and thus develop leadership and team building skills.

You will develop the skills needed to be a successful lawyer.

"Get involved in as much pro bono work as you can. It's a great way to develop material for the competency based questions on your application forms. Most universities have their own pro bono societies. If your university doesn't have one, speak to a law firm about sponsorship and think about setting one up yourself."

Joanna Pennick, Solicitor

"I worked with the Texas Defender Service in my second year, helping research petitions regarding death row inmates. Apart from contributing to answering questions about teamwork, leadership, etc. it gave me a broader view of legal research across different jurisdictions. It also gave me something to address in my interview, and the nature of the work meant that the interviewer was often interested and probed further. As such, because it was something I was comfortable talking about, it made part of the interview relatively easy."

LLB Law Undergraduate

OTHER WORK EXPERIENCE

Whilst some legal work experience is essential, non-legal work experience can be just as valuable in developing the key transferable skills that you will need for practice. This sort of experience will be helpful to illustrate your responses to competency based questions on application forms and at interview. It also demonstrates your ability to balance academic and paid work effectively, and shows that you are a well-rounded individual with experience of life outside the legal world.

"It is essential to secure work experience prior to applying to law firms as it demonstrates your commitment and dedication to a career in law. Not all work experience needs to be of a legal nature. Non-legal work experience can be beneficial as it is a great way of boosting your CV. The key is to demonstrate the transferable skills you have gained, e.g. working in a shop

> shows that you have communication skills from taking to the
> customers, a level of responsibility if you are handling the cash
> at the till, problem solving skills, etc. That said, there is no sub-
> stitute for legal work experience and the more you can secure,
> the stronger your application will be."
>
> *Cecily Holt, LPC graduate*

Part-Time Jobs

The key to getting the most value from your part-time job is how
you sell the skills you have developed. Think about the skills that
law firms are looking for in prospective trainees (see Ch.10 for
further guidance) and then consider how you have demonstrated
these skills in your work. For example, any role with a customer
facing element will require excellent communication skills and
possibly also the ability to negotiate with others or diffuse difficult situations.

Marketing experience can be very useful as can any job
that involves sales or working to targets. Remember that
law firms sell their legal services and time to clients and
therefore networking events and effective business development strategies are increasingly important to their businesses.
You will also have to get used to working towards fee targets
each month so anything that prepares you for this will be
invaluable.

> "I had a part-time job working in a call centre for a bank. In that
> environment, we worked in teams, we had to reach targets,
> and we had performance appraisals—all that gives you experi-
> ence of working in an office environment and having goals or
> targets to achieve. It's all good preparation for life in a law
> firm."
>
> *A Trainee Solicitor at a Regional Firm*

Industrial Placement Years and Other Commercial Experience

Many commercial firms, especially City firms, value commercial or finance experience, which makes sense given the focus of their practice areas and clients. This might include working for a financial institution, an insurance company, or a large corporation. You may be able to secure this independently, or you could consider taking part in a placement year if your university offers one as part of your degree.

> "Some of the really large, global firms would think that working in a commercial organisation is more useful and more appropriate than legal work experience in a small high street firm."
>
> *A Law Careers Tutor*

The value of a placement year will depend largely on the area of law that you wish to specialise in, the type of firm you wish to train with, and the organisation in which you choose to spend your placement year. Before committing to a placement, consider what you are going to get out of it and how effectively you can sell the experience to employers. You will certainly gain a sense of commercial awareness by understanding how a business works from the inside and you will acquire knowledge of a particular sector, which might be useful for future practice. You should also learn about effective team work, how to present information at meetings, how to draft professional correspondence and, depending on the nature of the placement, perhaps also develop your negotiation skills and ability to work towards targets.

TIPS FOR SUCCESSFUL WORK PLACEMENTS

Do not be distracted by the social events—you are there to make a positive impression on the recruiters, and to decide whether or not you could see yourself working for that firm. The firms are trying to impress you just as much as you are trying to impress them but it is possible to look past the gloss and make a reasonable assessment of the culture, working practices and quality of training that the firm offers. Think about the rapport between the trainees and also between the trainees and senior members of staff. What is the working culture like? How supportive does the training environment seem to be? What hours do people work? What sort of work are trainees involved in? Do they cover the practice areas that you are interested in?

Get involved—recruiters are looking for applicants with enthusiasm, confidence, a proactive attitude, and the ability to build relationships and work as part of a team.

> "You've only got a week or so to make a good impression on a firm during your vacation scheme. Candidates stand out when they are genuinely engaged in the whole process and when they make a real effort to get on with everyone, from support staff to lawyers, and become part of the team. Try to be as natural and genuine as you possibly can. Roll your sleeves up and get involved in everything, including the social events."
> *Sam Lee, Head of Recruitment, Bond Dickinson LLP*

Don't confuse aggression with drive and ambition—many applicants (particularly those applying to City firms) think that firms are looking for dominant, aggressive individuals. This is not the case. Do not feel that you have to adopt an aggressive personality or that you have to be incredibly domineering or always speak during negotiations or team building exercises. That is not what firms or clients want from their lawyers. Instead show that you are able to listen effectively as well as being able to drive things forward.

> "Although you are really focused and driven by what you are doing, you also need to be polite to others and supportive of their endeavours during the vacation scheme. Even though you want to succeed over others, you also need to show that you can build relationships and work as part of a team. If you are kind and generous towards others on the vacation scheme, it will reflect positively on you."
> *A Trainee Solicitor at a City Firm*

Treat the scheme as an extended interview—remember that your performance is being assessed by those around you, even when you least expect it. This means that you should project a professional and confident impression from the moment you set foot in the building. This includes being courteous to reception staff and exchanging a smile or even a few words with anyone you happen to meet in the lift. Do not underestimate the importance of this; you never know who you are speaking to nor how much influence they might wield in the recruitment process. With that point in mind, never underestimate the influence of current trainees.

> "Vacation scheme students shoot themselves in the foot when they are least expecting it to happen. In particular, they often underestimate the role of the trainee in the recruitment process and the fact that we are asked to provide feedback on their performance in the workplace and socially. As much as you want them to be relaxed and confident, they have to remember that they are there to be assessed and that people are judging whether they are likely to fit into the culture of that particular firm."
>
> *A Trainee Solicitor at a City Firm*

Show that you are a team player—those around you will be making an assessment about whether you have the potential to be a good trainee, whether you are likely to fit into the firm's culture, and whether you will be able to develop effective working relationships with colleagues and clients.

Concentrate on all tasks—it is not just the formal assessment centre tasks that are being assessed. Firms will be interested in how you perform in the workplace and how you approach the tasks that are allocated to you. Take every piece of work seriously and make sure you complete them within the agreed deadline. Pay attention to presentation and do not be afraid to use your initiative if supplementary questions or issues arise out of the initial task.

"The students who really distinguish themselves are those who take a pro-active approach to research tasks and are able to think laterally. They tend to go the extra mile to ask the natural supplementary question arising out of that research without actually being asked to consider it."

A Solicitor

Make sure that you attend all the social events, do not say that you have already made plans. People want to know that you are the kind of person who will make a real commitment to the firm and that you will put your personal plans on hold when necessary to get the work done. They want people who are prepared to roll up their sleeves and get involved, and this includes social events.

Good manners cost nothing—it might sound obvious, but do not forget about office etiquette and basic manners. It is easy to let your guard down while participating in an extended placement but you should not get involved in office gossip and you should be pleasant and courteous to everyone around you. Send a thank you email at the end of the scheme to the HR manager and any fee earners who supervised you. This is a sign of good manners and will also keep your name in the minds of key decision makers.

Do not text, email or use social media—do not surf the internet, access personal email accounts or use social networking sites during office hours: it is unprofessional and your internet usage might be monitored. If you are given a work email address, do not use it to email friends or family, and avoid frivolous email exchanges with other candidates or trainees. Your emails will probably be monitored during the course of the placement. Switch off your mobile and do not take personal calls during office hours.

Do not overindulge during social events—it is easy to let your guard down when you leave the office and head to the local bar with some of the trainees, but remember that you will still be watched and assessed even after you leave the office.

Dress to impress throughout the placement—invest in the best suit you can afford and make sure that your shoes are polished. Also, take care to ensure that your hair and nails are tidy and that any jewellery, accessories, and make up are appropriate to a professional office environment.

> "Try to stay on top of your assignments during the placement and don't get too enthusiastic and end up accepting everything that comes your way. Take things that you know are manageable and apply yourself fully letting the quality of the work do the talking. If you are confused, don't be embarrassed to ask for help or further instructions—it's better to get the work done right and to a good standard. Also make sure that you socialise and stay interested in the firm. If the firm holds interviews at the end of the placement, they will go over everything you have done over the time you were with them so it might be worth noting down things you did across the week, just so you can remember."
>
> *LLB Law Undergraduate*

OTHER WAYS TO ENHANCE YOUR CV

Hobbies and Extra-Curricular Activities

Do not focus on work experience at the expense of your hobbies or extra-curricular activities. These are just as important for your CV as they add colour to your applications and help paint a picture of you as an individual, rather than an anonymous applicant who ticks all the boxes but has no life outside work. They are also essential to maintaining a healthy work/life balance and will help you make new friends, reduce stress, and learn new skills.

Hobbies, Clubs and Societies

One approach is to develop your hobbies with one eye on your CV. For example, if you enjoy scuba diving, consider joining your university's scuba diving society. You could even think about standing for one of the positions on the management committee such as Social Secretary, Treasurer or even President. By choosing to join a society, you are demonstrating that you are the sort of person who gets on with others but you can indulge your passion for scuba diving at the same time. Thus, you are enhancing your CV in a more meaningful way than if you were taking a few lessons at your local outdoor centre or doing scuba diving with your family twice a year on holiday.

By joining a society, you are also demonstrating that you can manage your time effectively by balancing your commitment to the society against your academic and other work commitments. If you put yourself forward for the management committee, depending on your role within the committee and the activities you are involved in, you should also be able to demonstrate specific employability skills and have some good supporting evidence for application forms or interview questions. The table below illustrates some of the key skills which you might be able to demonstrate through various society events.

Example	Employability Skills
Organising sponsorship for new equipment	Negotiation skills, powers of persuasion, communication skills, networking skills.
Organising a fundraising event	Organisational skills, leadership, networking, project management, problem solving, flexibility.
Managing the society's finances	Integrity, honesty, budget keeping, numeracy, record keeping.

Whilst joining a society can be great for your social life, and a good indicator of a genuine team spirit, you don't have to join a society to develop key employability skills alongside your hobbies. If you love dancing or amateur dramatics, consider organising an independent show to raise money for a local charity. If you play a musical instrument, you may have gained a qualification which will indicate considerable commitment and dedication. You might also play in a band or orchestra, which would be a good example of team working skills and time management since you will have to balance individual practice and group rehearsals against your academic commitments.

You can also use your extra-curricular activities to develop areas of your CV that you think need improving. This would show a genuine commitment to self-development and a desire to embrace new challenges.

> "At university I knew that my presentation skills were not particularly strong so I pushed myself into situations where I would be forced to do that sort of thing because it was the only way I could get better. For example, I joined the mooting society and debating society although I was petrified! It was a good opportunity to practice these key skills and also to pick up different techniques from others."
>
> *A Trainee Solicitor*

Most law schools encourage students to participate in internal and external competitions for mooting, negotiating and interviewing. These provide fantastic opportunities to make new friends, learn new skills, boost your confidence, and enhance your CV at the same time.

> "By participating in activities such as negotiating, mooting and client interviewing, you will get the opportunity to develop genuine legal skills which will benefit you throughout your career. These skills will not only give you extra confidence when you enter the legal profession, they will also look good on your CV. Potential employers will be impressed by students who have proven practical legal skills as well as the academic skills normally associated with a law degree."
>
> *Third Year Law Undergraduate, University of Portsmouth*

Travelling

A period of independent travel is unlikely to impress recruiters unless you are able to show the skills that you developed as a result. For example, perhaps the travelling demonstrates your resilience, your ability to manage a budget, your fundraising skills, your ability to organise a group or plan an itinerary, and your ability to use your initiative when things do not go to plan. It might be even better if you could combine some independent travelling with a period of voluntary or charity work. American summer camps or conservation projects abroad are popular choices for those who want to combine work experience and skills development with some travelling. Teaching English as a foreign language is also popular as are internships with NGOs.

> "If you haven't secured a training contract and are looking to take a gap year, then ideally you need to get some relevant work experience, whether as a paralegal or in the voluntary sector. However, if you decide to go travelling, you need to show that you have used your time productively. At least then you can show that you are a balanced person who has managed a budget, planned your journey and accommodation, and built relationships with people."
>
> *Sam Lee, Head of Recruitment Manager, Bond Dickinson LLP*

Charity Work and Fundraising

This is likely to be a particularly useful experience if you plan to enter public service or specialise in an area of law where you will be exposed to social challenges or where you will come into contact with people at particularly difficult times in their lives. That said, charity and fundraising work is likely to be of interest to commercial law firms too because it will develop your ability to work as part of a team, to communicate with people from all walks of life, to negotiate on behalf of others, to persuade others of your point of view, and to work towards financial targets and common goals. These are all qualities that law firms want to see in their future trainees. Firms are likely to be particularly impressed if you have started a charity or fundraising programme of your own since this demonstrates initiative and entrepreneurial spirit.

If you are interested in a particular area of law, you might like to link your charity work to that area. For example, you could join Greenpeace if you are interested in environmental law, Amnesty International if you are interested in human rights, or Shelter if you are interested in housing law.

Appendix 2 (Further Reading) refers to several useful websites which provide access to volunteering opportunities in your area and beyond. One particularly useful website is Do It (*http:// www.do-it.org.uk*) which provides access to a database of volunteering opportunities and is searchable by reference to specific interests (e.g. Art and Culture, Law and Legal Support, Human and Civil Rights, Children, Education and Literacy, Disability, etc.) and/or by reference to postcode. Another excellent resource is *http://www.joininuk.org* which connects volunteers to sports-related projects. Again, you can search by reference to postcode which will make it easier to find volunteering opportunities close to your home or university. The site also connects volunteers to opportunities to support national sports events, such as the Olympics, the Invictus Games, Sports Relief and the Great North Run.

Law Commission Research Projects

The Law Commission is an independent body whose purpose is to review the laws of England and Wales and assess whether they are fit for purpose. Each year, the Law Commission recruits approximately 10–15 law graduates as temporary research assistants to work on specific projects reviewing and reforming the law. The recruitment process runs from December to January and the posts are taken up in September.

For more information on these opportunities, visit the Law Commission website at *http://www.lawcom.gov.uk.*

Enactus

Over 50 UK universities run Enactus projects, which provide another opportunity for students to develop commercial awareness and team building skills. Enactus is an international organisation which seeks to contribute to communities around the world by engaging students in community outreach projects while encouraging them to become socially responsible and entrepreneurial business leaders. For more information, and to read about examples of Enactus projects in the UK and overseas, visit the website at *http://www.enactusuk.org*.

12 DEVELOPING AND DEMONSTRATING COMMERCIAL AWARENESS

Written in collaboration with Valya Georgieva

Commercial awareness is a key element of the recruitment criteria of all law firms. So, what is it, how do you develop it and, crucially, how do you demonstrate to recruiters that you have it?

Legal advice is expensive so commercial clients expect their lawyers to add value to their businesses and transactions. Clients are unlikely to be interested in a lengthy account of what the law states. They are more interested in knowing whether they can achieve their commercial goals within the limits of the law; the risks they might face if they pursue their intended action (and the magnitude of that risk); how such risks could be managed or avoided; and whether any alternative action is available to them. A lawyer can add value by finding solutions where the law makes a particular course of action difficult or expensive; being able to apply the law creatively to achieve the client's goal; or by helping the client to carry out a risk/benefit analysis of a particular approach. A lawyer's ability to think commercially is often what sets him/her apart from others who can give the same technical advice but who are not able to offer such pragmatic solutions to problems, or potential problems, or are not as knowledgeable about the client's business or sector.

The advice above also applies to private clients to some extent since they will also demand practical, meaningful advice and value for money. Private clients are arguably even less likely to be interested in the detail of the law than commercial clients: they simply want to know where they stand, what risks they face, how those risks can be managed, what their final position is likely to be, and how much the legal advice will cost them. In this context, lawyers can set themselves apart by taking the time to under-stand their clients' individual circumstances, and by explaining their advice in clear and straightforward terms in a way that is helpful to their clients.

WHAT IS COMMERCIAL AWARENESS AND WHY DO LAWYERS NEED IT?

It is not easy to find a single definition of "commercial awareness". However, if you were to ask 10 lawyers to try to define it, you would probably see some common threads appearing in their answers.

Interest in Business & Finance—recruiters in commercial firms will expect you to be genuinely interested in, and curious about, business and finance. They will also expect you to understand the type of advice that clients want from their lawyers and, in the case of commercial clients, the importance of factors that affect the way they do business (including key economic, regulatory, and commercial drivers).

In terms of economic drivers, think about the effect of wider economic conditions on established businesses and on new start-ups. This might include the effects of changing interest rates, inflation, the availability of debt finance, and the strength of the pound against other currencies. Regulatory drivers will vary depending on the particular client(s) you are dealing with, but they might include issues such as competition laws, or new or existing regulatory frameworks and regulatory bodies in the client's sector. Commercial drivers might include the stance taken by competitors on a particular issue, or the company's short and long term strategic plan.

Knowledge of the varied working practices, culture and clients at different law firms—recruiters will also look for a sense of reality about the type of clients you wish to work for and the workload and culture of the particular firm you wish to join. You should also be able to demonstrate that you understand how and why a law firm structures its business in the way it does. This includes why the law firm has offices in locations that it does. For

City and commercial law firms, you should understand why the firm has chosen to have a global presence and understand the strategic decisions for having offices in certain countries and not others. Understanding why a firm has recently opened (or closed) certain offices is also crucial to demonstrating commercial awareness (for example, to meet client needs or to reduce costs).

You are unlikely to appear commercially aware if you tell the recruitment partner at a Magic Circle firm that you want to become a lawyer because you want to help people and make a meaningful contribution to your local community. The firm might offer pro bono opportunities, but your clients at the firm will be large, probably global, corporations whose main drivers are to generate profits and investment, attract talented staff, remain innovative and productive, and be alert and responsive to threats from competitors, the market and elsewhere. Profits and income generation are not dirty words to them so, whilst your commitment to public service is commendable, you need to demonstrate that you are in tune with the firm's commercial goals. Similarly, however strong your academics or work experience profile, you are unlikely to be selected for a training contract with a local authority without demonstrating a genuine commitment to public service. Lastly, a small local firm specialising in private client work is unlikely to want a trainee who is lacking in empathy or any commitment to helping individuals through sometimes difficult personal situations.

Appreciation of regulatory and commercial challenges—you need to demonstrate to recruiters that you appreciate the commercial challenges that face today's lawyers and the impact of regulatory reform on the structure and profitability of firms.

Some firms have started to offer legal advice online or outside of traditional working hours (in the evening and at weekends) in a bid to show that they are responding to their clients' needs. Others have started to abandon hourly charge-out rates in favour of fixed fee work in a bid to make billing more transparent, and to give clients more certainty in terms of how much a particular piece of advice or legal drafting or a specific transaction is likely to cost them. Some firms have reduced overhead (and thus the cost to clients) by outsourcing certain services (e.g. due diligence reporting, preparation of disclosure bundles, property management processes) to subsidiaries based in geographic areas where labour and property is cheaper. These operations tend to be resourced by a large team of paralegals who are supervised by one or two senior solicitors. This practice has become widely known as the "commoditisation of legal services". An awareness of these pressures, the advantages and disadvantages for law firms of the new approaches, and perhaps evidence of thinking about what the legal services model might look like in 10 years' time, would also fall under the umbrella of "commercial awareness".

Another key development is the Legal Services Act 2007 which came into force in October 2011. The Act provided for the creation of Legal Disciplinary Practices (organisations that only provide legal services but in which up to 25 per cent of the advisors are non-lawyers) and Alternative Business Structures (ABS) (legal practices owned by non-lawyers which may provide just legal advice or a combination of legal advice and other services). Co-operative Legal Services is a good example of an ABS: it is a legal advice service which is owned and operated by a non-legal commercial entity (the Co-operative Group). The introduction of ABSs in particular have paved the way for existing commercial organisations (often retailers) to apply their consumer centric business models to the provision of legal services by offering lower cost services based on fixed fees, greater accessibility and flexibility, and often the added comfort of being backed by household name. The success of such organisations has put consumer choice front and centre, and has been a major threat for some law firms, particularly smaller high street practices whose main source of fees come from the areas which these ABSs have targeted (residential conveyancing, personal injury claims, wills and probate, family law and employment advice).

You might find the following websites useful to keep an eye on developments in the legal profession and legal services market:

http://www.theguardian.com/law
http://www.thetimes.co.uk/tto/law
http://www.thelawyer.com
http://www.legalweek.com
http://www.lawgazette.co.uk

Awareness that law firms are businesses too—show that you appreciate the importance of "fee earning" and the timely creation and payment of bills to the success of that business.

During work experience placements, ask your supervisor/ mentor what their billing target is and also ask them how many chargeable hours they have to account for each day. Other terms like "utilisation rate" (the extent to which a fee earner is working to capacity against his/her chargeable hour target) and "billable hours" (hours which can be charged to a client (unlike hours which cannot be charged to a client such as training or housekeeping/admin)) are also worth discussion. Ask your supervisor to explain the firm's billing, time recording, and debt recovery processes to you. You need to be clear about the importance of these processes to clients and the firm. In particular, ensure that you are familiar with the "six minute unit" whereby you have to account for your time each day in units of six minutes rounded up. So, if you spent 15 minutes on a client telephone call, you would record three units of time. Perhaps you could also ask your supervisor to show you their time recording computer software and to explain the different parts of an invoice.

Accurate understanding of the work of a solicitor—life in a law firm is not just about applying the law. It also involves business development, marketing, networking, meeting billing and chargeable hours targets, client care and client management. You should be able to show that you are aware of this reality, and that you can draw on the necessary soft skills to excel in these other areas. Read Ch.14 which explores the importance of brand development to law firms, and how social media is being used to support this.

This is an important point and explains why firms are so keen to test your "soft skills" and ability to function as part of a team during assessment centres and placements. Demonstrating commercial awareness does not just revolve around understanding the issues in the financial pages. You can demonstrate commercial awareness by reference to extra-curricular activities such as organising a fundraising event, gaining sponsorship for a particular event or for equipment for a university society, or the experience gained by running your own small business enterprise whether on your own initiative or as part of a university-led scheme. Refer to Chs 10, 17 and 18 for more guidance on the transferable skills employers will be looking for and how they test them at assessment centres and interviews.

HOW DO LAW FIRMS TEST COMMERCIAL AWARENESS?

The individual and overlapping threads listed above can probably be boiled down even further into two main areas:

interest in, and enthusiasm for, business and finance (for those applying to commercial firms); and
a commitment to, and a realistic understanding of, legal practice and excellent client care (for all aspiring solicitors).

The remainder of this chapter will provide advice on how law firms test these two important areas, and how you can demonstrate your potential in each of them.

At this stage, it will be helpful to dispel some areas of misunderstanding concerning the development of commercial awareness:

you are not expected to demonstrate that you are an expert in financial and business affairs;
the development of this attribute cannot be taught or achieved by reading a financial publication every day; and
you cannot and should not try to fake it.

It is also important to remember your entry level to the profession. You are applying for a position as a *trainee* solicitor. The clue to your role, and the expectations of recruiters, is in the title: you are going to be training to become a solicitor; you are not expected to demonstrate that you are the finished article. Therefore, recruiters will be looking for candidates who show a genuine interest in, and enthusiasm for, commercial and financial issues and related news stories, who demonstrate an aptitude and enthusiasm for developing that interest, who demonstrate a good deal of common sense and excellent problem solving skills (the foundation of the commercial lawyer's skill set), and who are able to identify and explain where they have demonstrated or developed commercial awareness from their own work experience and/or extra-curricular activities.

As you might imagine, it is not particularly difficult for firms to test the first aspect of commercial awareness (knowledge of business and finance). One way in which they might achieve this is by asking specific questions on application forms (e.g. "tell me about a recent commercial issue that has interested you" or "tell me about an issue that you have been following in the business press"). They might follow up on this issue during the interview to test the depth of your knowledge or they might ask you to comment on any issues that you can spot in a specific case study, press release or newspaper article. The second aspect of commercial awareness is more difficult to test but firms will begin by asking you why you want to be a lawyer and work for that type of firm and by trying to find out if you have the soft skills that will be needed to become a successful, commercially aware lawyer.

DEVELOPING AND DEMONSTRATING COMMERCIAL AWARENESS

Making Use of Your Experiences

It is quite likely that your CV will be similar to many of the other applicants, e.g. similar work experience, similar extra-curricular experiences, similar knowledge of the key issues in the financial and general press, etc. However, your ability to explain the relevance and value of those experiences could set you apart from the rest. The depth of self-awareness and a candidate's ability to reflect on what has been learnt from an experience is often as important as the quality of the experience itself. Think seriously and deeply about the experiences on your CV and look for opportunities to highlight your commercial awareness to employers. In other words, show that you are sufficiently well-informed about the role of a commercial lawyer, and the workings of a modern law firm, to be able to understand and explain the significance of your own experiences and why they demonstrate that you have the potential to become a good commercial lawyer.

Use your legal work experience to gain an understanding of how law firms work, the role of a solicitor, and the key regulatory and commercial issues affecting law firms and their clients. You might think that everyone who completes a work experience placement should have gained an understanding of how law firms work and what solicitors do but, perhaps fortunately for you, this is not the case. It is not enough to simply sit in the office and take it all in: you need to think actively about what is going on around you and ask questions.

Questions to ask/things to think about during work placements in law firms

What is the flow of work like in the office? Does it vary from department to department?
How do lawyers deal with the quiet times?
What seems to be the biggest cause of frustration for the lawyers in the office?
How is time recorded?
Is all the time recorded on a file actually charged to a client? If not, how is the final bill calculated and by whom?
How is billing managed?
What happens about late payment of invoices?
What happens when a client queries his/her invoice?
What seem to be the most effective strategies for generating new clients or new matters for existing clients?
What happens at networking events?
Why do lawyers attend networking events, and how do they make sure they get the most out of them?

Also remember that non-legal work experience can be useful to gain an understanding of how businesses are structured, the impact of the law on the services and products they supply, and the challenges they face within their sector. You might also get an opportunity to sit in on a meeting or telephone conference with the client and its lawyers. This would be a great opportunity to find out what the key decision makers in that business expect from their legal advisors, what frustrates them about dealing with lawyers, and where they feel lawyers can, or should, add value. If the opportunity to develop this knowledge is not forthcoming, make sure you ask. There is nothing to be gained in playing the wallflower during work placements and most people are willing to help if they sense a genuine desire to learn.

As discussed above, another important part of demonstrating commercial awareness is to show an employer that you have the soft skills to deliver legal advice in a way that will be meaningful to clients, and to support your firm by generating new business. Look for examples on your CV which show that you have those soft skills, using the examples below as a starting point.

Ability to think laterally and find practical solutions to complex problems—this could include: Duke of Edinburgh challenges; experiences from travelling; solving problems associated with the planning of a large event; dealing with an unexpected problem while working as a student advisor at an open day.

Skills in marketing, business development, and customer service—this could include: working in the hospitality industry; working in a call centre as a customer service operator; organising a charity event; setting up a new society at university; or organising the sponsorship for your netball team's kit.

Experience of working towards group or individual financial targets—this could include: organising a fundraising event; or working in a sales role.

Negotiating experience—this could include: CAB advice work; negotiating with a landlord over rent or repairs to your student house; negotiating a favourable deal when buying a new laptop or car or on behalf of a student society for a social event; or you might have demonstrated good negotiation skills in a sales or customer service role where you have to appease difficult or dissatisfied customers.

Remember that the employer wants to know that you have developed, and have a natural aptitude for, the relevant skills to excel in a commercial environment; there is no requirement that you must already have gained exceptional levels of actual commercial experience so taking examples from your everyday life, your extra-curricular interests, or your non-legal work experience is absolutely fine.

Getting to Grips with the Financial Pages

It is probably unrealistic for you to pledge to read the Financial Times from cover to cover each day, and in fact the net gain in terms of your commercial awareness development would probably not be proportionate to the effort and time you would have to invest. As a student, it may be useful to start by reading about business stories on BBC news online for a general background, before delving into the deeper analysis provided by the financial press.

Developing commercial awareness and knowledge of current affairs is a gradual process and not something that can be achieved in a week or even a month. To demonstrate real depth of understanding, you must show a genuine interest in the world around you and develop your knowledge layer by layer. If you do this, you will be able to apply your wider knowledge to a case study, article discussion or interview question even if you do not know about the specific matter at hand.

Whilst there is no doubt that it would make sense to keep abreast of the main stories in the legal, business and general press (see below and Appendix 2 for some suggested publications), you also need to engage in deep and active learning in this area which will not come by skimming each and every story. Instead, once you have had a quick read of the paper, focus on a couple of stories each week and analyse them closely. Then, make an effort to follow up on any stories of interest: keep an eye out for follow up stories and, if specific companies or agencies are involved, have a look for press releases on the relevant website.

As well as tracking particular news stories, perhaps you could track a couple of companies in a particular sector so you gain a good understanding of what challenges that sector is facing, or has or will face, and also what opportunities might arise or have arisen. It may be useful to focus on a client (or a key sector) of the law firm that you are applying to, to demonstrate that you have both commercial awareness and an interest in that particular law firm's practice.

Another approach might be to develop an in-depth knowledge of three financial news stories each week and keep updating that knowledge. Make sure that you understand the significance of the stories and the background to them, and consider whether there are any parallels with other stories or issues. You should be able to articulate an informed opinion on the issue, and show an understanding of other points of view. This is as important, perhaps more important, than reading the newspapers daily and taking the stories at face value. There are two dangers with the latter approach: you are likely to forget the content of most of the stories because you are simply reading them, rather than thinking actively about them; and you are not going to be able to demonstrate an in-depth knowledge of the story nor hold your own in a serious conversation or debate about it.

> "Some people view the interview as being almost like a test so they think they just have to revise everything that's been in the papers in the last two weeks and reel it off and that's it. But I think that's where you can become unstuck at the interview because you might be able to mention something in your application form but the interviewers are likely to want to engage in a full discussion about that particular issue. You probably need two or three key stories that you've actually followed closely and researched."
>
> *A Trainee at a City Firm*

Advice when reading news stories

Keep asking questions of yourself and others. Do you really understand what the article is about? Do you understand all the terms and language used in the article? If not, ask someone or look it up.

Do not just accept articles at face value; analyse them as you would a journal article for an academic essay.

It is not simply a question of knowing what is happening, or has happened; it is about being able to explain why those things happened and what impact/significance they have had. You need to develop your skills of analysis and application rather than just being able to re-tell the news stories. Employers will probably ask an open-ended question inviting you to tell them about a news story which interests you and why, rather than asking you if you saw the main news story on the front page of the Financial Times that day.

Identify key buzzwords, understand them, and be able to use them. Using the appropriate language helps to make you appear more commercially aware (as long as you actually understand it and can use it appropriately!).

Think about all the different facets of the story, not just the main focus. For example, if you read a story about a company buying another business, you should concentrate on all the other affected areas (such as whether employees, real estate and intellectual property will be transferring, the tax implications of the sale and the market perception of the sale (e.g. if it is a competitor buying the company), not just the main corporate law issues.

Listen and Learn

Whilst learning about important stories in the financial press is important, there is no substitute for getting out there and speaking to people. You will be amazed by how quickly your commercial awareness will develop simply by listening to people speak about their business, the challenges they face in their day-to-day working life, and any commercial issues that they see developing generally or in their specific sector/industry. Try to attend as many guest lectures and workshops as you can, even if the speaker is from a firm or sector or profession that you are not necessarily interested in. You could also look out for talks given by speakers in other faculties or departments within your university.

For example, you might not see any relevance in a talk given by a marketing manager from Vodafone, but perhaps he/she will discuss some of the challenges and opportunities facing the tel-ecoms industry, or some of the deals that Vodafone has been involved in, which might well be very useful if you attend an inter-view, or fill in an application form, for a firm which has Vodafone as its client or who acts for other companies in the same sector.

Also, make an effort to follow blogs or tweets published by law firms as they will be writing about issues that affect their business or their clients' businesses. These resources can help you to pin-point relevant issues, rather than making your own assessment about what might or might not be relevant.

With social media gradually becoming the "go to" resource for seeking and sharing information, you have the unique opportu-nity to not only pinpoint relevant "hot" topics in the legal indus-try, but to also follow discussions on those topics and form your own opinion along the way. There are two kinds of information that you are likely to see on a law firm's Twitter feed: internal news and external news. Internal news would include head-lines from the firm's press releases, news about successful client engagements and awards, and new appointments within the firm. External news would include links to the firm's news page, newsletter or external news headlines which affect its clients.

Although not all law firms are active on Twitter, the ones that are can give you an insight into the key issues that affect both themselves and their clients. This is a good starting point on which you can build up your commercial awareness.

In addition to following law firms' tweets to keep up with their news and updates, you should also ensure that you follow some of the general media accounts such as BBC News (**@BBCNews**), Guardian Law (**@GdnLaw**) and Sky News Business (**@SkyNewsBiz**), as well as the legal press accounts such as Legal Futures (**@legal-futures**), Law Society Gazette (**@lawsocgazette**), The Lawyer (**@TheLawyermag**) and LawCareers.Net (**@LawCareersNetUK**). These are all excellent accounts to help you with your general commercial awareness and training contract applications as well as developing your knowledge of the legal market place.

Although there is a lot of "noise" on social media platforms such as Twitter, there are also a lot of very useful accounts. The best way to get started is to find a few good accounts to follow and then to look at who they engage with, who they follow and who follows them. Below is a suggested list of recommended accounts to get started with.

Useful Twitter Accounts

@CAwareSociety — Commercial Awareness Society at the University of Law. They share current news which could help improve your commercial awareness.

@chambersstudent — A comprehensive student careers guide to training contracts, pupillages and law schools. They share law firm and chambers vacancies, including vacation schemes, pupillages, training contracts, as well as tips and advice from the industry.

@CityAM — Free daily business newspaper. They share breaking business news, commentary and features from *http://www.cityam.com*.

@inhouse_trainee — Chris is a First class LLB graduate, currently studying the LPC whilst training with a FTSE100 company. He shares tips and advice for prospective solicitors, insight into his role as an in-house trainee, as well as news and opinions from the legal industry.

@JackofKent — David Allen Green is a Financial Times blogger. He also blogs in a personal capacity at *http://jackofkent.com*. He shares critical views and opinions about law and policy. His personal account is **@davidallengreen**.

@Jezhop — Jeremy Hopkins is an ex-practice manager at a leading Chambers, currently a Head of Operations at an award-winning Alternative Business Structure, Riverview Law. He blogs at *http://www.clerkingwell.co.uk* about legal practice matters.

@JohnHyde1982 — John Hyde is a deputy news editor and reporter for the Law Society Gazette. He shares views and opinions about legal and political matters.

@lawcampus — This is an academic community provided by LexisNexis UK. They share legal news, blogs and research tips.

@LawCareersNetUK — This is a comprehensive online tool for future lawyers and law recruiters. They share tips and advice, as well as other useful insight from the legal profession to help students find a training contract or pupillage.

@LawTrainee — The Twitter account which accompanies this book and the companion website.

@lawsocgazette — The Law Society Gazette. They share the latest legal news and analysis, tailored for solicitors, barristers and lawyers to be.

@Lawyer2Bmag — Lawyer2B is an essential comprehensive guide to a career in law. They share news, analysis and features from the legal industry.

@legalbrat — Tim Bratton is an ex-General Counsel of the Financial Times, currently a Practice Development Director at an Alternative Business Structure, Lawyers On Demand. He shares views and opinions about the legal industry and profession.

@LegalBusinessUK — Legal Business is a leading magazine providing business news, opinions, commentary, analysis and features from the legal industry.

@legalfutures — Legal Futures is a news resource providing daily news on alternative business structures, new market entrants, regulatory change and innovation for lawyers and law firms.

@legal_luke — Luke Murphy is a finance solicitor in the London office of a global law firm. He is a mentor to students willing to enter into the legal profession and a speaker on the subject of employability.

@LegalTony — Anthony Lyons is a paralegal at a law firm in London and a future trainee solicitor. He is well regarded on Twitter for his tips and advice to prospective solicitors through **#AskaTrainee**—a hashtag campaign where legal recruiters and aspiring lawyers come together for an hour-long Q&A session on Twitter.

@LexisNexisUK — LexisNexis UK shares news, opinions, analysis, commentary and blogs from the legal industry.

@Schroders — A global asset management company. Shares mainly business and financial news.

@SJ_weekly — Solicitors Journal. A weekly legal news journal for solicitors.

@TheLawLounge — Sharing news, discussion and jobs from the legal industry.

@TheLawyermag — Top UK legal magazine. They share debates, features, blogs, analysis and jobs from the legal industry.

@TheLex100 — The Lex100 is a comprehensive guide to a career in law for students.

@tobyhornett — Toby Hornett is a Clifford Chance trained in-house lawyer providing careers coaching to aspiring lawyers.

@TraineeSurgery — Trainee Solicitor Surgery is a specialist career service providing expert careers advice on getting a training contract, vacation scheme or paralegal role, as well as the latest job vacancies.

@TSL_Tweets — The Student Lawyer is an online resource providing careers and study advice to law students as well as the latest news, commentary, and opinions on legal issues.

@YLawyer — Young Lawyer is an online magazine provided by the Solicitors Journal team. It is aimed at prospective and new legal professionals and provides tips, advice and insight from the legal profession.

"Use lists. List people into key areas that you're interested in, whether it is other lawyers in a specific field, newsfeeds from governing bodies or the area of law you work in, or general media."
Emma Daly, External Communications Manager,
Blake Morgan LLP

Once you have found a few relevant accounts to follow, the best way to keep them organised is to create lists with the different types of accounts. So, for example, you can have a list for law students, a list for lawyers in different areas of law, and also a list for news accounts that will help you with your commercial awareness. Thus, you can get an easy access to all tweets from the relevant group of people, instead of having to scroll down through hundreds and thousands of irrelevant tweets. Whenever you see a headline or a discussion that is of interest, you can add it to your "Favourites" and read it at your leisure.

You can also use a Twitter application, such as Hootsuite or Tweetdeck, and set up a search for a particular keyword such as "training contract" or a particular hashtag such as **#commerciala-wareness**. Then you could have all tweets with those words at your fingertips so you can catch up with them at a glance. Whilst you need to accept that there is no possible way in which you could ensure that you read absolutely everything, the more time you spend on Twitter the easier you will find it to filter out the accounts which do not add any value to your newsfeed and to follow more of the interesting and valuable accounts. The best way to do this is to experiment. Start following people who you think will be of interest, but don't be afraid to "unfollow" them as soon as you see that they are not as relevant or useful as you first thought. Over time, you can build your own network of "trusted" professionals whose opinions are important to you.

People on Twitter will often engage with topics in the news by sharing their own opinion about them. This is another good way to improve your commercial awareness by simply "listening" to what people have to say about a particular issue. For example, if you know that there is an upcoming legal reform or another current issue in the news, use Twitter to search for conversations and discussions on that issue. People are constantly talking about current events and, whilst their opinions might not always be helpful or well-informed, they will allow you to see the issue from a different perspective and eventually to form your own opinion which you can express at an interview.

> "The goal should be to find people to follow who are regularly sharing the sort of information you are interested in or need to know about. For example, following the **@CityAM** twitter account will mean that every day you will receive links to a multitude of business stories—even keeping track of the headlines of many of these is a good starting point for commercial awareness. The aim should then be for the candidate to choose a small number of stories that genuinely interest

them which are likely to continue for a while and follow those in more depth over an extended period."

Matt Oliver, Career Coach For Lawyers,
The Legal Careers Group

FINAL THOUGHTS

Hopefully, this chapter has demonstrated that you must take an active and serious approach to your pursuit of commercial awareness development, and that this cannot be achieved overnight. It should also have shown you that a broad, superficial understanding of stories that have been reported in the commercial and financial press is not enough; you must understand the background to the stories and the practical impact of the events/ issues that have been reported. Without this, and without really understanding the background to, and impact of, the commercial issues that you have chosen to discuss, you will certainly not survive the sort of intensive, commercially driven interview that you can expect at a City or commercial law firm. It is not a good strategy to try to give an impression of commercial awareness which you don't actually have. First, you are unlikely to be able to pull the wool over the eyes of an experienced legal recruiter and, secondly, you are highly unlikely to enjoy your work or career, or be able to stick at it long term, if you don't have a genuine interest in business. There are, of course, areas of legal practice that are less commercially driven, but even so you will still need to understand how your own business works, how business/revenue is generated and how client relationships are managed so commercial awareness will be necessary in some guise or other even if you intend to practice in other areas.

"Commercial focus to me is all about being practical. It's about understanding what your clients want, understanding the markets that your clients operate in, and being able to practically apply business solutions. It's not just about being able to apply the letter of the law; it's about looking at what the law is and how that will affect your client. It's about understanding finance; it's about understanding the sector that we as a firm operate in . . . it's so many things. It's difficult to demonstrate commercial focus in an application form although we do ask specific questions to try to draw it out. It's obvious when students have done their research and are able to draw effectively on their work experience. They need to be aware that being a commercial lawyer is about being a business advisor and building relationships with clients and, crucially, it's about bringing in fees."

Sam Lee, Head of Recruitment, Bond Dickinson LLP

13 MAKING CONNECTIONS AND OPENING DOORS

WHAT IS NETWORKING AND WHY IS IT IMPORTANT?

There is no place for modesty or shyness when it comes to applying for training contracts. The marketplace is incredibly competitive and effective networking is essential to a successful outcome. You probably already have a small network of contacts so make the most of them all and invest effort in expanding your network. Never miss an opportunity to ask for work experience or to speak to someone about their career path and ask for any advice they could offer you. You will often find that people are only too happy to talk to you because they remember how difficult it was when they were trying to secure a training contract. Even something as simple as asking your best friend's mum to put you in touch with her friend who is a solicitor can pay dividends in the end as you never know where a chain of related contacts will lead you.

> "Networking is establishing a network or circle of professional relationships—people you would be able to email and ask questions of. The way that you make first contact with these people can be incredibly varied but students need to be ready to take down names and email addresses and to think about how the contact could develop. It won't always work, but the worst that can happen is someone will say that they can't help because they are too busy."
>
> *A Law Careers Consultant*

> "One of my students had a weekend job at a hair salon and managed to secure work experience by approaching one of the clients. He was a solicitor and took an interest in her

> because he was impressed by her perseverance and powers
> of persuasion. It's essential to make the most of every single
> contact because you never know where they might lead you."
> *Law Careers Advisor, University of Portsmouth*

Networking does not end once you have secured a training contract; it is an increasingly important aspect of legal practice in its
own right. Therefore, recruiters want to know that you will be a
good ambassador for their firm and that you will have the confidence and skills to attend business development events to win
new work and clients, and raise your firm's profile. They will have
this in mind when they meet you at interviews, assessment days,
or other careers events. That said, do not worry if you are not
someone to whom these things come naturally, networking is a
skill like any other and it can be developed and improved if you
persevere and practise. It really is worth the effort to develop
this invaluable business tool and it does get easier the more you
do it.

   This chapter will give you advice for effective networking, and
will show you how you can get the most out of law fairs and other
networking events. However, my advice can only take you so far.
There is no substitute for stepping outside your comfort zone and
investing time and effort in preparing for, and attending, as many
networking events as you can in order to see some results. If you
don't make this commitment, you are wasting your time and,
potentially, damaging your chances of a training contract if you
meet a recruiter and appear unprepared.

NETWORKING EVENTS

Your university or law school might arrange networking events
for you. These could consist of guest lectures, careers workshops,
law fairs, drinks receptions, or mentoring schemes. You should
make every effort to attend these events. The guests will be volunteers who have given up their time to help students with career
planning and this will make the networking process even easier;
they are there to help you so it will not be as difficult as trying to
warm up cold contacts. I have included some general tips below

for easing nerves and making a good impression at networking events such as drinks receptions or conferences. Tips for getting the most out of law fairs follow separately since they are probably the most common and significant form of networking event for law students and deserve special attention.

> "You have to make the most of every contact. If you meet trainees at networking events or other careers events and they give you their card, make sure you follow it up and don't be afraid to ask for some help or guidance when it comes to preparing your application forms. As long as you don't over-step the mark, they are likely to be the kind of people who are happy to help applicants because they've volunteered for these careers events."
>
> *A Law Undergraduate*

Tips for Making a Good Impression at Networking Events

Try to find out who will be attending the event—and think about what you might like to talk to them about or what you might have in common. This should give you a clearer sense of purpose when you arrive (for a start, you can focus on looking out for the individuals you have targeted) and will mean that you have some possible topics of conversation in mind if nerves get the better of you.

First impressions count—so pay attention to your appearance. If possible, check the dress code beforehand but, if you are in any doubt about what to wear, it is usually safest to dress up rather than down. Recruiters will be looking for people who know how to dress appropriately in a business environment and who will give a polished and professional appearance when introduced to clients or prospective clients. Seemingly small details can make all the difference so make sure that your shoes are polished, your nails and hair are neat, your clothes are pressed, and any jewellery is kept to a minimum. Women should ensure that make up, necklines and hemlines are appropriate for a business event, rather than a nightclub.

Consider eating before an event—that way you do not have to worry about holding a conversation while balancing a plate of food and a drink. This can be trickier than you might imagine, especially if you are nervous.

Arrive early to avoid the fear of entering a large crowd of people—if you do arrive to a packed room, take a deep breath and look out for someone who is on their own. They will probably be just as relieved to speak to someone as you are. If everyone seems to be in groups already, make your way to a busy area such as the drinks table or registration area and try to break into a group of people who have also just arrived. This should make it easier to start a conversation, rather than trying to break into a group where conversation is already well established. Remember that everyone else is in the same boat and you will be surprised at how easy it is to make conversation once you have attended a couple of these events.

Prepare some key points to use when you meet someone new—this will give you confidence and ensure that you make a positive first impression. Do not waste the opportunity by simply giving your name; tell the other person something about yourself and perhaps why you are attending this particular event. Obviously, you need to strike the correct tone here to avoid sounding as though you are reeling off your CV or placing an advert in a lonely hearts column, but it will help to have a few key points in mind and should help you to project confidence when you are asked about yourself.

Avoid spending the whole event with friends—this can sometimes be counter-productive if you cling to each other nervously and fail to embrace the opportunity to make new contacts. By all means, spend the first 10 minutes with a friend while you get a feel for the event and the people who are in the room, but then try to move off in your own direction for the remainder of the event. You can always arrange to meet up halfway through to exchange notes if you feel that you need a bit of extra security for your first event.

Try to make people feel valued when they are speaking to you—do not cast your eyes around the room to see if there is anyone else worth speaking to. Make an effort to be attentive and ask questions to show that you are interested in what they are telling you. If you really do not feel that the conversation is going anywhere, you can excuse yourself politely after a reasonable time and pretend that you have seen someone else you need to speak to, or that you are going to get another drink.

Always follow up any contacts as soon as possible after the event—if someone has offered you work experience or an informal chat about their career, send them an email the day after the event to thank them for their offer and to try to set something up. The email should be formal ("Dear John" rather than "Hi John"), concise and professional. I have included an example below but obviously you should write yours in your own words and style.

Dear John,

It was a pleasure to meet you at Jane Blogs' event last night, and to have the opportunity to discuss her ideas on mentoring and coaching with you after the lecture. I hope you had a safe journey back to London.

You said that you would be willing to meet with me to discuss my career plans and some possible work experience opportunities. I am very keen to take you up on your very kind offer and wondered whether we could try to find a mutually convenient time to meet. My diary is fairly flexible so perhaps you could suggest some possible dates? I can travel to your offices in London if that is most convenient for you.

I will look forward to hearing from you.

Yours sincerely,

Charlotte Harrison

Law Fairs

Law fairs are arguably the most important networking events for law students. Most universities and law schools host an annual law fair where students can meet representatives from law firms and other legal employers at a single event on campus. These events are useful because they allow students to find out more about particular firms, make contact with those involved in recruitment, and take the first step towards securing a training contract. However, a law fair is only useful if you take the event seriously and put in the preparation beforehand. You need to decide which delegates you wish to target, and produce a list of questions to ask them. There is absolutely no point just turning up on the day and wandering aimlessly around the stands.

> "It helps if you can do a little preparation in advance of attending the event. If you know who is attending, look at their profile on the firm's website, Linkedin or Twitter. If you know something about the person you'll be meeting, you'll feel more comfortable and come across as confident and knowledgeable."
> *Samantha Hope, Graduate Recruitment Manager, Shoosmiths*

To decide which firms you wish to target, you should review the list of delegates and read each firm's profile in the Chambers & Partners Student Guide or the Law Society's "Training Contract and Pupillage Handbook". There is also a very helpful feature on *http://www. lawcareers.net* called "Meet the Recruiter". You could look through previous editions and see if recruiters from these firms have been interviewed. You should also look at each firm's website to find out about the size and culture of each firm; the type of clients they work for and the practice areas they specialise in; the location of the firm's offices; the average trainee intake each year; and any recent high profile cases or transactions that the firm has been involved in. Try to narrow down your targets to three or four firms so you can spend quality time with each representative, make a good impression, and really find out more about the firm's culture.

Good research will help you project the image of an informed and motivated student and should also provide ideas for intelligent questions. Try to think of one or two specific questions for each of the firms or organisations that you are targeting. Make a note of the questions on the list of delegates so that you have them to hand as you make your way around the stands. Do not ask questions which you could answer yourself by reviewing the firm's website, e.g. "what kind of work do you do?" or "do you have offices in London?". Instead ask questions that you really want to know the answer to and which demonstrate that you are a serious candidate who has done their research and is prepared to invest time and effort in their career planning. Read through the sample questions below as a starting point, but remember that this is your opportunity to ask the questions that are important to you.

Questions to ask law firms and other legal employers at law fairs

You might want to ask about one of their practice areas or find out more about the type of clients they work for.

How is the training contract structured (if this is not clear from the website) and what type of work are trainees exposed to? You might also want to know how much choice trainees have in terms of the seats they visit, and whether any seats are compulsory.

Are there any opportunities for commercial secondments or secondments to overseas offices? If you ask this question, you should be prepared to be asked why this is important to you so make sure you think about this beforehand.

If you have the opportunity to speak to current trainees, you might want to ask them why they chose to train with that particular firm; what they feel differentiates that firm from others that they applied to; what seats they have completed so far; whether the training contract has been as they expected; what they like most about working for that firm; and/or what advice they would give you in terms of navigating the recruitment process.

What qualities are they looking for in prospective trainees? What is their average retention rate (i.e. the number of trainees they retain on qualification)?

> Do they advise students to study particular options at university or during Stage 2 of the LPC?
>
> Do they have a list of preferred LPC providers?
>
> How many trainees are recruited while completing the LPC, rather than while still at university?
>
> What is the firm's unique selling point?

Although you might feel overwhelmed by the thought of approaching people at these events, it does get easier the more you do it. You will also find that most people are very approachable and once you have broken the ice with your first question, conversation should flow more easily.

> "The best conversations I've had at events are just that—conversations. It is important to build a rapport with someone, so if you know they are passionate about baking, strike up a conversation about that—and try turning it into a question about the firm. For example, you could ask: "I read that you are interested in baking. Does Shoosmiths give you opportunities to get involved in social and corporate responsibility events that allow you to use your hobbies?
>
> At any event you attend, be yourself; it's the one unique quality you have that no one else does!"
>
> *Samantha Hope, Graduate Recruitment Manager, Shoosmiths*

The general networking advice applies equally to law fairs, but this section includes some specific advice for navigating law fairs.

Try to get hold of a list of delegates a couple of days before the event—take some time to think about why you are going, who you would like to speak to, why you wish to speak with them, and what questions you could ask them. Make a list of the three or four firms that you are especially keen to target and write out your questions to avoid forgetting them. This will help to focus your thoughts and prevent you from wandering aimlessly at the beginning of the event and wasting time or, even worse, approaching someone without any idea of what you want to say to them.

Arrive on time—and certainly not in the last 10 minutes of the event. Sometimes law fairs will finish early if the rush seems to be over (in which case you might well miss your chance if you arrive too late) and it is usually the case that everyone gets hotter, more tired, and perhaps a little less enthusiastic as the hours roll on.

Make a good first impression—you never know where it might lead. Project an air of confident professionalism and maintain eye contact when speaking to people. A good candidate will appear professional, polished, well prepared, and confident (but not arrogant). Do not be afraid to take the initiative by introducing yourself to representatives and remember that a firm handshake and a warm smile will help to project a confident appearance (even if you don't feel so confident underneath!).

Check the dress code—they vary so make sure that you check with the event organiser beforehand. If there is not a dress code, it is up to you to decide what would be appropriate. For most evening law fairs, it is usual to wear a suit but there is often more flexibility for daytime events. If you do not wear a suit, you should wear something smart and take care to ensure that your hair, shoes, and any accessories are polished and appropriate for a business event. You should give the impression that you are prepared fully for the event and didn't just drop by after a lecture because all your friends headed in that direction.

Do not adopt the snatch and run approach—avoid the temptation to grab the free merchandise from each stand without even speaking to the representatives. This is a waste of your time and theirs, and, frankly, it is very rude and immature.

Act professionally and be courteous to other visitors—do not jump in if there is a queue of people waiting to speak to someone at a particular stand; avoid interrupting other people's conversations to ask your own questions; and know when your time is up (do not monopolise the recruiters' time).

Treat all representatives with respect—do not dismiss the trainee or graduate recruitment officer in favour of the recruitment partner. In fact, discussions with trainees will often be far more insightful and relevant than those with other representatives.

Do not use the representatives as careers advisors—they will expect you to know about the recruitment process, different types of firms and training providers, and to be aware of key deadlines, etc. The purpose of the law fair is to find out more about particular employers or education providers, not to get a crash course in the route to securing a training contract.

Collect business cards if they are offered—make a note of who you spoke to and what was discussed, and, if appropriate, follow up your discussions after the event. Even if they didn't offer work experience, or any formal assistance, it would still be appropriate to send a short email telling them that it was a pleasure to meet them, thanking them for their advice, and advising them that you will be making an application to their firm in the coming cycle (but obviously only add the last item if you actually will be applying to them).

If you take my advice, you should be able to use your time more efficiently, give the impression of a focused, organised and well-prepared individual when you meet potential recruiters, and hopefully walk away with some useful contacts, information and advice. On that note, remember to take a notebook and pen with you to note down any important details.

After the law fair, reflect on whether you are still interested in the same firm or type of firm. Also think about whether you would like to investigate alternative career or training opportunities. In terms of skills development, you should reflect on what you did well in terms of your performance, and what you would do differently at future networking events. Finally, set some action points in terms of any new firms you wish to investigate, new issues or questions which you need to research, applications you will be making, and future events that you will attend.

"The application process starts before you even pick up an application form: go to the careers fairs; do your research beforehand and target firms carefully; introduce yourself to representatives from your chosen firms and tell them that you want to work for their firm and why. Create a positive impression there. In short, you must take every opportunity to meet the recruitment people so that when your application arrives, those firms will recognise who you are. It's this level of pro-activity that convinces me that you have a genuine interest in working for my firm. Also, make sure you actually make reference to these meetings in your application and follow up on any offers of help—if there is a half open door, push it open (it's amazing how many students fail to follow up on these meetings or make use of my contact details if I give them a business card)."

Training Manager of a National Law Firm

"You will know in advance what firms are going to be at the law fair so make sure that you do your research. Approach it in the same way that you would prepare for an interview. Make sure you know about the firm and have an awareness of the type of work that it is involved in. Be ready to ask sensible questions—not just "tell me about your firm"—and dress smartly. We remember good (and bad) candidates from law fairs and I'm always really impressed when students actually email and say thank you for taking the time to speak to them at the event."

Sam Lee, Head of Recruitment, Bond Dickinson LLP

Having read this chapter, you should be in no doubt about the fact that professional networking is an essential skill in a solicitor's (or aspiring solicitor's) tool kit. This chapter has focused largely on developing your professional network through face-to-face events. However, you also need to be alive to the opportunities to develop your professional network and individual profile through social media. You can find more advice on this in the second half of Ch.14.

14 BRAND DEVELOPMENT AND SOCIAL MEDIA

Written by Valya Georgieva

In recent years, the legal profession has become increasingly crowded and this has generated fresh challenges for solicitors, aspiring solicitors and law firms not least in terms of how they differentiate themselves from their competitors. This chapter will explore the importance of brand development to individuals and law firms, and explain how and why social media is used to support brand development and professional networking.

BRANDING AND SOCIAL MEDIA FOR LAW FIRMS AND THEIR SOLICITORS

The impact of increased competition amongst law firms can be divided into three main areas: retaining clients; winning new business; and talent recruitment and retention. In order to succeed in each of those areas, law firms are striving to differentiate themselves from their competitors. In theory, there are three key ways in which such differentiation could be achieved. These are discussed below.

Price—for clients, one of the key factors in choosing a legal service provider is the cost. Law firms are therefore under increasing pressure to offer better services at a lower price. Nevertheless, competing on price is not always a viable option, especially in areas such as litigation where it is extremely difficult to predict the cost at the outset of a dispute.

Service—although this is a good competition model for niche firms with narrow areas of specialism, it is not such a good option for medium-sized full-service law firms, which offer essentially the same services as other firms in the same market. You will probably have noticed that if you visit a full-service law firm's website, they often describe themselves as "a leading law firm" and "best in their field". In practice, you will not be able to vouch for this until you gain some experience with the firm in question. The same applies to clients who would rarely be able to compare law firms solely based on the services provided, until they actually use those services.

Brand—in practical terms, the best way for law firms to differentiate themselves is to develop their own brand. On the one hand, this is the firm's vision about itself; the values they place at the heart of their business; the quality of the services they strive to provide to their clients; the contributions they make to their community; the work environment they provide for their employees; and the experience and expertise of the firm's employees. It is based on this vision that a law firm would make a "promise" to their clients about what they should expect from the firm were they to use its services. This "promise" is usually articulated through the firm's website, social media activity and press releases about the firm. On the other hand, the brand is the client's expectation and perception of that law firm based on its website, reputation or the quality of services previously received. Ultimately, the brand is about building trust with the firm's clients so that they know they will receive the same quality of services every time.

> "The brand represents the values of the firm as a business, the values of the people who work in the firm, the behaviour of the people internally and externally, the quality of the work that the firm does, the relationships the firm has with its clients, the tone of voice used to speak to the press or to clients, the tone of voice in all communications."
> *Emma Daly, External Communications Manager,*
> *Blake Morgan LLP*

The first impression that a law firm would usually make on prospective clients, or those who may wish to work for the firm, is via its website. Look at the websites for three law firms in your local area. The impression that you get from each website will probably be quite different. They might all be full service law firms but each of them will stand for something different and each of them will have developed their website to reflect their image and key values.

Clients will often shop around before they select the law firm whose services they would like to use. Whether they are looking for a divorce or advice on a personal injury claim or contractual dispute, it is the perception of a particular law firm, the contents of its website and the presentation of its solicitors that makes or breaks a client's decision to instruct that law firm.

Individual clients often look for a solicitor who is personable, down to earth and speaks in plain English. This has increased the need for solicitors to get inside their clients' heads, speak their language and demonstrate that they cater for their needs. There are a number of ways in which this could be achieved but one of the best ways to do this nowadays is by creating relevant content and ensuring that clients, and prospective clients, have quick and easy access to the information which they need and are searching for. This is what has prompted solicitors to maintain a presence on the channels and platforms which their clients use, with social media being one of the most powerful tools. With every new tweet, retweet and blog post, clients are becoming increasingly empowered to make an informed choice about their legal service provider. At the same time, solicitors are given the unique opportunity to engage with their clients and prospective clients by listening to what they have to say on social media and responding to their needs.

"People use social media increasingly to find an answer to their question or their problem. There is so much free information online that solicitors can't afford to be as 'smoke screen' as they used to be. If your firm does not provide guidance or information other firms will."
Emma Daly, External Communications Manager,
Blake Morgan LLP

In terms of branding, social media is a tool which allows solicitors and law firms to communicate their message to their audience and help create an image, a perception and a feel for that particular law firm. There are four key ways in which social media could be used by law firms and solicitors.

Communication and broadcasting tool—most law firms usually use social media channels to share content from their website and others which are relevant to that firm's services and activities. This is the first and very basic step of using social media. It can be useful as it increases the likelihood of the firm's website content being read by their target audience. In order to be effective, content sharing has to be timely and on point. So for example if there is a change in the law today or if a judgment is being handed down which sets a precedent that affects a law firm's clients, it would be expected that the firm which provides services in that area of law should "talk about" it and share content that will be of interest to their clients.

Graduate recruitment tool—many law firms have at least two accounts on Twitter, one being their general corporate account, the other being an account for graduate recruitment purposes. With more and more students starting to use social media, Twitter is often one of the best places for law firms to create an image for themselves and to show what it means to be working with that law firm and why students should apply. There have been a number of training contract campaigns on Twitter with law firms and career advisers sharing "top tips" for completing training contract applications. Law firms have a chance to differentiate themselves from their competitors by joining the conversation and helping students make an informed decision about whether or not they can picture themselves working with that law firm. Shoosmiths is one example of a law firm which has really spent time developing its online presence. With their **#AskShoos** hashtag campaign running throughout the year, students are given the unique opportunity to get some first-hand guidance from the graduate recruiters at Shoosmiths before making a decision to apply for a training contract.

"Our presence on social media is incredibly important in maintaining client relationships and attracting potential trainee solicitors to join our firm.

Being social enables us to engage with students in a variety of ways. We use Facebook and Twitter to answer questions instantly and share relevant legal updates with our audience. We also share photos and videos of activities our people are involved in such as fundraising, volunteering, and diversity initiatives like career workshops in schools.

Being social also gives us a platform to talk openly about applications, interviews and careers advice.

Our Twitter account is not managed by a marketing team, but by the trainees themselves, supported by the recruitment team. Trainees tweet directly from **@ShoosmithsGrads**, enabling them to reach a much wider audience than they would just by attending events."

Samantha Hope, Graduate Recruitment Manager, Shoosmiths

CSR activities—corporate social responsibility (CSR) has become an increasingly important ingredient of every law firm's brand. This is a process whereby the law firm (or any other business organisation) assesses the impact of its business operations on the environment and the community in which it operates, and aims to make a positive contribution to them. It involves taking an active part in local communities and having a vision that goes beyond profitability. This in turn encourages clients to be more willing to engage and work with that firm. That is why most of today's law firms invest a considerable amount of time and other resources in promoting their CSR activities. Social media is one of the best channels to use for this purpose. With most local organisations and charities having a social media presence, law firms have the opportunity to engage with them on another, more personable level, whilst creating a warmer image of the firm overall.

Trusted advisers and leaders in their field—finally, social media can and should also be used by the solicitors themselves, in conjunction with the law firm, in order to raise their profiles as trusted advisers and leaders in their field. Solicitors and law firms have a real opportunity here to show their audience that they know what they are talking about by blogging and writing articles about current issues in their field, as well as by engaging in discussions on social media platforms such as Twitter and LinkedIn.

As well as a branding tool, social media can help law firms win new business, again in conjunction with other strategies.

> "Social media can bring in new business but I don't think you should look at it as a silver bullet. Social media is just one piece of the puzzle . . . Buying legal services, it's a very complex decision. Is someone going to hire you just because of your tweet? Almost certainly not. But is it possible that they'll hire you because of a series of factors including the fact that you are always on top of the legal issues in your industry, I think that's a very different question. It positions you as a thought leader and it really shows your expertise level."
>
> *Adrian Dayton Esq., Social Media Consultant and author of the book 'Social Media for Lawyers'*

Social media is good for reinforcing the law firm's message. It is like seeing an advert on the television a few times. Whilst you won't necessarily remember and buy the product the first or second time, it would often influence your final decision to buy a product. We tend to buy things which are familiar to us and which we know or think will be of good quality. The same applies to choosing a legal service provider, especially if we are looking for a local regional law firm. The more that law firm pops in our news feed and the more we hear about it, the more likely we are to remember its name and choose its services when we need them. The same applies to what is known as word of mouth marketing. Buying legal services is a daunting experience and people would often seek recommendations and reassurance that this is the best firm in the area.

> "I've seen it on Twitter. The conversation started 'I need an employment lawyer in Southampton area, don't know the

area very well, our company's just relocated, who shall I ask?'
Somebody independently replied 'I would try Max Craft at
Blake Morgan; he's always been fantastic for us'."
Emma Daly, External Communications Manager,
Blake Morgan LLP

As well as the law firms themselves, solicitors too have an opportunity to really raise their profile by engaging in discussions and
answering questions online. In order to be able to achieve that,
one must have a real interest in, and commitment to, social
media as it requires the investment of a good deal of time and
effort if you wish to do it properly. The early adopters of social
media platforms such as Twitter have managed to become influ-
ential and recognised by their peers for their expertise in their
area of law. There are no hard and fast rules on how this could
be achieved. The best way to do it is to really take the time
to understand how the ethics of social media work. Start by
listening first, then broadcasting, and eventually engaging in
conversations.

In order to make the most of platforms such as Twitter and
blogging, solicitors must realise that the best way to use them
is to add value. This means going far beyond broadcasting and
self-promotion. It means sharing a view and opinion as an expert
in a particular area. Whilst Twitter is only limited to 140 characters, which makes it somewhat difficult to express a valuable
opinion, regularly sharing content in one's area of expertise will
make a solicitor stand out as keeping on top of the issues that
could potentially affect his/her clients. So for example, imagine
that there is a debate in the House of Lords about a prospective change in the law which would affect the financial industry.
Banking Solicitor A writes a blog or an article addressing the issue.
He writes in plain English, without using legalese, and explains
the implications of the change on his clients and the financial
industry at large. He engages in discussions about the issue and
expresses his opinion on its potential impact on Twitter and
LinkedIn. Banking Solicitor B writes a blog simply stating that the
change in the law is happening and providing a link to a general
news website without adding any analysis of that news from his

client's perspective. Banking Solicitor C writes a long article providing background to the law including case law. He then moves on to provide a detailed analysis of the legal change. All other things being equal, if a client was to choose a solicitor based on this, Solicitor A would clearly stand out from Solicitors B and C. This is because a banking solicitor would be expected to not only follow the debate through and to know the nitty-gritty of the law, but to be able to advise his/her clients on the potential practical and commercial implications of it.

> "Social media enables people to find information quickly in bite sized pieces and in plain language. Users access their social media in down time usually on train journeys, commutes in the morning, at lunch time, maybe last thing at night."
> *Emma Daly, External Communications Manager,*
> *Blake Morgan LLP*

People will usually spend 10 seconds on a web page reading an article before they decide if they want to keep reading or if they are looking for something else. That is why clients usually want to read something which gives them the gist of an issue within a few paragraphs, in plain English without any jargon or legalese. And that is what has motivated solicitors to move slightly away from the standard lengthy legal articles and start blogging.

PERSONAL BRANDING AND SOCIAL MEDIA FOR STUDENTS

With social media becoming commonly used by law firms and solicitors, you could benefit from gaining an understanding of it early on in your career. Although social media on its own is not a magic key which could unlock the door to a training contract, there are a number of ways in which it could help you expand your professional network online and progress your career.

> "[T]he lawyers that really have put some attention to [social media], will absolutely stand out from their peers. Because

> it's a signal to the law firm that this lawyer is willing to do the work, to brand themselves within the firm."
>
> *Adrian Dayton Esq., Social Media Consultant and author of the book 'Social Media for Lawyers'*

In order to be able to make the most of social media, you should start by realising that platforms such as LinkedIn and Twitter are not the equivalent of Facebook. Facebook is a strictly personal networking platform. LinkedIn is a strictly professional networking platform. Twitter is somewhat in the middle. You should take the time to understand the etiquette of each of those platforms in order to ensure that they work to your benefit rather than your detriment.

> "Social media use is one great way to develop a personal brand. However, it needs to be done with some thought rather than just spending every waking hour on the social networks. I still see way too many students and firms alike using social media in a poor and ineffective way. A small amount of time spent researching how to use the different social networks to build a personal brand will reveal plenty of advice to get them starting on the right foot. My advice is to choose one social network and to focus on that one only until they become familiar with it and understand how to use it to their advantage. Often it's just a case of spending a small amount of time each day and observing how others are using it and then modelling those people who are clearly doing it well."
>
> *Matt Oliver, Career Coach For Lawyers, The Legal Careers Group*

Facebook

Facebook is currently one of the most popular social media networks for students. It is also the most dangerous if it is not used with caution. Founded in 2004, Facebook is now the largest social media network with over 1.3 billion users. As such, it is one of the first search results on a Google search for your name. This means that your Facebook profile is easily accessible to your current and prospective employers. Not many people consider this when setting their profile up and when updating their status. However, we have already seen examples of people being dismissed over the content of their Facebook updates so this is an issue which is worth taking seriously. The points below set out a few steps which you could take to ensure you are not one of those people who are left vulnerable at work as a result of your Facebook settings.

Adjust your privacy and profile visibility settings—by default, everything you post on Facebook is set as public which means that it can be viewed and accessed by everyone, whether or not they are your "friend". The minimum you should do is to restrict everything to "Friends only" in order to ensure that you have control over who sees your posts and photographs. The next step would be to split your friends into different lists to include "Friends", "Acquaintances", "Colleagues" and "Close friends". This would allow you to select the relevant group of friends you wish to share each post with.

Control your Facebook timeline and tags—one of the most dangerous features of Facebook is the fact that other people can tag you in posts and photographs which would automatically appear in your profile by default. There is an option to restrict tags so that they do not appear in your profile until you have approved them and the advice is to take advantage of this feature in order to avoid being tagged in some embarrassing photos.

Keep it personal—Facebook is a network for connecting with friends and relatives. Few people tend to keep it that way. The danger of adding colleagues to your Facebook is that you might forget that you have done so and post something which they should not read. It is not difficult to imagine a situation where someone ends up being dismissed, or at least disciplined, for complaining about their job and manager on Facebook whilst forgetting that their manager is a "friend" on Facebook.

Think before you update your status or add a friend—even if you take the steps above, you never know who might read your status and share it with someone else. The advice here is two-fold: think before accepting a "friend" request; and think before you update your status.

LinkedIn

LinkedIn is a social media network which allows you to build your professional identity online, whilst expanding your network of professional connections and contacts. It is often misunderstood or overlooked by students and I can therefore not emphasise enough the importance of setting up your profile and understanding how it works early on in your career.

> "Every lawyer should have a LinkedIn account. And I think that a good LinkedIn profile is the new resume."
> *Adrian Dayton Esq., Social Media Consultant and author of the book 'Social Media for Lawyers'*

There are three key ways in which you could use LinkedIn.

Networking—imagine the following situation. You attend a networking event, such as the annual conference of the Junior Lawyers Division of the Law Society. You meet and network with a number of professionals. Some may give you their business card, some might not. The best way to establish a connection and start building a professional relationship with them is to connect with them on LinkedIn following the event. If you do that, make sure to include a short message explaining where you know them from and why you want to connect. Other people may not remember you as well as you remember them, especially if it was a busy event. The default LinkedIn message is "I'd like to add you to my professional network". Never use this on its own. An example of an introductory message would be as follows:

Dear [insert name here],

It was a pleasure to meet you at the [insert event title here] on [insert date here] at [insert venue here]. I would like to add you to my professional network because [insert reason here]

Many thanks and I hope to hear from you soon.

[Insert your name here]

Connecting to classmates, lecturers and colleagues—the other reason for using LinkedIn is to keep in touch with people you have met at university as well as colleagues you have worked with. Once again, you should include a personal message every time you send someone an invitation to connect to ensure that they accept your request. You should also only add those people whom you have actually worked with in your professional capacity, rather than every single person you have ever seen walking in the corridors. This will ensure that your connections are limited to those who know you personally and who can vouch for you as a professional.

Job opportunities—more and more firms and organisations are starting to advertise their vacancies via LinkedIn. There are also a number of legal recruiters and head-hunters who are constantly searching for people to connect with. If your profile is complete, you will start receiving recommendations for legal opportunities based on the words used in your profile. You could also use the search facility to find paralegal or other opportunities of interest.

So, now you know why LinkedIn is useful, you should read the following key tips on using LinkedIn effectively.

Complete your profile—there is nothing worse than an incomplete profile without a photograph. You should therefore set aside at least half an hour to ensure that your profile is up to date and complete. Your "headline" is the first thing that someone will see about you—make sure it is relevant. If you are still at university you might want to use something such as "A penultimate year law student looking for a training contract with a medium to large corporate/commercial practice." Treat your LinkedIn profile as a CV and make sure that all your relevant experience and skills are included.

Add a professional photograph—your LinkedIn profile is usually the first or second result when someone searches for your name on Google. Your LinkedIn profile is one of the first image results for your name. Do remember that LinkedIn is not Facebook and you should therefore not use a photograph that you wouldn't want seen by a prospective employer. A good photograph will be a clear head and shoulders shot of you against a neutral background. Since LinkedIn is a professionally oriented network, make sure you are dressed as professionally as possible. Keep the photograph simple and avoid wearing too much make up or distracting jewellery and hair styles. Avoid adding a photograph with other people or with an inappropriate background, such as a beach or a party.

Add connections—once you have set up your profile, start connecting to people you have worked with.

Ask for recommendations—one of the best features of LinkedIn is the opportunity to request a recommendation. The etiquette is that you can request a recommendation from employers you have worked for but not your current employer. If you are still at university you may want to request a recommendation from a lecturer that has worked closely with you, such as your dissertation supervisor. Make sure that you include a personal message when requesting the recommendation explaining why you consider this person to be in a position to write a recommendation for you.

Update your profile as you progress your career—ensure that your profile is kept up to date and that all your relevant experience and achievements are included for completeness.

Twitter

Twitter is the next step to completing your online presence. It is a social media network which is not for everyone and before deciding to use it you should ensure you have a real interest in and an understanding of the way it works. When Twitter was first created in 2006, it was intended as a platform for sharing your moods and day-to-day activities with your friends. Today, with over 240 million users, it has grown to become the key medium for receiving news and information as well as building relationships online. Using Twitter allows you to achieve the key objectives listed below.

Expand your professional network—Twitter is a relatively relaxed social media channel which allows you to speak to professionals who you would not usually have the opportunity to meet in person. Use this opportunity to your benefit by engaging in discussions with them or even reaching out for advice. If you find a solicitor who specialises in an area of law which you are interested in, don't be afraid to ask them questions about it. You will be surprised at how approachable people on Twitter usually are.

Raise your online profile—if you use Twitter in the right way you will end up attracting followers who will be interested in what you have to say and will reach out to you for your opinion. If you share anything of value and if you engage with the right people and in the right conversations, you may easily be noticed by law firms who are on Twitter. This can be beneficial if you were to apply for a training contract with those law firms.

Engage with professionals on a more personal level—a lot of professionals will be using Twitter from both a personal and professional perspective. You might have a common interest in cycling or cooking with a solicitor on Twitter. Use this as an opportunity to engage with them. This would make them much more willing to give you advice if needed at a later stage.

Get answers to your questions—people ask questions on Twitter all the time to include anything from "Can anyone recommend any good dressmakers in Berkshire?" to "Does anyone have any tips on writing a legal dissertation?" There are also a number of hashtags that could be used by students to ask questions particularly relating to training contract applications, such as the **#AskAtrainee** hour-long Q&A session for solicitors-to-be organised by **@LegalTony**. In addition to sending a question to your whole network of followers, you can find people who are best placed to answer your question and ask them personally.

Learn about new conferences, publications and research in your areas of interest—if you are following the right people who work in your areas of interest and are well established professionals, chances are they will be talking about new conferences and publications in that area.

Know things well before they reach the news—for example, the news about the Boston marathon bombing in 2013 broke on Twitter before it reached any of the news channels.

Listen to what people are saying on a particular topic—if you are interested to know people's opinion about a trending issue in the news, one of the best sources to use is Twitter where you can track discussions by using a relevant keyword or a hashtag.

Have personally-curated updates—news, information, stories you care about are available at your fingertips. Over time, you will develop your own network of people who share information which is of interest to you and you will be able to browse through this information on the move.

There are no hard and fast rules on using Twitter effectively. The best way to get started is to find a few relevant people who share content of interest and start following them as well as the people they engage with. Once you gain some confidence and understanding about the Twitter etiquette, the next and most important step is to start engaging. There are discussions on every single topic you can think of every second of every minute of every day. The difficulty is in finding the relevant conversations and having something clever to say in response. That is how relationships are built online.

There are hundreds of thousands of professionals on Twitter. Some are quite active, some less so. But most of them would be quite willing to respond to a query you may have, be it about their profession, their career path, or simply asking for some advice on an issue in their area of expertise. Twitter is a relatively relaxed platform which in a way takes the pressure away from having to write a formal email to a professional asking a question.

> "There have been various articles shared over the internet which promote the benefits of creating a 'personal brand'. Personally, I used the concept of developing a following on Twitter and LinkedIn in order to gain authority and engage with those in the legal profession who might otherwise be less interested in discussing a career in law. I did this by developing a 'voice', i.e. a consistent approach to conversation on social media. My advice to students wishing to develop their own voice is to share honest, thoughtful and interesting content— be it their own or, where having acknowledged the author, others."
>
> *Anthony Lyons, Paralegal at King & Wood Mallesons*

Key Tips on Using Twitter Effectively

Content is king—if you decide to give Twitter a go, the best way to make the most of it is to decide what image you want to create for yourself and to share content which would be of interest to your target audience accordingly. For example, you might be a final year law student wishing to motivate and inspire other law students by telling them about your journey and the challenges you face. Your target audience would be other law students who are searching for training contracts. You might therefore share tips and advice on successful training contract applications as well as blogs on how to balance a busy final year of university with other activities such as a part-time job. Or you might have a real passion for sports and healthy eating. You might therefore create a blog sharing tips, advice and recipes on healthy eating. Your target audience would be others who share the same interest in sports and healthy eating.

Engagement is queen—once you become more comfortable with the Twitter etiquette, the next step would be to start engaging with others and joining in discussions on topics that are of interest to you. Finding the relevant conversations does take time but once you manage to do that, the benefits are considerable. By reading what others say and engaging with them, you would develop relationships online and people would start reading and paying more attention to what you have to say online too.

Be consistent and persistent—if you want to develop your own personal voice and brand, you should plan your tweets accordingly and ensure that the content you post is consistent. People who start following you would do so because they have found the content you share interesting. If you suddenly change your voice, chances are that you will lose a number of your followers.

Answer questions—people ask questions and look for solutions to their problems on Twitter all the time. If you see a question that you know the answer to, respond.

Add value—there is a lot of "noise" on Twitter and in order to be able to stand out from the crowd and get people to follow you, you should make sure to add value to the content you share. This means sharing your thoughts and opinion, joining in discussions, commenting on issues you are interested in and passionate about. Twitter needs more people who are knowledgeable, approachable and share interesting content. With time, practice and persistence, you could be one of those people.

Be professional, yet personal—be yourself—Twitter is a networking tool above anything else, and people want to connect to other people who are personable, approachable and down to earth. Nevertheless, if you are to use Twitter in order to connect to other professionals, the advice is to be professional too. Treat

Twitter like a never-ending networking event. Think before you tweet, never say anything that could be considered offensive or ignorant and find the right balance between your personal and your professional self. Remember that Twitter is an open network and so you wouldn't want to share anything that you wouldn't want read by a potential recruiter.

> "The biggest risks of social media are completely avoided as long as you refrain from saying something stupid. The only people that have ever gotten into trouble have said something or done something that on its face clearly shows poor judgment."
>
> *Adrian Dayton Esq., Social Media Consultant and*
> *author of the book 'Social Media for Lawyers'*

BLOGGING

As a solicitor-to-be, one thing that you should learn to be particularly good at is writing. Every solicitor should be able to write in a way that is easy to understand by their clients, without the use of jargon and legalese. This is where blogging comes into play. With a number of blogging platforms which are free to use (e.g. WordPress and Blogger) everyone can get published today provided you have something clever and interesting to share with the world.

Whilst blogging is not for everyone, there are a number of reasons why you might want to consider blogging. These are discussed below.

Personal branding/authenticity—the use of social media and blogging is not a fast route to creating a personal brand. However, if you are looking to create a personal image and a "voice" online, a good place to start is to create your own blog and start sharing your thoughts and opinions on issues that are of interest to you. Your blog does not have to be a legal blog. It could be about something you are passionate about, such as healthy eating or cooking. Law firms are usually looking for well-rounded individuals who have interests outside of law so an interesting and impactful blog could be an excellent way of demonstrating this to potential employers. If you mention in your application that you are writing a blog on a particular topic, this would really make you stand out and give you something different to talk about at your interview.

Networking—there are hundreds of thousands of blogs written on every single issue you could think about. One good way to expand your social network is to find people who blog in the same area as you do and start exchanging thoughts and opinions with them.

Professional and intangible skills—blogging requires a considerable amount of time, motivation and persistence. Once you start blogging, and depending on how good you are at it, your audience will expect to see more and more from your posts online. Blogging teaches you to be disciplined, consistent and persistent and those are professional skills which would be invaluable during your legal career. Blogging also makes you a better, and arguably more engaging, writer.

People will hear about you—if you are good at it, people will share your content and spread your thoughts and opinions. It does take a considerable amount of time but if you take the time to develop your blog and your personal brand you will be on your way to becoming an "influencer" of your audience online.

Get published—last but not least, blogging is the easiest way to have your thoughts published online. This of course comes with its risks, as once you share something online it is very difficult to completely remove it. You should therefore spend some considerable amount of time planning your blog and ensuring that what you say online does not show poor judgment.

> "Whilst I don't think that being on Twitter and blogging on their own will help law students stand out, they certainly help as part of the general mix. They represent another way for a

student to connect with their target law firms and to develop their personal brand. If done in the right way then it is relatively easy to get onto a firm's radar and have your name recognised when it comes to the application and interview stages. It is also a great way to seek out targeted advice which can be used to gain a competitive advantage in the recruitment process."

Matt Oliver, Career Coach For Lawyers,
The Legal Careers Group

Tips on Getting Started with Blogging:

Define your niche—before you create your blog, you should take the time to think about who you want to be online and what you want to talk about. The most successful bloggers are those who have clearly defined their niche so that their audience knows what to expect when they come back.

Know your audience—once you define your niche, you should think about who your target audience is. Your blog posts should be targeted at that audience and so they should be written in a way that would be interesting for them.

Be consistent—you should be consistent in your approach and in the voice which you choose for yourself. This is the best way to ensure that people who read your blog once will want to read more.

Promote your posts—Use other social media channels such as Twitter and LinkedIn to share your blogs to your target audience.

Read and link to other blogs—one good way to ensure that your blog is read and discovered is to read other people's blogs, link to them and comment on them if you have an opinion.

Be yourself—people who read blogs expect the writer to be themselves and to express their real opinion on the issue in question. Make sure that the image you create for yourself is a genuine one and that you will be able to comment on and answer questions about the issues discussed in your blog.

Give people a reason to return—last but not least, the content you post must be unique and interesting in order to ensure that people will return and will want to hear from you again.

Making social media work to your benefit is a time consuming task that comes with its risks and responsibilities. You must therefore ensure that you are committed to it and that you understand both its potential benefits and its potential pitfalls. The above is not a comprehensive guide on using social media but some general advice on the key considerations which you should keep in mind when using Facebook, LinkedIn, Twitter and blogging to your advantage rather than detriment whilst progressing your professional career.

PART III
THE TRAINING CONTRACT

Section 2
The Application Process

15 EFFECTIVE CVS AND COVERING LETTERS

WHY ARE CVS SO IMPORTANT?

Most law firms now use online forms for training contract applications. However, some still request a CV and covering letter and you can also use them when making speculative applications for informal work experience. Therefore, it is well worth investing serious effort in creating an impressive legal CV and one that is tailored to the type of firm you are targeting.

At a basic level, a CV documents your education, background and work experience but it is so much more than that if you use it correctly: it allows you to demonstrate how and why you have the potential to become an excellent solicitor. Do not just say that you have excellent organisational skills, give evidence to prove the point. Think of the CV as helping you to build a case to demonstrate why that firm or organisation should employ you and remember, like any good lawyer, you must have evidence to support your claims.

> "Producing a standard legal CV is fine but it still needs to be tailored for each application. The key is to do your research and to use that research to change the CV slightly. For example, you might change the emphasis on your work experience or mention different modules that you took at university. Certainly, the covering letter should be targeted to that particular firm."
>
> *Law Careers Consultant*

WHAT SHOULD YOU INCLUDE IN A LEGAL CV?

To ensure that your CV focuses on the skills that demonstrate your potential to become a good solicitor, you need to think carefully about what experiences and achievements to include, and how to document them. Before you start writing, take a moment to think about your work experience, extra-curricular and academic achievements, and any voluntary work that you have been involved in. What have you learnt from each one and why might they be relevant to a future employer? You might like to look back at the Map of Experience which you prepared in Ch.10 and draw on some of those experiences in your CV. It is worth dedicating plenty of time to this exercise as it will ensure that you draw on the most appropriate material for each section and that you sell your skills effectively.

A standard CV will tend to cover the areas listed below. You can use this list as a guide when structuring your CV but there are no definitive rules as long as the document is clear, concise and easy to read. Your careers service will be able to provide detailed advice on CV writing and you can also download templates from law careers websites.

Personal details—including name, address, landline number, mobile number, and email address. If you have a different term-time address, you should make this clear and state when you are contactable at each address. You do not have to disclose your gender, nationality, date of birth or marital status.

Education and qualifications—you should state where you studied and when, and list your qualifications and grades. This information should be presented in reverse chronological order (i.e. most recent first). If you have not yet received your final degree classification, you could include a breakdown of your first and second year grades at university. If you are not comfortable disclosing the individual marks you could give an average percentage for each year but be aware that firms will probably request confirmation of the individual marks at some point.

Details of any previous careers—if you are a mature entrant to the profession, make sure you draw out the key skills from your previous careers and map them against the skills that legal employers are looking for. Also draw out any experience of a particular sector which might be relevant to the firm's clients.

Work experience—set out your work experience in reverse chronological order and consider dividing it into paid work (i.e. your employment history) and work experience placements. In each case, you might like to use bullet points to make the information more accessible. For each period of employment, you should state your role within the organisation and make it clear how long you worked there. Remember to sell your skills to the prospective employer but do not dismiss part-time jobs just because they did not involve legal practice. The key is demonstrating that you have the essential skills that firms are looking for; it is not about demonstrating that you are already a competent legal practitioner. For example, think about the skills you would need for a part-time job in a shop or a customer service call centre. These could include your ability to diffuse difficult situations with customers; work within a team; communicate effectively; work productively under pressure; meet financial targets; lead a team effectively; and balance a rigorous academic degree with paid work.

Additional achievements or scholarships—this could include prizes or scholarships at sixth form, university or law school, Duke of Edinburgh Awards, mooting or negotiation competitions, selection for overseas placements, fundraising efforts, positions of responsibility such as student council representative or roles within the student law society, and/or sporting achievements.

Interests and hobbies—mention any qualifications that you have gained through your extra-curricular activities and demonstrate the skills that you have developed. It is better to pick one or two hobbies and demonstrate a genuine enthusiasm for them, rather than listing several activities with little or no detail to support your interest in them. For example, if you have been travelling, you could talk about your most memorable experience or something interesting that you learnt about the culture of a particular country. If you enjoy a particular sport, you could mention competitions that you have entered, or challenges you have been involved in, and whether you raised any money for charity in the process.

References—you should include contact details (full name, job title, address, email address and, if possible, telephone number) for at least one, and ideally two, referees. It is usual to provide one academic and one employment related reference but make sure that you have asked the person's permission before including his/her details. Consider giving your referees a copy of your CV so that they have a list of your achievements to hand when writing your reference. This will be particularly helpful for tutors who might be called upon to write several references in the same week.

OTHER TIPS FOR WRITING EFFECTIVE CVS

The CV should be clear, concise, and no longer than two sides of A4. Consider using bullet points rather than paragraphs to show the skills you have gained from each experience. This will make it easier and quicker for recruiters to pick out the relevant information.

Use a sensible font (e.g. Times New Roman, Arial, or Calibri) and ensure that the text is easy to read and not too small. Justify the text and make use of bullet points, bold font, italics, and headings to present the information as professionally as possible.

If possible, give specific examples to demonstrate the skills you have developed through particular experiences. For example, if you were appointed to a position of responsibility, give an example of something you achieved during your term of office.

2013–2015   University of Portsmouth Dance Society

As the Social Secretary, I coordinated the organising team for the Dance Society Summer Ball. Main responsibilities included preparing a budget, identifying suitable venues and narrowing down entertainment options to present to the social committee. I was the main point of contact for all event bookings, which involved negotiating discounts and paying monies. I was also responsible for co-ordinating the sales team and designing the marketing material. The 2014 Summer Ball sold 300 tickets—an increase of 30 per cent on previous years.

Avoid breaks in chronology: they are likely to make employers suspicious and might lead to your application being rejected if they do not have time to clarify the reasons for the gap. If there is a gap on your CV, use the covering letter to explain what you were doing during that period.

Make sure you proof read your CV at least twice and correct any spelling or grammatical errors and any typos. It is amazing how many people fail to do this. Employers are looking for candidates who care about their work and can demonstrate attention to detail; they do not want people who cannot be bothered to proof read their own CV, or who do so and miss the mistakes.

Ask someone you trust to review your CV and give you feedback. However, do not feel that you have to adopt all their suggestions. A CV is a very personal document so it is important that you are comfortable with it and that it reflects you as an individual.

Make sure you can actually talk about the things that you mention on your CV and avoid the temptation to embellish any of the details. There is always the possibility that you will find yourself being interviewed by an expert in something you have expressed a passion for. This could be a wonderful coincidence if you are able to hold your own during the discussion, but it will be incredibly embarrassing if you have exaggerated your interest and/or expertise. Partners and clients need to be able to rely on, and trust, their solicitors and trainees so any lies or exaggerated statements will severely affect your employment prospects if they are discovered.

WHAT ARE EMPLOYERS LOOKING FOR WHEN THEY REVIEW YOUR CV?

When assessing a CV you need to put yourself into the shoes of the employer. Imagine that you will be receiving hundreds, or even thousands, of CVs and will only have a very short time to sift through them. Non-verbal communication is just as powerful in the process of reviewing CVs as it is during an interview situation so presentation and a professional image are crucial. Recruiters will assess CVs on presentation, layout and clarity even before they engage with the content. At this stage a CV can be rejected if it is messy, confusing, or if seems as though little thought has gone into the overall appearance of the document. Make sure you use clear headings, a sensible structure, accessible information, and make effective use of bullet points to break up text and other formatting tools like bold/italics/underlined to highlight certain areas, etc. Finally, it should go without saying that employers will pay keen attention to spelling and grammar and will not expect to see any typos. Above all else, they will be questioning whether the candidate is likely to be a good fit with the culture and philosophy of their firm/organisation.

Questions which employers might be asking when reviewing the content of your CV

Does the applicant satisfy the academic standards we require? If not, are there any relevant extenuating circumstances?

Are there any gaps in the education or work history? Have they been accounted for?

Does the applicant have the skills required in the person specification/job description? Is there evidence to support their assertions?

Does the applicant have any unique selling points?

Has the applicant demonstrated that they are capable of managing their time to balance work, study and other interests?

What is the extent of the applicant's work experience?

Does the applicant demonstrate that he/she is genuinely motivated to be a solicitor?
What are the applicant's interests? Is the applicant a team player or does he/she have solo pursuits? What character do their hobbies and interests suggest?
Is this candidate likely to fit into the culture of our organisation?

HOW TO WRITE AN EFFECTIVE COVERING LETTER

It is very tempting to run off a stack of standard covering letters in a bid to get through as many applications as possible. However, this is likely to be counter-productive because recruiters are skilled at identifying a standard "cut-and-paste" letter. It would be a far better use of your time if you made a few well written and targeted applications to firms that genuinely interest you.

A covering letter is the first opportunity you have to introduce yourself to the reader. Think about how many other CVs and letters that partner or recruitment officer has to sift through—you may only have a minute or two to prevent your application from going into the rejection pile so do not waste it. The letter should explain, clearly and succinctly, why you are applying to that firm and why they should consider you for a training contract or work experience. You must demonstrate that you have made an informed decision to pursue a career as a solicitor, that you are aware of the realities of legal practice, and that your interest in that particular firm is genuine. It is essential to address the question "why us and why you".

Encourage the reader to look at your CV in more detail by picking out some interesting facts about your work experience or relevant extra-curricular activities. Tell them about the skills you have developed and why they should take your application further. This is not the time to be modest!

Example:

You will see from my CV that I have been a part-time volunteer fundraiser for Barnardo's for the last three years. This role has helped me develop excellent organisational and team working skills as I work with other fundraisers to organise fundraising events throughout the year. The role also requires excellent communication skills as I have to liaise with members of the local business community to seek sponsorship and generate ticket sales for our events.

Your careers centre will be able to advise you on structuring your covering letter and might even produce standard templates for you to use as a starting point. You should also consider the guidance notes below.

Personalise your letter—try not to address the letter "Dear Sir/ Madam". If you are replying to an advertisement, you will normally be given the name of a particular contact. If you are making a speculative application, call the firm or company and find out the name of the person to whom you should address your letter (e.g. a particular HR advisor, or the Head of Legal, etc.).

Set out your stall—explain why you are contacting the firm and what you are looking for. Also state where and what course you are studying.

Demonstrate interest and enthusiasm—show that you are genuinely interested in working for that firm. This is your opportunity to target your application to the relevant employer. Perhaps you have completed a work placement with the firm (or a similar firm) or perhaps you met some of their trainees at a networking event or perhaps you have become interested in one of their specialist practice areas since you studied it as an option at university or law school. For local or regional firms, try to demonstrate links to the surrounding area and explain why you want to work for that firm in that area. Show that you have researched the firm by referring to their website or the firm's entry in Chambers & Partners. You could also mention some of the deals or projects that they have been involved in (look at the news section of their website).

Sell yourself—show the recruiter what sets you apart from other candidates, i.e. why they should find out more about you. Draw out relevant points from your CV and show how they are relevant to this role. If the selection criteria have been provided to you, make sure that you match this discussion to the skills that are identified in those criteria. It is not just about explaining why you want a job with that firm or company: you must also explain why they should employ you.

Key skills or qualities—consider highlighting any specialist skills in languages or some other area that you feel is relevant to the employer. For example, if you are applying to a specialist IP firm, your background in pharmaceuticals or your degree in science might be of particular interest and if you are applying to a global law firm, your ability to speak fluent Mandarin is likely to be a key selling point.

Availability—provide a note of your availability for interview and, if appropriate, your contact details for term and vacation time.

Presentation and style—presentation is extremely important so print your letter on good quality paper and think about how it looks on the page. Format the letter carefully so that the text is not too squashed up or spaced out too widely. Also remember to justify the text and use a sensible font style and size. You should adopt a professional tone and use short, concise sentences and simple language. Lastly, try to keep your letter to one side of A4.

Pay attention to details—make sure you proof read your letter at least twice and correct any spelling or grammatical errors and any typos. Before you send it, ask someone you trust to review your letter and provide you with honest feedback.

16 APPLICATION FORMS: HOW TO WRITE WINNING RESPONSES

Students often ask how many applications they should make. The answer is as many as you can manage without sacrificing quality and without jeopardising your academic work. You should resist the temptation to run off a stack of application forms with answers that have been cobbled together using standard phrases and some creative cutting and pasting. It would be a far better use of your time to make a few well-written and targeted applications to firms that genuinely interest you. For your key target firms, you could expect to spend three or four days researching the firm, reviewing your evidence, identifying examples, composing answers, re-drafting answers, and finessing an application form.

Since City firms and most national and regional firms recruit two years in advance, if you want to start your training contract straight after the LPC, you should start to apply for training contracts during your second year at university if you are a law undergraduate and during your third year for all other undergraduates. Please refer to Chs 3 and 8 for more details of the route to qualification and the recruitment timetable.

Training contract applications close between March and August each year with the majority of firms having a 31 July closing date, and only a handful running into August. Note, however, that some firms review forms on a rolling basis while others review them all after the closing date. You should check the policy of each of your target firms to avoid missing out because the places have been filled before you have submitted your application. Even if firms do wait until the closing date to review applications, consider the impression that you will give by submitting an application on the stroke of midnight, rather than several days, weeks or months in advance. The earlier the application is submitted, the more likely it is that a candidate has specifically targeted that firm.

You will need to research individual firms for exact details of their application processes and submission deadlines. The Chambers Student (*http://www.chambersstudent.co.uk*) has some useful information on applying for training contracts, including a table setting out the key deadlines and a table which compares the salaries (first year trainee, second year trainee and qualification), sponsorship and benefits offered by each firm. There is also a useful diary feature on *http://www.lawcareers.net* which highlights key dates in the recruitment calendar. It also has a useful feature called "MyLC.N" which enables you to save key dates into your own personalised career planner.

> "You can tell the people who have just applied for 50 training contracts and not really focused on who you are and what you do. A good application will answer all of the questions (and every part of each question), and will demonstrate effective communication skills and attention to detail. It's difficult to do on an application form, but try to demonstrate an understanding of the firm you are applying to. Also try to appear enthusiastic without going over the top. You're looking for someone who stands out . . . you're looking for a bit of sparkle on an application form."
>
> *Sam Lee, Graduate Head of Recruitment, Bond Dickinson LLP*

QUESTIONS IN APPLICATIONS FORMS

Application forms usually contain two types of questions: fact based questions and competency questions.

Fact based questions—these would include questions about your qualifications, personal details and work experience. These do not tend to pose too many difficulties; it is simply a question of completing the boxes with the relevant information.

Competency questions—these are trickier to answer but they provide your opportunity to shine if you can master the technique. The questions will ask you to demonstrate that you have a specific skill or attribute with reference to a specific example.

In other words, you have to draw on your bank of experiences in order to demonstrate your competence in certain areas. Everyone has to answer the same questions so it becomes easier to differentiate between candidates. Employers will be able to evaluate your writing style and how effectively and persuasively you can communicate on paper. They will also be interested in how you substantiate your answers and how well you are able to reflect on your experiences.

Examples of competency based questions

Give an example of a time when you found yourself outside of your comfort zone and explain how you responded to that situation.

Give an example of a situation when you demonstrated your ability to work effectively as part of a team. What role did you play and how did you contribute to the success of that team?

Give an example of a time when you had to demonstrate your ability to work effectively under pressure.

Illustrate your ability to communicate effectively in a challenging situation.

Give an example of a time when you had to take the lead or use your initiative in order to achieve a particular goal.

Illustrate your ability to negotiate a successful outcome to a challenging situation.

The key to giving an effective answer to these questions lies in your ability to reflect on your performance in a particular situation. You need to use that example to illustrate the skills you relied on to achieve a particular result. Therefore, before you even begin to draft a response, you need to identify the skill that the employer is looking for and choose the most appropriate example to demonstrate your competence in that area. This is where the Map of Experiences at the end of Ch.10 really comes into its own. If you take advantage of the advice in that chapter, and have a good bank of experiences to draw on, you should be well-placed to answer these questions.

"More people fail to get through because of the content of their application form than for any other reason. For many of them, it is not that they don't have interesting and relevant experiences to draw on, but rather that they haven't learnt how to sell them effectively to employers."

Training Manager of a National Law Firm

"Competency questions are designed to elicit information about your previous experiences. They give you the opportunity to analyse your performance and demonstrate how you could do a good job in the future. Use a variety of examples from different areas of your life to demonstrate the breadth of your experience. Always think 'why is the recruiter asking me this?' and link your experience to what you learned, the skills you developed, and how this will add value to your future role."

Samantha Hope, Graduate Recruitment Manager, Shoosmiths

Having identified a suitable example from your Map of Experiences, your next task is to compose the answer. Many employers recommend using the "STAR" model to encourage effective reflection. This model is explained in detail below with some worked examples to get you started.

THE STAR MODEL

Situation   Put the example in context, but keep it brief: what happened/what was the problem/where were you?

Task   What were you asked to do? What did you decide to do? What did you decide was the key issue or priority? Why?

Action   How did you approach that task? What were your options? What action did you take and why? This section should document your thought processes and emphasise the key skills that you had to rely on or develop.

Result   What was the end result? What did you achieve? Illustrate with evidence where possible. Also discuss what you learnt from the experience and/or what you might do differently next time.

To illustrate the process, I have included a completed Map of Experiences at the end of this chapter (see Ch.10 for more advice on how to create your own version). Then, using the STAR approach, I have prepared two responses around the examples given in the chart.

Give an example to demonstrate your ability to work effectively under pressure

[Situation] During the summer between my first and second year of university, I worked as a legal secretary for a small law firm in Bath. [Task] One of the other secretaries had to take sick leave unexpectedly which meant that I had to work for three fee earners. I had to find a way to juggle the competing needs of the various lawyers whilst the firm sought additional cover. [Action] I initiated meetings with each fee earner at the beginning and end of the day so I could get a clear sense of their workload and prioritise work accordingly. This also meant that I could make effective use of the evening secretary where appropriate or plan to work late or come in early if necessary. I made good use of the electronic diary to set reminders for each fee earner, and I kept a rolling "to do" list which was updated each evening to ensure that I didn't miss any key tasks or deadlines. [Result] The other secretary returned to work after two weeks and I was given a small bonus to reflect my performance during her absence. I learnt the importance of open channels of communication and excellent time management to maintain good output in a pressurised environment.

Give an example of a time when you have contributed to the success of a team

[Situation] I participated in a 24-hour sponsored relay bike ride event with three friends to raise money for Cancer Research. [Task] This required a concerted commitment and a strong sense of team spirit to ensure that we finished the course and made a significant donation to the charity. [Action] I committed to a rigorous training regime for six months before the event because

I didn't want to let down my other team mates. We also worked hard as a team to generate sponsorship to make our training pay off for the charity. We organised a rota to seek donations from members of the public at various places in our home town and we set up a fundraising website. The event itself was gruelling: we had to pull together as a team to overcome the physical and mental challenges which we faced. [Result] Our hard work paid off in the end: we managed to complete the event and our combined efforts raised £2,225 for the charity. Through this experience I learnt that I have the resilience to survive a physically and mentally gruelling challenge, and I was reminded of the power of team work to achieve something which at first glance seemed impossible.

Do not feel that answers to competency questions need to demonstrate super human stamina or unusual experiences. You can frame a very good answer around a fairly commonplace experience as illustrated by the example below.

[Situation] I participated in an internal negotiation competition during my first year at university. [Task] This involved working as a team with my partner to score the highest possible marks in the competition. Our goal was to progress to an external competition and win a place to compete at the regional heats. [Action] We had to work together to research the case study and plan the strategy for the negotiation. Since the negotiation competition clashed with various coursework submission dates, we divided up the research into different parts to ensure we used our time efficiently and to reflect our individual areas of expertise. We also divided up the roles during the negotiation—I was the lead negotiator and my partner kept a close eye on the budget and took a careful note of the points we had covered. This kept things moving at a good pace and ensured that we remained on track. [Result] We were successful in the internal competition and were praised in the feedback for our excellent team work. We were delighted that we managed to progress to the regional competition which was held at the University of Law but, sadly, we narrowly missed out on a place at the national final. However, we will be competing again next year to try to

*improve our performance by starting our preparations earlier
and joining the negotiation club to practise our skills before the
competition begins.*

> "An outstanding CV or application is one that refers to a variety
> of experiences and skills—we are looking for individuals with
> broad experience. We don't want an application form that
> just focuses on legal experience or someone who uses the
> same example to answer all the questions. Try to draw on all
> your experiences and show you have gained something from
> each of them whether that is netball coaching, mooting com-
> petitions, legal work experience, a Saturday job, or travelling
> experiences. If you use the same example all the way through,
> you are not picking up any extra points in the scoring process.
> Show that you are a balanced, well-rounded person who has
> achieved success in more than one area of their life."
>
> *Lynn Ford, HR Manager, Blake Morgan LLP*

OTHER THINGS TO CONSIDER WHEN COMPLETING APPLICATION FORMS

Preparation

Spend time planning your answers carefully. If possible, keep
coming back to the questions over several weeks to see if any
fresh ideas come to mind.

Use the Map of Experiences in Ch.10 to make sure you illustrate each question with the most effective example from
your CV. It would be sensible to carry out this exercise as
early as possible in the academic year since it will help you
to identify any gaps in your experience and you might be
able to address them by joining particular societies, entering
competitions, or volunteering for pro bono work. The earlier
you identify the gaps, the better your chances of addressing
them before the submission deadline.

It is easy to put off application forms in order to concentrate
on coursework deadlines and revision, but bear in mind that

it will probably take much longer than you think to complete each form. Allow yourself plenty of time to avoid a last-minute panic and to make sure that the form reflects your true potential.

Read the form thoroughly before you start filling it in to ensure that you have followed the instructions correctly. This will include complying with any stated word counts.

Composing Your Answers

As you answer each question, keep referring to the individual job specification and the generic list of qualities that firms are looking for (see Ch.10) to ensure you demonstrate as many as possible in your responses.

Read the question carefully: if it asks for one example, only give one even if you can think of several. However, if it asks for examples of a particular skill, you must give a range of different examples.

Your application should demonstrate genuine enthusiasm for that particular firm and your research must shine through. The best applications will incorporate research in a sophisticated way to add weight to the statements being made, without sounding too rehearsed or clumsy.

The fact that the application is online does not mean that you can adopt a casual tone or that it is acceptable to use text or email abbreviations.

Do not repeat the question in your answer as it wastes valuable space.

Good communication skills and a professional attitude are essential for a successful career as a solicitor. Your application form should reflect these attributes. Structure each answer carefully, adopt a clear, concise style of writing, and make sure you have actually answered the question.

Think About Your Evidence

A key skill for any aspiring lawyer is an ability to substantiate your claims. This means that you must provide examples of how you have demonstrated particular skills and attributes, rather than simply making general statements.

Firms are looking for well-rounded individuals with breadth of experience so try not to use the same example more than once.

Submitting Your Form

Proof read your work carefully before submitting the form. If possible, ask someone else to review it for you and provide feedback.

Submit the form before the deadline to avoid any last-minute technical hitches arising from failed internet access or other computer problems. Keep a copy of the form for interview preparation.

Competency	Situation	Task	Demonstrate the Competency
Attention to detail	*Secretary at a small Surveying Practice*	*Taking minutes at the weekly business development meeting*	My role includes taking minutes at the weekly business development meeting and circulating those minutes to the rest of the team. I have to record the discussions accurately, including making a note of any agreed action points and stating who has been allocated responsibility for that task. This role requires excellent listening skills and attention to detail as I cannot afford to miss any important details and I have to make sure that I write up the notes accurately at the end of the meeting.

Fig.4 Completed Map of Experiences

Competency	Situation	Task	Demonstrate the Competency
Excellent oral and written communication skills	*Mentoring scheme*	*Mentoring school children who were interested in studying Law at university*	I met with the children in a small group and also organised one-to-one sessions to discuss individual career plans. This role required good listening skills and the ability to relate to children who were studying at a very different level to me. I had to explain things in a way which was meaningful to them without patronising them and I also had to explain certain concepts to them clearly and accurately (e.g. university fees, student loans, living costs, etc.).
Excellent organisational skills and ability to prioritise/manage time effectively	*Social secretary*	*Arranging talks and demonstrations. Arranging stall at Freshers' Fayre*	I am the social secretary of the Boxing Club. This year, having made a note of the availability of key committee members, I coordinated the rota for the Freshers' Fayre stand to ensure it was fully covered for the whole event. I also arranged a series of talks by guest speakers throughout the year and arranged catering and venues for the talks.

Fig.4 (continued)

Competency	Situation	Task	Demonstrate the Competency
Ability to act on your own initiative	*Student represen-tative*	*Achieving extra computer facilities at university in response to student complaints*	Students were frequently expressing their frustration at the fact that there was a shortage of computers in the IT labs. I contacted the other Student Representatives and we worked together to canvass the opinions of students. I then coordinated a written report which was submitted to the Dean of the Business School and the Students' Union. I discovered that a library refurbishment was planned for the end of the year so we used the report to make several suggestions about changes which could be made to the IT resources during the refurbishment, e.g. installing some "quick access stand-alone" computers to use only for printing, checking timetables, or checking emails, and the installation of a larger IT lab with more computers. These changes were implemented as part of the refurbishment.

Fig.4 (continued)

Competency	Situation	Task	Demonstrate the Competency
Resilience and Ability to work under pressure	*Summer work as legal secretary*	*Covering at short notice for another secretary who was on sick leave*	One of the other secretaries had to take sick leave unexpectedly. I had to work for three fee earners and balance their competing workloads and expectations for two weeks. I had to adapt quickly to the different expectations of the new fee earners and get up to speed quickly with their files and key deadlines.
Ability to work effectively within a team	*Sponsored bike ride*	*Completing the course and raising money for charity as part of a team*	Training and fundraising for a 24-hour sponsored relay bike ride event with three friends to raise money for Cancer Research. I trained regularly for six months because I didn't want to let the others down. We shared the fundraising by taking it in turns to visit local supermarkets and town centres to raise money. We had to motivate each other during the bike ride because it was a very challenging course and we all struggled to keep up the pace at one point or other.

Fig.4 (continued)

Competency	Situation	Task	Demonstrate the Competency
Excellent research skills	*Employment clinic volunteer*	*Researching cases*	At the Employment Clinic, we offer advice to students and members of the public on any aspect of employment law. The client visits us for an initial meeting during which we take a note of his/her problem or query and ensure that we have the necessary background information. We then work in a small team to research the issue and prepare a letter of advice to the client. This experience has enhanced my ability to break down an issue into its component parts and has also increased my knowledge of Westlaw and LexisNexis as we use those databases on a weekly basis to research the clients' problems.
Excellent problem solving skills	*Local football team*	*Obtaining sponsorship for new kit from local businesses*	As captain of our local football team, I could see that morale was low because we didn't have a team kit. The problem was that we did not have the funds to pay for a new kit. We started a fundraising campaign but it was not

Fig.4 (continued)

Competency	Situation	Task	Demonstrate the Competency
			particularly successful and I was worried that the season would end before we got the new kit. I realised that it was not going to be possible to get someone to pay for the kit as a goodwill gesture so I decided to address the problem commercially. I asked each player what household chore they would be willing to donate to raise money for the kit. Then I organised an auction in our local pub and the customers bid for the different players, e.g. cutting the garden hedges, mending broken fences, fixing guttering, etc.). The auction was successful and we raised enough for a new kit with some money left over.
Ability to negotiate effectively	*Student housing*	*Choosing a student house*	I was looking for a student house to share with three friends in my final year of university. We narrowed it down to two houses but there was a 50/50 split between each house. We had to find a way to make a final choice.

Fig.4 (continued)

Competency	Situation	Task	Demonstrate the Competency
			Eventually, I managed to persuade the others to vote for my preferred house. I achieved this by asking each housemate to identify their two key requirements. I then drew up a list of the pros and cons of each house against the groups' key requirements. The house which I preferred ticked more of the group's requirements than the other house so we went with that one in the end.

Fig.4 (continued)

17 PREPARING FOR INTERVIEWS

You should be extremely proud of yourself if you are called for a training contract interview. Given the fierce competition for places, this is an enormous achievement. It also means that you have convinced the recruitment panel that you have the potential to succeed as a trainee solicitor in their firm. The interview provides an opportunity for them to test their decision, clarify any queries, and make sure that you are as good as they first thought. By this stage, you are more than halfway there and have everything to play for. All you have to do is reinforce the messages in your application and convince them in person that you are worth investing in.

> "Do your research on the firm, the lawyers who work there and the practice areas they cover. Practice talking about yourself and the skills and qualities you possess; most people find it really difficult to talk about themselves. Ask yourself why the firm would employ you rather than anyone else and make sure you can answer the question."
>
> *Lorna Sansom, Associate, B P Collins LLP*

> "The magic is in getting an interview. If you get that far, don't even think about being nervous. All you can and should do is be yourself. But do make sure that you are extremely well prepared and have researched the firm thoroughly."
>
> *Training Partner at a Regional Law Firm*

WHAT TO EXPECT FROM A TRAINING CONTRACT INTERVIEW

The tone and format of any interview will depend on the type of firm and the personality of the interviewers. Therefore it is impossible to provide a definitive guide to training contract interviews. The one thing you can be sure of, though, is that preparation, practice, and personality will make all the difference to your chances of a successful outcome.

Your interview might be a single partner interview, or there could be a panel of interviewers. It is worth finding out in advance who will be interviewing you so that you can research their career history and current role within the organisation. If you are faced with a panel interview, make sure that you direct your answers to the whole panel, rather than just the person who asked the question.

During the interview, the interviewer, or interview panel, will be trying to find out five key things. I have listed them below.

Why do you want to be a solicitor and is that the result of an informed decision-making process?
Why do you want to work for this type of firm and for this firm in particular?
Do you have the skills and qualities that they are looking for?
Why should we employ you? What sets you apart from other candidates?
Would you fit into the culture of our firm?

The interview will probably begin with some "warm up" questions, e.g. "tell us about yourself", or "tell us why you have applied for this role", or "tell us about your university experience". Do not be put off by the apparent simplicity of these questions. Their purpose is to allow you to settle in and to put everyone at ease before the interview begins in earnest. If you are asked open questions, make the most of the opportunity to direct the conversation onto areas that you are comfortable talking about. Sometimes you can also use the time to expand certain aspects of your application form or to mention something which you forgot to mention earlier. This is your opportunity to create a positive first impression, and to develop a rapport with the interviewer(s).

After the "warm up" questions, the interviewer(s) might wish to clarify some details from your application or they might try to find out more about something that you have mentioned on your form. These questions will then lead into the main body of the interview when you can expect to be asked questions on your choice of degree, choice of training contract provider, future career aspirations, personal interests and achievements, and your potential to become a good solicitor.

You should also expect some competency based questions. These will probably be based on the key competencies which were tested in the application form since these are the skills that the firm values most highly. Use the STAR model to approach these questions (as you would do in an application form) and try to support your examples with evidence. For example, if you mention your success as a telesales operator, give an idea of the number of sales you made in the last quarter and how that compares with your colleagues. If you won a client interviewing competition with your partner, explain how many pairs were in the competition as a whole.

Do not be put off if there are a few unusual or particularly challenging questions during the course of the interview. Often the interviewer(s) will be just as interested in how you handle such questions as with the content of your actual answers so remain calm, project confidence and do not let a difficult question fluster you.

Some Interview Questions to Consider

Why Us/Why You?

Why do you want to become a solicitor?
Why do you want to work for a firm like this one?
Why should we offer you a training contract?
What sets you apart from other candidates?
What do you think makes a good training contract provider?
What do you think differentiates a City firm from a regional firm?
What do you think clients want from their lawyers?

Getting to Know You

What motivates you?
How would your best friend describe you?
Which work experience placement did you enjoy most and why?
What have you enjoyed most about your degree?
Where do you see yourself in five years' time?
Tell me about a current issue in the news and why it interests you.

Some Tricky Questions

What is the worst decision you have ever made and what did you learn from it?
Which historical figure would you most like to be stuck in a lift with?
Name two of your weaknesses.
Which of your characteristics would you most like to change?
Are you a good loser?
What challenges lie ahead for the legal profession?
Are you proud of your A Level results?

Competency-Based Questions

Tell me about a time when you had to work effectively under pressure.
Give an example of a time when you have had to negotiate on behalf of someone else.
Give an example of a time when you led a team to achieve a particular goal.
Give an example which illustrates the strength of your communication skills.
Tell me about a time when you were faced with a problem, and how you resolved it.
Give an example of a time when you had to demonstrate your organisational skills.

Tell me about a time which illustrates the strength of your attention to detail.

> "The interview form is just one part of the half-day that candidates spend at a Shoosmiths' assessment centre; there are a number of skills and behaviours that we look for throughout the process. During the interview, candidates should demonstrate their key strengths using a variety of experiences, all of which should help to show them as a well-rounded individual with the potential to be a successful solicitor.
>
> It's even better if their strengths match the firm's values, which are: taking initiative, being within reach and responsive, talking business sense, and pulling together."
>
> *Samantha Hope, Graduate Recruitment Manager, Shoosmiths*

Presentations

Your interview might include a short presentation in which case you could be given a choice from a selection of titles, or allowed to choose your own topic. You will usually be given information about the presentation a week or so before the interview. Generally speaking, recruiters will be more interested in your ability to engage an audience and present information clearly, rather than topic that you have chosen.

The interviewers will be looking for:

interesting, appropriate and accurate content;
a sensible structure and logical thought processes;
an ability to keep to time;
eye contact with the audience;
effective (but not distracting) use of body language;
confidence; and
an ability to communicate concepts clearly.

Case Studies

You might also be asked to respond to a case study at some point during the interview. You will be asked to explain to the interviewers how you would advise the client or what your next steps would be. You will usually receive the case study when you arrive for the interview and you will be given a short time (perhaps 10 minutes) to review it. You should also be prepared to comment on any potential professional ethics issues arising from information given in the case study.

Generally speaking, the interviewers will not expect candidates to demonstrate significant knowledge of any legal issues arising from the case study. Instead, they are likely to judge candidates on their ability to:

> think on their feet;
> demonstrate reasoned thought processes and develop a sensible strategy;
> demonstrate a logical approach to the problem and an ability to prioritise tasks appropriately;
> identify the key issues in a given scenario;
> disregard any information that is irrelevant or which distracts from the key issues;
> identify areas where further information or clarification is required;
> identify and deal with any ethical issues;
> think commercially (where appropriate); and
> explain the key issues and their course of action or strategy in a clear, concise and accurate manner.

The interviewer(s) might ask you to defend your position on a couple of points, or might even challenge you directly. If this happens, do not adopt a defensive attitude, just be prepared to listen to their ideas, justify your position and your reasoning, and illustrate your thought processes.

Example
You are a trainee in the corporate department. Your supervisor is on sick leave and you are left in the office alone one evening. A client calls you and demands some advice in relation to an indemnity provision in the share purchase agreement that you have been working on with your supervisor. He says that he needs

the advice this evening as he wishes to sign the agreement. He is fairly aggressive towards you when you tell him that you are a trainee and cannot give him advice immediately. You know that this is one of the firm's most important clients and you are keen to make a good impression. You put the phone down and do some initial advice which suggests that this is not as straightforward as you first thought but you are confident that you know the answer. What do you do now?

Things to think about:

What is your goal here? Are there conflicting priorities? How will you balance them?

What is the obvious ethical issue? Make sure you explain the risk explicitly and show how and why this has influenced your strategy.

Demonstrate a methodical approach when explaining your strategy.

Remember the importance of keeping clients informed.

Telephone Interviews

Telephone interviews can be used as a means of shortlisting candidates after the initial review of application forms. They will tend to be shorter than a face-to-face interview, and the interviewer will be interested in your ability to engage in a conversation and to create a rapport with them.

You should treat telephone interviews in exactly the same way as other interviews. Follow the same advice in terms of preparation and make sure you find a quiet place to sit (or stand) while you are being interviewed. If possible, try to use a landline rather than a mobile phone to avoid problems with poor signal or low battery. Lastly, make sure you factor in some time to gather your thoughts before the interview (rather like the time spent in the reception area of a firm before a face-to-face interview). You do not want to pick up the phone immediately after a mad dash home from a busy morning at university or a rugby training session.

PREPARING FOR INTERVIEWS

Practice Makes Perfect

You should try not to become someone different for any interview. The interviewers obviously liked what they read in your application form and the interview is an opportunity for them to find out more about you as an individual. Therefore, over-prepared answers are unlikely to be helpful and will probably irritate your interviewer(s) in the end. It can, however, be extremely useful to attend a mock interview to practise your responses to standard questions and to receive honest feedback on your performance. Speak to your tutors and careers advisors to find out what support your university or law school offers.

Alternatively, rather than engage in a formal interview, you could run through a list of possible questions with your careers advisor and discuss how you would approach each one. This can be particularly helpful because you will receive guidance on what employers are looking for and you can practise using your experiences to illustrate particular competencies, but you avoid the risk of reeling off over-prepared and stilted answers. This approach might also mean that you are more likely to address the issues being raised by the interviewer(s), rather than trying to shoehorn your pre-prepared answers into their questions without really listening to what is being asked.

Ultimately it is a balancing act: you want to come across as someone who is polished and prepared, but you do not want to deliver a set of anonymous, scripted answers. The interviewers have already decided that you look good on paper so now is the time to let your personality shine through. They will also be interested in whether you can think on your feet and respond appropriately when you are challenged or faced with something unexpected, so perfectly prepared answers will only take you so far.

"Mock interviews can be useful if you are very nervous and you're not good at articulating your ideas and need help structuring your answers, but I think there is a danger that you can be too coached."

A Trainee Solicitor

"I prepared for interviews by thinking about the top 10 questions and about how I would structure my answer. For each one, I put down the three main points that I would cover but I didn't want to over prepare."

A Trainee Solicitor

Do Your Research

Your first research task is to try to find out what to expect from the interview. Speak to your careers advisor and find out if they have received any feedback from other students who have had interviews with that firm. If so, perhaps you could arrange to speak to them. Also, speak to your tutors and make use of any contacts that you have made through mentoring schemes or work experience placements. Lastly, have a look at law careers websites, such as *http://www.lawcareers.net* and *http://www.chambersstudent.co.uk*. At the very least, these resources will offer general advice on training contract interviews but they might also have specific information about the recruitment processes at the firm you are hoping to join.

You must also ensure that you are in a strong position to produce a credible answer to the question "why do you want to train at this firm?". Revisit the guidance in Ch.9 about researching law firms and targeting applications, and update your research by reviewing the firm's website and keeping an eye out for relevant stories in the legal and general press. You should also ensure that you are attached to the firm's social media network.

Revisit your application form and make a note of the key skills that were tested in the questions. If a firm has asked about these skills in the application form, it is highly likely that they are the ones they are most interested in. Therefore, the interviewer(s) will probably pick up on those skills during the interview and take the discussion forward. Re-reading your application form will also remind you of the examples you gave in your answers. Try to come up with some new examples to use during the interview to avoid repeating yourself, and to show the breadth of your experiences and achievements.

> "Go back to your answers to the questions in the application form—those skills are obviously the ones that the firm is interested in but have some more examples ready and be prepared to expand on the detail that you've already given."
>
> *A Law Careers Consultant*

Whilst reviewing your form think about any challenging questions that might arise from information you have given. Is there anything in the application that could be viewed in a negative light? This might include limited work experience placements, poor A Level results, or inconsistent marks for degree modules. If so, think about how you could respond to those questions to reassure the interviewer that they should not affect your potential to be a good trainee.

Lastly, make sure that you keep up to date with current affairs and legal news by reading a quality newspaper and legal trade publications on a regular basis. In particular, look up any recent deals or cases that the firm has been involved in and be prepared to discuss them in detail. At City firms, be prepared for a commercially driven interview. The partners will want to know that you have a genuine interest in commercial affairs. They will be looking for candidates who can demonstrate depth of knowledge, rather than those who have simply skimmed the headlines of the Financial Times for the two weeks immediately before the interview. Revisit Ch.12 for further guidance on developing commercial awareness and keeping abreast of events in the legal press, the financial and commercial press, and the general press. Appendix 2 (Further Reading) also suggests some useful resources to help you keep up to date with current affairs and legal news.

Think of Some Sensible Questions to Ask

At the end of the interview, there will usually be some time for you to ask questions. It is worth taking some time to think about these in advance since your question(s) will reveal a great deal about you, and possibly also your level of preparation and commercial awareness.

"It shouldn't just be a clever question to show off your research; it needs to be one that is relevant to a decision about whether you would want to train at that organisation or not. The interviewer wants you to show a real interest. Don't just ask the question and sit back; try to ask a small follow up question while the interviewer is talking to emphasise that you are still engaging with them."

A Law Careers Consultant

It is difficult to give specific advice on what makes a sensible question, but essentially it should be something which demonstrates that you are a well-prepared and well-informed candidate who is genuinely motivated to become a solicitor and work for that particular firm. Therefore, you need to target your question to the firm you are applying to, and firms will not be impressed if a question in this book is regurgitated by hundreds of interviewees. Rather than giving some suggested questions, I have listed below some prompts which might help you to formulate your own.

You might be interested in what drew the interviewer to the firm and whether it has met his/her expectations.

You might be interested to know more about a particular deal which you have read about in the press.

You might be interested in the interviewer's opinion on the impact of recent regulatory changes in a particular sector (if they have clients in that sector) or in the legal profession.

You might be interested in what differentiates this firm from others of the same size and profile.

If the firm has a tailored LPC, you might be interested in why it has taken that option, and how and why it selected its dedicated provider.

You might have some observations from the vacation scheme or open day which you can use to frame a question.

FINAL INTERVIEW TIPS

Always dress smartly for an interview—you should wear a suit even if the firm's dress code is smart casual or if you are being interviewed on a "dress down" day. Make sure that your shoes are polished, your hair is neat, and your make up (if appropriate) and any accessories are appropriate to a business environment.

Arrive on time—if you have not been to the firm's offices before, it would be worth having a trial run before the interview to check how long it takes you door-to-door and to make sure you know exactly where you are heading on the big day. Then add some time for transport delays or bad traffic. If the worst happens, you might need to call ahead if there is any risk that you might be delayed so take the firm's contact details with you.

Be polite and friendly to everyone you meet—you never know who will be asked to provide feedback on you. Do not be afraid to talk to other candidates if you meet them in the reception area; they will probably be relieved to see a friendly face. However, keep the conversation within professional limits because you never know who might be listening.

Create a positive first impression—first impressions are crucial because they set the tone for the rest of the interview. It is much easier to build on a positive beginning than to try to make up ground after a bad start. This starts as soon as you approach the building; try to project an air of professionalism and calm confidence (even if you don't feel it!). Then, as you enter the interview room, make sure you smile, make eye contact, and shake hands with the interviewers. Put them at ease as soon as you enter the interview room. Give the impression of a calm and collected professional who can deal with anything life (or a client) throws at them.

It might be helpful to consider the impression you would create if you were appearing before prospective clients at a pitch for new work. A strong candidate is one who puts the panel at ease from the moment they enter the room, who is dressed professionally, who offers a strong handshake and smile, who pitches his entrance appropriately given the situation, and who is able to engage in the initial pleasantries in a relaxed but appropriate manner. A weak candidate would be one who appears nervous, who offers a weak handshake, who is dressed inappropriately and/or untidily, who fails to smile, who finds it difficult to engage in initial pleasantries, or who gives the impression of a lack of confidence or competence.

> "It's about being positive, pleasant, polite, at ease (but not cocky), and demonstrating good judgement both in terms of their choice of language and decisions about when to use humour, when to be firm, when to sit back, etc. You want to know that someone is calm, sure-footed and reliable."
>
> *Training Partner of a Regional Law Firm*

Body language—think about your body language throughout the interview. A strong candidate is someone who maintains eye contact, uses body language effectively to communicate his points (without being distracting), and who creates an impression of confidence (but not arrogance) throughout the interview. Sit up straight, do not cross your arms in front of you, and keep control of any distracting or irritating hand gestures.

Evidence of motivation—competition for training contracts is fierce and the best firms have the pick of the best candidates. Strong candidates will demonstrate their genuine enthusiasm for the particular role supported by evidence of prior research. They will tailor their responses to the particular organisation and, in doing so, will demonstrate evidence of informed decision making. In short, they will give a persuasive explanation of why they want this role and why they are a strong candidate.

After the interview—reflect on your performance and do not be afraid to seek feedback if you are unsuccessful. Interviewing is a skill like any other. It takes time and practice to get it right so treat each interview as a separate learning experience and do not give up.

SOME CASE STUDIES

"The final stage of my training contract assessment with a large regional law firm involved a panel interview comprising a 10 minute prepared presentation, discussion of a case study supplied on the day and the main interview. I was very nervous while waiting to go into the interview room because at the time it felt like everything hinged on that one interview. In hindsight, although it's good to be a little nervous, it's also important not to lose sight of the task at hand and to try and keep things in perspective. The assessment stages are as much for the firm to get a feel for you as a person, as they are for you to get a feel for the type of firm it is and whether you fit the environment. Although it sounds cliché, firms are all different and it's important to find the right fit for you. The more relaxed you are, the better you will come across. Practice interviews with family members and lecturers certainly helped me prepare and feel more at ease in the interview environment and with how to structure answers to more challenging questions. The main interview focussed on my application form and my key competencies (such as communication skills and ability to think on my feet). The case study was a typical 'what would do if no one was in the office and your client wanted to do X . . .' There was also discussion about key legal reforms which were in the press at the time. In total the interview lasted around an hour and fifteen minutes and was very detailed. The panel (consisting of a senior HR representative, and two partners) were friendly but asked direct and sometimes challenging questions about my opinions on current topics and were very focussed on discussing my skills, therefore it was important that I could draw on different examples from those already used in my application form."

A Trainee Solicitor

"I attended an interview with an international telecoms company as part of the assessment process for obtaining a summer scheme with the company. The interview was with two firm employees; the senior solicitor who would have overall responsibility for me during my vacation scheme and a representative from HR. The interview was focused towards the differences of working in-house compared to private practice, key legal and current affairs topics which may affect a company such as this and a more in depth review of my application form. We sat around a table in an internal meeting room in one of the offices and, although the atmosphere was fairly informal and the interviewers were very friendly, some of the questions were intended to challenge, show I could form reasoned opinions and had a solid understanding of the environment in which they worked. The interview lasted around an hour and I found out I had been successful in obtaining the placement a couple of weeks later."

A Trainee Solicitor

18 PREPARING FOR ASSESSMENT CENTRES

Assessment centres or assessment days are a common feature of the recruitment process. They usually involve spending a day or half a day at the firm's offices with a group of other candidates to allow the firm to see how you interact with others and how you perform in a variety of skills-based activities. You will probably find that your first assessment centre is a fairly daunting experience but try to think of it as your opportunity to showcase the breadth of your skills and a good way to find out more about the culture of the particular firm. This chapter sets out general guidance on what to expect from assessment centres and some advice on how to approach the different types of exercise.

ASSESSMENT CENTRE ACTIVITIES

Firms spend considerable time and money designing their assessment centres across a range of specific competencies so each assessment centre will be slightly different to the next. However, you should expect to encounter any number of activities from the list below.

Interaction with trainees and partners (usually over coffee or lunch)
Drafting exercise
Individual presentation
Negotiation exercise
Role play exercise
Group exercise
Aptitude tests
Interview

Presentation about the firm from a partner or recruitment officer
Tour of the firm's offices

If a task comes up unexpectedly, try to remain calm and professional. Employers want to see that you can work well under pressure and very often your initial reaction to such unexpected tasks can be just as revealing as your overall performance. You are in the same boat as all the other candidates so think of it as an opportunity to shine, rather than something to be anxious about.

> "My assessment centre involved completing an in-tray exercise, writing a letter relating to a claim, making a presentation, and participating in a negotiation exercise. This was followed by an interview with the graduate recruitment manager and a second interview with two partners."
>
> *A Trainee Solicitor*

Icebreaker Exercises

You might encounter a short icebreaker exercise at the beginning of the assessment centre. This is likely to be similar to the sort of exercise you have experienced at university induction events. For example, you might be asked to spend five minutes talking to the person next to you and then to introduce your partner to the rest of the group outlining what you have learnt about them. What is the point of this exercise? The recruiters will be interested in the strength of your verbal communication skills; how quickly you can build a relationship with someone; how well you listen to and retain information; and how effectively you can package and present information to a group of people.

Group Exercises

You can almost certainly expect at least one group exercise at every assessment centre. You might be asked to complete a practical task (e.g. building something from a set of given materials) or to engage in a group discussion or role play exercise. In all these exercises, firms are looking for commercial thinking; creativity; good listening skills; strength of character (without being over-bearing); and an ability to build relationships quickly; to work productively and effectively within a time constraint; to think quickly; to communicate ideas clearly and effectively; to be per-suasive but also flexible; to work as a team; and to be considerate towards other team members.

Examples of group discussions might include the following:

> you are asked to pitch a new service to a potential new client;
> you are asked to pitch a new marketing brand to the manag-ing board;
> you are given a list of items and must convince the recruit-ment manager what three items he/she should take to a desert island;
> you are given a list of people and must convince the recruit-ment manager which three people should be saved in the event of a nuclear disaster.

Questions which recruiters might be asking when observing a group activity

How well do they interact with others?
Was one person the natural leader?
Did anyone dominate the discussion?
Did everyone make at least one contribution?
Did anyone try to bring out quieter members of the group?
How well did they listen to each other?
Did any conflicts or disagreements arise? How well did they handle them?
Did anyone keep an eye on the time?
Did they work well as a team?

At the outset, you may need to clarify the instructions and ensure that everyone understands what is expected of the group. You might also need to prioritise issues and, if appropriate, consider setting an agenda. After that, you could ask the group whether anyone has any thoughts as to how to approach the task. Then you can disclose your own views and try to achieve a consensus on how to move forward. If you disagree with someone's suggestion, first acknowledge their contribution and then provide a counter argument by saying "I appreciate your suggestion, however I believe . . .". If someone else in the group has made a good idea or suggestion then acknowledge and praise them without being patronising.

You do not need to be aggressive or domineering to impress recruiters. It is much more important to demonstrate good listening skills and the ability to form effective working relationships quickly. Recruiters will be looking for candidates who can listen to and support others, bring new people into the conversation, and ask for opinions to try to reach a group consensus. Try to involve quieter members of the group who are not contributing by asking them what their thoughts and opinions are on the matter. That said, it is perfectly acceptable to challenge other people's ideas as long as you do so professionally and with respect. Equally, you may need to manage dominant personalities effectively to ensure that everyone has an opportunity to contribute. This may require good diplomacy skills and resilience if someone is being particularly competitive (do not be tempted to respond to such behaviour defensively or aggressively).

Think about time management and make sure you complete the task within the time that has been allocated to you. If you take on the role of timekeeper, try to suggest to the group how you might organise the time from the beginning and then keep the group on track for the remainder of the task. Don't be afraid to make people move on, or push the group for a decision, if time is getting tight.

You might prefer to avoid being the note taker if it takes you outside of the discussion but do make sure that someone keeps track of the group's progress, any decisions that have been made, and the reasons for those decisions. This task might be made easier if you have been given a laptop or white board so think carefully about how to make the most effective use of any resources which you are allocated. If you are nominated as the note taker, don't just write the notes down at random; think about how it would look best to jot down ideas (i.e. spider diagram, putting ideas into decision-making tools, etc.)

As the task unfolds, try to reflect on and evaluate your performance and make adjustments accordingly. For example, try to encourage others to speak if you think you are being too loud, or try to get more involved if you realise that you have not made any meaningful contributions yet.

In-tray or E-tray Exercise

These exercises are paper based or electronic simulations of office life through which candidates are given an opportunity to demonstrate their ability to think quickly and prioritise work effectively. You will be given a scenario, a stack of documents relating to that scenario, and a list of key members of your team. For example, you might be told that you have just returned from a two-week holiday and have found the following emails in your in-box:

> a telephone message asking you to call your sister;
> an email from one of the associates in your team asking you to attend a meeting this morning;
> an email from one of the solicitors in your team asking you to take some documents to court this afternoon;
> an email (marked urgent) from a client asking you to speak at their annual conference next month;
> an email from a client asking you to call him about a claim form he has just received;
> a memo from a senior partner asking you to carry out some research for him;
> an email from another trainee asking you to join him for lunch;
> an email from a senior partner asking for information for a new client pitch;
> an email from an existing client asking you to call him in relation to some new work;
> an email from one of your supervisor's most important clients asking you to call him about a new contract; and
> a reminder that you have a training session at lunchtime today.

You must decide what action to take in relation to each document: delegate the work to someone else (and if so to whom); deal with it now; deal with it at the end of the day; deal with it tomorrow; or ignore it. In an exercise such as this, recruiters are testing the following skills: your ability to read and understand instructions; your time management skills; your planning and prioritising skills; your written or verbal communication skills (if you are asked to report back to the HR Manager); your ability to work to a deadline; and your ability to digest information in a pressurised environment.

The trick with these exercises is not to panic and to work your way through the paperwork methodically once you have read the instructions carefully. Remember that the recruiter is testing your resilience and your ability to work effectively in a pressurised environment so prove to them that you are up to the challenge. It is likely that the exercise will be timed so keep an eye on the clock and make sure you have some time left at the end to review your decisions and make any last-minute adjustments.

Review all the paperwork to start with so you have a clear idea of what you are working with. Prioritise tasks as you go through this review process using a numbering or colour coded system. Then go through the paperwork again making decisions about how to deal with each task in light of the others in the pack and the level of priority of each one. You might find it helpful to make notes as you go through so you can refer to them when you report your decisions later on.

Drafting Exercises

Through these tasks, employers will assess your written communication skills and your ability to produce a professional document or letter (e.g. a letter of claim, a letter of complaint, or a letter of advice).

Keep in mind these tips when preparing for a drafting exercise:

think carefully about the structure of your document;
sift out any irrelevant information or "red herrings" in the instructions;

adjust the tone according to the type of document you have been asked to produce;

remember that employers are looking for logical thought processes and an ability to write clearly and succinctly.

Aptitude and Personality Tests

In today's increasingly competitive graduate recruitment market, these tests are often used by employers as an additional filter during the application process. Given the type of work undertaken by lawyers, verbal reasoning tests are more likely to be used in the legal recruitment process than numerical reasoning although some employers use a combination of the two. Some employers also ask candidates to complete a personality test. The tests might form part of an interview process, or as one of a selection of activities at an assessment centre. However, some employers ask candidates to complete online tests at home before the interview stage.

Aptitude Tests

Aptitude tests measure your ability to reason (in other words to draw conclusions from particular information) usually either numerically or verbally, although some also test your lateral thinking or problem-solving abilities. Aptitude tests are normally completed under timed conditions and generally employers will set a minimum performance level for each test.

Verbal reasoning tests are similar to the comprehension exercises you might remember from school. You will be given a short written passage followed by a series of statements commenting on, or drawing inferences from, the content/meaning of the passage and you will be asked to assess the accuracy of those statements. You might also encounter questions that ask you to look for patterns or connections in lists of words.

Numerical reasoning tests ask you to draw conclusions from a set of statistical data but do not panic if you feel you are poor at maths; you are unlikely to have to get to grips with anything more complicated than basic addition, subtraction, multiplication, division, and percentages. For this reason, it is worth revising some basic GCSE guides to polish up your skills in these key areas.

Abstract reasoning tests require you to demonstrate your problem solving abilities. For example, you might be given a series of symbols followed by a new group of symbols underneath. Your task is to decide which of these new symbols naturally follows the pattern and would therefore be next in the series.

There is generally only one correct answer for aptitude tests and you are often under a time constraint (although you will not necessarily be expected to answer all the questions on the paper). Try to keep moving through the questions at a steady pace and, if you are struggling with a particular question, move on and revisit it later.

Personality Tests

Personality tests measure a person's behaviour, motivation levels, values, interests, personal qualities and the way they are likely to react to a particular situation or challenge. In short, they provide a snapshot of an individual's personality and key characteristics. For this reason, they are often used by employers as part of the graduate recruitment selection process because they enable them to assess how a candidate is likely to perform in certain situations, whether they are likely to suit a particular role, and whether they are likely to fit into the culture of the organisation.

Unlike aptitude tests, there are no right or wrong answers in personality tests. These tests aim to build up a picture of you as a person so there will be no pre-determined set of answers and you will not normally be under any time constraints when completing the questionnaire. However, in order to avoid unnecessary stress on the day, it would be worth practising a selection of aptitude tests and personality tests so you know what to expect.

When completing a personality test, try to answer each question as honestly as you can and, although there is often no time limit for these tests, try not to over-analyse each question (remember that there is no right or wrong answer).

"You will spend half a day at a Shoosmiths assessment centre. It's an opportunity for you to get to know the firm, as much as it is an opportunity for us to get to know you.

You can expect to network with assessors (made up of trainees, associate solicitors, partners and HR staff) on your arrival, before receiving an introduction to the day by Shoosmith's CEO, Claire Rowe.

You will take part in a group exercise and a written exercise, as well as presenting for five minutes on a pre-prepared topic. And of course, you'll attend an interview. There will also be a session where you can ask trainees anything over a coffee.

You can prepare for the assessment centre by researching the firm and your interviewers. Think about the experiences you may want to talk about during your interviews, which should demonstrate your strengths.

On the day, be yourself and don't let nerves get the better of you. If you don't feel like you performed well on one section of the day, try to do your best on the next exercise, as one bad exercise won't necessarily rule you out. You'll feel the pressure, like in any interview or exam situation, but use it to your advantage to demonstrate your resilience."

Samantha Hope, Graduate Recruitment Manager, Shoosmiths

19 MAKING USE OF FEEDBACK

Training contracts are very difficult to secure so do not be disheartened if you fail on your first attempt. Instead, reflect upon your performance, identify and learn from your mistakes, and use the extra year to your advantage by gaining as much additional experience as possible.

That said, you need to be realistic about your applications. If you make lots of applications to a similar type of firm and are rejected by all of them, consider whether that is because there is something wrong with your technique, or whether you have pitched your applications incorrectly. It might be that you do not fit the profile for that type of firm. Re-visit the advice given in Chs 9 and 10, and reflect seriously on your approach. You could also consider taking advice from a trusted careers advisor or tutor to see if they think you are making appropriate applications.

SOME FINAL WORDS OF ADVICE FROM THE EXPERTS

"Do not give up! If you are sure you want to be a solicitor, keep going and you will get your training contract. However, you must be true to yourself about the kind of law you are interested in and set yourself a realistic goal. Interviewers can tell whether or not your heart is in it. If you really want to do family or crime, don't apply to commercial City firms for the salary alone and then be surprised if you don't get offered a position. I started making applications for training contracts before I started the GDL and made approximately 50 applications over three years. I was confident that I would secure a training contract as I had good grades and, as a more mature student, I had plenty of life/work/client experience. However, I made a serious mistake—I was not honest with myself about the type of firm I wanted to work for. I only applied to large firms with huge salaries who specialised in corporate law. I had many interviews but was rejected each time. I could not understand why and began to lose confidence. After I finished the LPC, I stopped worrying about salary and made a few well-researched and well-considered applications to firms I was genuinely interested in. I interviewed at one particular firm that I was very excited about and where I could see myself being very happy. I found it remarkable that I could be myself at the interview and did not need to feign an interest in corporate law, or pretend that I read the Financial Times every day. I was very comfortable during the recruitment process and I actually quite enjoyed the assessment day and the interview. I felt instantly 'at home' and was delighted to be offered a training contract. In hindsight, I am extremely pleased that I did not get offered a training contract with any of the firms I applied to initially. I have no interest in corporate law and I am not surprised that the interviewers could see that."

A Trainee Solicitor

"If you are consistently failing to get through the first stage of the application process, it's absolutely crucial to get some feedback. If you don't know where you are going wrong, you won't know how to improve and you might be making the same mistake time and time again. It might be something that you can rectify quite easily."

A Graduate Recruitment Manager

"If you are getting assessment centres but not getting any further than that, you need to think seriously about what you are doing wrong and the best way to do this is to ask for some feedback from firms."

Graduate Recruitment Manager

"I applied for training contracts during my second year at university but didn't get anywhere so I reapplied in my third year and found that my applications were far more successful, possibly because, on reflection, the first time round I applied to firms that I wouldn't actually have wanted to work for. My applications were far more targeted second time round. I had also volunteered to help at the university's listening service and I had completed three vacation schemes so I had a lot more on my CV second time round."

A Trainee Solicitor

"If you know that you really want to become a solicitor, just keep trying. Maybe the right firm finds you in the end and those rejections are just part of the process of sifting out the ones where you wouldn't actually be happy in the long term."

A Trainee Solicitor

PART III
THE TRAINING CONTRACT

Section 3
The Training Contract and Beyond

20 THE TRAINING CONTRACT AND QUALIFICATION

Putting academic credentials aside for a moment, what makes a good trainee and how can you get the most out of your training contract? No two trainees are the same, but there are certain attributes that some of the best trainees have in common.

Keep an open mind when starting each new seat—Commercial Property might not be your ideal practice area, but the people in your department have chosen to make a career there; do not insult them by moaning every time you are given work, or by making it clear that you are only there to "tick a box" before moving onto a more interesting area of practice. Equally, a training contract can be full of surprises: you might find that the land law you hated at university suddenly becomes fascinating in the practical context of commercial property deals. It has also been known for even the most narrow-minded of trainees to forget his prejudices towards a particular seat when he is desperately seeking a permanent position on qualification so do not burn your bridges.

> "As I approach qualification, my qualification choices have changed partly as a result of changes in the market and the availability of jobs, which meant that I have had to consider other options. My advice would be to try to keep an open mind and work hard in each seat. In today's market, you have to have four good appraisals otherwise even the department that you perform excellently in won't take you on because the competition is so strong."
>
> *A Trainee Solicitor at a City firm*

Adopt a positive attitude—it is far nicer to work with positive people rather than those who do not integrate and make it clear that they would rather be somewhere else. Loyalty to the firm and to your department can go a long way and might be the key to successful retention if there is a choice between you and another candidate on qualification. You want to be remembered as the trainee who was always willing to help, even when asked to undertake the most menial tasks. Be enthusiastic and maintain a sense of humour. You will be given some difficult tasks to complete during your training contract ranging from the excruciatingly boring (e.g. proof reading 100 leases or scheduling bundles of completion documents) to the downright frightening (e.g. your first solo completion meeting or client interview). A sense of humour and thick skin will help see you through, and remember every job has its drawbacks and one day you will be able to delegate these tasks to another unsuspecting trainee!

Respect and be courteous to everyone—you never know who you are going to need in the future. Even if you are certain that you will not want to qualify into a seat, you might well find yourself working in larger, cross departmental teams with many of those solicitors in the future and, therefore, forming good relationships during your training contract will pay dividends in the end. Also remember that office politics are omnipresent and people have a tendency to talk. The partner in your commercial property seat may have a close working relationship with the partner in your preferred seat of corporate and a good word from the property partner may help your chances of securing the much sought after corporate seat. Equally, you should never underestimate the support staff who will often know far more about a particular practice area than you can possibly imagine. They will also be able to help you with practical issues such as ordering stationery, finding templates on the computer system, and showing you how to record and bill time to particular clients. Life will be far more difficult for you if you do not make an effort to form a good relationship with them from the outset.

Support your fellow trainees—you will find that they provide a source of much needed encouragement and guidance during your training contract. They know just how frightening that Partner in Commercial Litigation can be, and they probably have a template disclosure letter that you might need when your supervisor asks you to prepare one at short notice on your first day in a new seat. They can probably also give you some tips on how to sweet talk the difficult secretary in the Family Law team, and will bring you a coffee and sandwich when you have been asked to check a stack of verification notes and will not make it home before midnight. However, remember that it is a two-way process and you need to invest in them too. It is particularly important to remember this when you are all vying for the same newly qualified positions during the final stage of the training contract. Trainees can become very competitive and can go to great lengths to secure positions on qualification. However, it is worth remembering that partners and recruitment managers are very experienced at placing trainees and they will not be fooled. You should resist the temptation to treat other trainees unfairly or unkindly: it will be noticed and it is unlikely to reflect well on you.

Work hard in every seat—the hard work does not end once you have secured the training contract. From then on, you have to prove that you can survive in the real world and persuade senior colleagues that you are worthy of a permanent position on qualification. Quite often firms will judge you on your performance in your least favourite seat as an indicator of your strength of character and professionalism. We all have to do jobs we do not like from time to time, but firms want people who are happy to roll up their sleeves and get on with the task in hand.

> "We often judge people on how they cope in the seat that we know is not one they particularly want to do because that is a good indicator of how they will cope in difficult times."
>
> *Former Training Partner at a Regional Law Firm*

Know when to ask for help and when to use your initiative—your supervisor will not mind you asking questions (that is the whole point of having a supervisor), but you must learn quickly how to get the right balance between using your initiative and seeking advice from others. There will be times when your supervisor is not available to answer your question. In that case you will need to do your own research, look back over the correspondence to see if you can find the answer to your question, or perhaps ask another colleague.

> "It can be difficult to know where the boundaries lie when dealing with clients because different supervisors have very different expectations. You can spend several months with someone who prefers to limit your exposure to clients and then move to sit with someone who wants you to do everything. It can make you question yourself."
>
> *A Trainee Solicitor*

> "If in doubt, ask someone. I felt a very strong pressure to show that I could do everything already. Although people do respect your ability to take the initiative, you don't always have to do that and there are some things where you should check whether it's OK to send something out. You don't have to go straight in and say 'I don't know what to do', but you could offer some solutions or options and ask how they would like you to proceed."
>
> *A Trainee Solicitor*

> "It's far better to get told off because you happen to be knocking on someone's door at the wrong time, rather than make a huge mistake that could result in a law suit. I've had a couple of experiences where partners have been a bit short with me but they usually come back later and apologise for it. You can't take things too personally."
>
> *A Trainee Solicitor*

Do not be too sensitive—lawyers are often forced to work very long hours under extremely pressurised conditions and this can make people short tempered and intolerant. Do not take this personally, just get on with the job and know when to keep quiet. Equally, learn how to take criticism constructively and to reflect on the strengths and weaknesses of your performance at work. If you make a mistake or are given advice on how to improve your performance in a particular area, take it in and learn from it. If you were expected to be the perfect solicitor from day one, there would be no need for the training contract.

> "One day you can have a great day and everything goes well and the next day you can feel completely useless."
>
> *A Trainee Solicitor*

> "On my first day in a new seat, I sent out an invoice that had been prepared by the previous trainee relating to a file I had inherited from him. The client was furious and made things very difficult for me. It was difficult to learn how to deal with that even though I knew I had done nothing wrong. You just have to learn to rise above it."
>
> *A Trainee Solicitor*

Accept that it will take time to settle into each new seat—many trainees find it rather unsettling to move between seats but this is an inevitable part of the training process so you need to learn to deal with it.

> "One of the biggest challenges of the training contract is moving seats because you've just got comfortable, everyone knows you and what you are capable of, they know they can trust you and then you have to go somewhere else in the firm and start again. You also have to get to know the culture and working practices of the new department and how they like things done."
>
> *A Trainee Solicitor*

"I was in corporate for my first seat and it was such a sea change moving to my real estate seat where you are really thrown in at the deep end. In real estate you're running files from day one and suddenly you've got all these calls and emails coming in from clients whereas in corporate you stand behind maybe two or three people up the food chain from you."

A Trainee Solicitor in a City Firm

Try to think commercially—this is a difficult one for trainees, many of whom will arrive fresh from university and law school, but it is one of the keys to a successful career. Make an effort to think about the commercial context of a particular transaction or instruction and discuss it with your supervisor. Also, make an effort to keep up to date with current and financial affairs and think about how they impact on clients' businesses and/or the projects you are working on. Even if you are not going to specialise in commercial law, you will need to keep in mind that solicitors are there to make money for their firms and to learn the importance of effective time recording and timely billing—this is as much about commercial awareness as anything else.

Manage your time and remain organised—as a trainee you might find yourself working for several different people in the same department and this can sometimes lead to problems with balancing conflicting interests. Although you must show that you can cope with competing demands on your time and are able to manage your workload effectively, this is a skill to be developed over time and you should always feel that you can ask for support from your supervisor. At the very least you should keep people informed of progress on a particular file and do not wait until the last minute before asking for help or telling them that you are not going to be able to complete the work within the timeframe. If you really cannot get something completed by a deadline, consider asking another trainee to help you (if your supervisor is happy with that).

Make a note of key dates and deadlines on files and do not be afraid to remind your supervisor of them if you think he has forgotten—they are only human too and can sometimes forget things and, even if they have remembered, they will probably be very impressed to see that you have used your initiative.

Keep an up-to-date record of all the files you are working on—your record should include the particular tasks you have been allocated for each one and the relevant deadlines. This will help you prioritise matters and manage your time and it will be useful when other fee earners ask about your capacity to help with a new matter, or if your supervisor asks for an update on your workload. It will also act as a useful record of the work you have been involved in during your training contract. All trainees have to complete a Record of Training in order to qualify as a solicitor (reg.14 of the SRA Training Regulations 2014) so it is worth devoting some time to this at the end of every month to avoid getting caught out.

> "Never go into someone's room without taking a pen and paper. Even if you are just popping in for a chat, you can come out with a load of new instructions!"
>
> *A Trainee Solicitor*

Learn to deal with sleepless nights—if you are thinking of specialising in corporate or banking work, you need to learn how to operate effectively on very little sleep.

> "Unless you are really lucky, there are going to be points where you will go home at 2 o'clock in the morning and come back in at 9 o'clock for about a week."
>
> *A Trainee Solicitor at a Magic Circle firm*

Get used to being out of your comfort zone for much of the time—the training contract provides a steep learning curve and you will often be asked to carry out tasks at short notice with very little background knowledge.

> "One of my most challenging experiences as a trainee was when I said I would cover for a trainee who was going on holiday and help with a completion meeting. I was responsible for all the

> document management on a huge multi-jurisdictional deal. It
> started on Friday and we completed the following Thursday
> at 3am."
>
> *A Trainee Solicitor at a City Firm*

QUALIFICATION

Upon qualification, many trainees will be offered permanent
positions by their firm, although this is dependent on market conditions at the time and should not be assumed to be a guaranteed
outcome. When deciding which area to qualify into, you need to
reflect honestly on your performance in each of your seats and
what you want to achieve from your career in the long term.
Think about your wider career aspirations; where you would like
to be in five and then ten years' time; the type of clients you
want to work for; the culture of particular departments and your
response to that culture; the type of work you enjoyed most
during your training; how much money you want to earn; and
perhaps also how important family and leisure time is to you.

For some trainees, the last few months of the training contract
can be a very stressful time indeed. While for many the transition
from trainee to newly qualified solicitor seems to work out seam-
lessly, others will face an uncertain future as they find that they
are not being retained by their firm or that there are no positions
available in the department of their choice. If you find yourself
in this position, you need to keep an open mind, remain positive
and proactive, have faith in your ability and, above all, keep
going. Hopefully, you will have taken the advice given above and
approached all your seats with a positive attitude and an open
mind. This will at least put you in the best possible position when
it comes to selection. If you find that you are not being retained
by your firm, or that it does not have any opportunities in your
chosen practice area, get in touch with some well-established
recruitment consultants, keep a close eye on firms' websites and
the Lawyer jobs pages, and don't be afraid to send some speculative letters and CVs to firms to see whether they will be recruiting
at NQ level if they are in your practice area.

Time for Celebrations

At the end of the long and, for many, very expensive journey is the prize of being admitted to the Roll of Solicitors. It can seem rather surreal to arrive in the office on your first day as a qualified solicitor and wonder what really is so different to yesterday! The first few months as a newly qualified solicitor can be daunting and rather stressful as you adjust to life as a professional and start taking responsibility for your own workload and clients. Take things slowly and remember that you are not expected to be running your own practice immediately. You can, and should, still ask senior colleagues for guidance. One of the most rewarding aspects of this career is the continual learning curve so you are not expected to know it all on day one!

Try to build up a broad range of work experience during your first few years as a qualified solicitor and, if possible, work with several different solicitors or partners. This will ensure that you have plenty of inspiration when developing your own approach to practice and client management and the more varied your workload, the more confident you will be when dealing with new matters in the future.

You will be invited to attend an admissions ceremony (normally some months after actually qualifying) to celebrate your achievement with family and friends. I would encourage you to make every effort to attend this ceremony. It is a wonderful achievement to have qualified as a solicitor so enjoy the limelight for a couple of hours at least before the hard work begins again!

21 A WEEK IN THE LIFE OF A TRAINEE SOLICITOR

Written by Annabelle Harrison, Trainee Solicitor, Blake Morgan LLP

I am a second year trainee at a large regional law firm and am currently undertaking the third seat of my training contract within the Built Environment team. Built Environment is one of the biggest teams in the firm comprising several areas of commercial real estate including social housing, agriculture, landlord and tenant, development, and corporate support work. It is December, which means I am halfway through the seat with mid-seat appraisals looming and the (scary!) reality of final seat choices and the prospect of qualification now not too far away.

Monday morning comes and I am in the car at 07.45 ready to begin my commute to work. I only live about 18 miles away from the office, but between there and my house lies a stretch of motorway named "one of the worst in Britain" for accidents and commuter traffic. I plug my iPod into the car radio and turn the volume up—only Beyoncé will do when stuck in Monday morning commuter traffic!

I arrive at the office for 08.45 and head to my desk where I power up my computer, grab a hot drink and catch up on emails that have come in over the weekend. At 09.30 it is time for the team meeting. I head over with a couple of colleagues and catch up on everyone's weekend on the way. The team meeting varies in length, but usually lasts for around 25 minutes and focuses on a review of the team's figures and target to date, details of new work and upcoming tenders, capacity within the team and general business development news. There is a tray of bacon rolls, fruit salad and yoghurt with granola at the side of the room and after the meeting everyone helps themselves to some breakfast and heads back to their desks.

Every Monday I also have a meeting with my supervisor, where we discuss my workload and any legal points from the previous week which I would like to review with him. This weekly session has proved to be an invaluable learning opportunity. One-on-one time with supervisors can sometimes be more sporadic depending on the working practices and environments of various teams and the demands of clients. You need to learn to be flexible during the training contract because supervisors operate in many diverse ways and you need to adapt to their differing expectations. I think it makes you a better lawyer in the end because you learn different things from each relationship.

On Monday nights I play netball in the firm's team and tonight we have a 19.00 game in the local league—let's hope for a win.

On **Tuesday** I spend the morning making amendments to a draft lease for one of our large commercial retail clients who is taking a lease of a shop unit within a shopping mall. The partner I am working for has allowed me to have a go at the initial amendments. He will then review my draft before it is sent over to the landlord's solicitor for their comments. It is soon lunchtime and I head down to the cafeteria with a number of other trainees from my intake. One of my favourite things about working in a large firm is being one of a several trainees. We all support each other and many of the trainees have now become good friends of mine. We try to organise regular trainee social events outside of work, such as dinners at local restaurants and drinks evenings. Talking to other trainees is also a great way to get the lowdown on seats you may hope to try at some point during your training. On Thursday night the Corporate and Built Environment departments are hosting Christmas drinks for the firm's key corporate clients and I have been tasked with organising a team of trainees to host the event. When I get back to my desk after lunch I send an email to the other trainees who have volunteered to help, setting out the timings for the evening and designating each trainee with a task. Some trainees will be doing "meet and greet" duties on the door, others will be taking coats and there will also be a couple hosting at the bar. The rest of my day is spent proofreading engrossment's, chasing up documents from the other side on various matters and reviewing and amending an option agreement.

Wednesday passes in a blur. I get to the office for 08.00 in order to attend a breakfast seminar from the Construction team. The session details key points regarding collateral warranties. I then get asked to assist on a large project and have to sift through six boxes of documents and prepare a corresponding deeds schedule. This is one of the more mundane trainee tasks, but it is still an important job that must be carried out correctly. I lunch at my desk today whilst finalising some research and a letter of advice to a client regarding stamp duty land tax. 19.00 rolls round and I decide to head home for the evening.

Thursday is the corporate client drinks night. I will need to be extra organised today to ensure I complete my work before leaving my desk at 17.30 to set up for the drinks event prior to the guests arriving at 18.00. I sit in on a client conference call in the morning with a partner. We review various documents relating to a proposed purchase of a development site which includes a transfer, option agreement and lease. I also have to review a 100-page agreement for lease and mark it up against the agreed heads of terms sent over by the client and some other smaller drafting tasks. At 17.30 I head downstairs to help set up for our client Christmas drinks event. The evening goes well, with many clients attending and a performance from the firm's choir singing a medley of Christmas carols. I enjoyed the experience of attending an event with many of the firm's key clients and at the end of the evening the partners thanked all the trainees for helping out. Getting involved with firm events such as this is a great way to get your face known in the wider firm and is an important part of the training experience.

Friday arrives and I am asked to assist with reviewing collateral warranties for a development project and am also given an urgent research task relating to land transfers between local authorities and faith schools. The research is complex and it takes a couple of hours to prepare a detailed note for the senior associate. The rest of the day is spent chasing up on various ongoing matters, undertaking a land registry registration and preparing a draft SDLT return form for a matter which is due to complete shortly. Every Friday the firm welcomes staff to head downstairs for a drink to network internally and relax at the end of the week. This is another great opportunity for trainees to interact with senior fee-earners in other areas of the firm and to find out more about other areas.

And it will all begin again next week!

22 FINAL THOUGHTS

KEY THEMES

I hope you have found this book useful as you plot your course from student to solicitor. It should be clear to you by now that there is a significant preparatory stage which must be taken seriously if you are to have any hope of securing a training contract. Spend time researching your options, developing your CV and targeting your applications. It is not a race, and time invested in the preparatory stage will be time well spent in the long run.

It should also be clear that work experience is essential to demonstrate that you have made an informed decision to pursue this career path and as a way of developing your commercial awareness. In addition, you should now have a much clearer understanding of the importance of networking and developing your own brand. Make the most of every contact in your existing network and invest time in making new ones because you never know where they might lead you.

Finally, and perhaps most importantly of all, believe in yourself and maintain your focus. Yes, it is a gruelling process, but that is what makes the prize worth having.

DEVELOPMENTS AND EMERGING ISSUES

We have witnessed considerable and unprecedented change in the legal services market since the first edition of this book was published: punishing legal aid cuts; increasing commoditisation and outsourcing of legal services; greater flexibility in the route to qualification as a solicitor; the application of the National Minimum Wage to training contracts (rather than the higher minimum salary which was previously set by the SRA); the introduction and increasing popularity of legal apprenticeships; the increase in ABSs and confirmation from the Legal Services Board that accounting firms are permitted to offer legal services. Is it only a matter of time before the Big 4 Accounting firms enter the legal services market and what impact will that have on City firms?

No doubt there will be considerable change to come following publication of the second edition. It is impossible to capture all the developments and emerging trends in one place which is why it is essential that you keep an eye on the ones that have been identified in this book and remain alert to new ones which unfold in legal education, the legal services market and beyond. This is especially important as you begin to prepare for training contract interviews.

Good luck!

APPENDIX 1: MONEY MATTERS

Qualifying as a solicitor is an expensive undertaking. Fees for the LPC alone can be up to £14,700 (at the time of writing). If you add to that the cost of completing a law degree, or non-law degree and GDL, plus living expenses throughout your studies, you will get an idea of the level of financial investment that is involved.

Some firms fund the cost of the LPC for their trainees and others will fund both the LPC and GDL for any non-law graduates in their trainee intake. However, for many aspiring solicitors the cost of qualification must be borne privately since, unlike university studies, you are unlikely to receive any funding from your local education authority. This appendix outlines a selection of funding sources, but your careers department might be able to suggest others.

The information contained in this appendix was correct at the time of writing but you are advised to make your own enquiries since bursaries, scholarship schemes and other sources of funding are subject to change over time.

You should also be aware that not all offers of funding are legitimate so do be alert to scam emails. Be vigilant and get in touch with the SRA if you have any doubt over the legitimacy of offers which are made to you.

Law School Scholarships and Bursaries

Some law schools offer scholarships, which usually take the form of a reduction in fees, rather than a cash award. They might also offer limited bursaries for students who are struggling to meet the costs of the course. Contact your provider for further details.

Law Society Diversity Access Scheme

The Diversity Access Scheme supports individuals who would otherwise be unable to fund their LPC fees. The scheme provides funding to cover LPC course fees. The package includes funding for up to the full cost of the LPC, a professional mentor, and work experience opportunities. For more information, visit *http://juniorlawyers.lawsociety.org.uk/ funding-studies#lsschemes* or *http://www.lawsociety.org.uk/ law-careers/diversity-access-scheme*.

Other Awards and Scholarships

HRLA Bursary Award

The Human Rights Lawyers' Association (HRLA) bursary scheme enables law students to undertake work placements in the field of human rights. For more information on this scheme, go to *http://www.hrla.org.uk/*.

The Inderpal Rahal Memorial Trust

The Inderpal Rahal Memorial Trust makes one, or occasionally two, awards of £2,000 per year towards legal training for women from an immigrant or refugee background who intend to practise or teach law in the UK. Candidates are required to complete an application form and those shortlisted will be asked to attend an interview. You should note, however, that awards will not be made to those taking a first degree in law.

Contact the trust administrator for further details, either by email *irmt@gclaw.co.uk*, or by writing to:

Inderpal Rahal Memorial Trust
Garden Court Chambers
57–60 Lincoln's Inn Fields
London WC2A 3LJ

The Graham Rushton Award for Visually Impaired Law Students

This award is a grant of around £7,000 for which blind and partially-sighted people can apply. The fund is paid from a legacy left to the RNIB by Graham Rushton, a blind lawyer, who wanted his legacy to assist blind and partially-sighted law students who are studying English Law in the UK.

For more information visit *http://juniorlawyers.lawsociety.org. uk/funding-studies*.

Vernon Cade Fund

This fund was established by the widow of a Cambridge solicitor, Vernon Cade, to provide financial assistance to those who are training to become solicitors and having a connection with the county of Cambridgeshire. For more information, visit *http://juniorlawyers.lawsociety.org.uk/funding-studies*.

Datalaw Scholarship

This scheme was launched in 2015. Datalaw pledged to pay up to £12,000 towards LPC tuition fees to the winner of its competition. Applicants were asked to write or film a blog explaining why they deserve to win an LPC scholarship. For more details visit *https:// www.datalawonline.co.uk/lpc-scholarship*.

Snowdon Trust Grants

These grants are administered by the Snowdon Trust and are open to students in post-16 education who have a physical or sensory disability. The Trust offers support for additional disability-related costs that are not fully provided from available statutory funding. For more information visit *http://www.snowdontrust.org/grants*.

Government Funding

Full-time and part-time students on undergraduate courses can apply online to Student Finance England for help with finance. For more information visit *https://www.gov.uk/studentfinancesteps*. At the time of writing, plans are being implemented to offer student finance for postgraduate courses from 2016. Keep an eye on the website for further details.

Disabled Students Allowances

These allowances are available to undergraduate or postgraduate students who are enrolled on a course which lasts more than one year, and who have a condition which affects their ability to study. They are paid on top of any other student finance and do not have to be repaid. The allowances aim to help students to pay the extra costs which may be faced as a result of the student's condition. They are calculated according to individual needs, rather than by reference to household income. For more information visit *https://www.gov.uk/ disabled-students-allowances-dsas#overview*.

Discretionary Local Educational Authority (LEA) Awards

Some LEAs offer awards for people who are starting professional courses. However, awards for the LPC and GDL are discretionary and awards are limited. Your LEA will be able to provide you with details of its discretionary award policies.

Professional and Career Development Loans

These are commercial bank loans for between £300 and £10,000 which are offered to help pay for work-related learning. Loans are usually offered at a low interest rate and the Government will pay the interest on the loan during your studies, and for one month afterwards. However, you will then need to start repaying the loan regardless of your earnings. Also note that these loans are not available to fund the GDL.

For more information, visit *https://www.gov.uk/career-development-loans/overview*.

Commercial Bank Loans

This is an expensive, but for many students inevitable, source of funding. Make sure you research your options carefully before entering into a loan agreement to ensure you choose the most competitive option and are aware of your obligations and liabilities under the agreement. Also remember that, unlike Student Loans, these commercial loans have to be repaid regardless of the level of your earnings at the end of the course.

Bespoke Professional Studies Loans

Some GDL and LPC providers have entered into partnerships with particular banks to offer students a bespoke professional studies loan to help with course fees and living costs. Look at providers' websites if you want to find out more about these schemes.

Bank Overdraft

Some banks provide an interest free overdraft facility for students, but this will only cover a fairly small proportion of the GDL/LPC fees, and interest will become payable eventually.

Part-Time Study

Some providers offer part-time study routes for the GDL and LPC. This can be a useful option for some students as it allows them to combine their studies with paid work.

Payment by Instalments

Many LPC and GDL providers now offer the opportunity for students to spread the cost of their studies by paying course fees in instalments. Contact individual providers for more details of these schemes.

Delay Study

If you are funding your studies privately, you could consider taking a year or two out before starting the LPC so you can save money to pay your course fees and living expenses. Working as a paralegal is a useful option because it allows you to gain legal work experience while building up your savings.

Other Sources

Keep an eye on legal careers websites for competitions which offer free LPC or GDL places, e.g. Lawyer2b (*http://l2b.thelawyer. com*).

Visit the Law Society's "Funding your Studies" webpages for details of grants, scholarships, bursaries and other sources of funding *http://juniorlawyers.lawsociety.org.uk/funding-studies*.

The website Scholarship Hub provides a database of funding for UK and EU students. You can find the website at *http://www. thescholarshiphub.org.uk*.

APPENDIX 2: FURTHER READING AND OTHER RESOURCES

The following list is to help you locate further information which may be helpful to you as you embark on the training contract recruitment process. The contact details and web addresses were correct at the time of writing.

WEBSITES

Professional and Regulatory Bodies

http://www.cilex.org.uk — Chartered Institute of Legal Executives
http://www.lawsociety.org.uk — The Law Society
http://www.sra.org.uk — The Solicitors Regulation Authority
http://www.theiop.org — The Institute of Paralegals

Training for Tomorrow

http://letr.org.uk — Legal Education & Training Review
http://www.sra.org.uk/trainees/period-recognised-training.page — SRA changes to training contract
http://www.sra.org.uk/sra/policy/training-for-tomorrow.page — SRA Training for Tomorrow
http://www.sra.org.uk/students/training-contract.page — SRA student pages

Apprenticeships

http://www.cilex.org.uk/study/apprenticeships.aspx
http://www.gov.uk/legal-services-apprenticeships
http://www.gov.uk/government/organisations/skills-funding-agency

Legal Directories

http://www.chambersandpartners.com — Chambers & Partners
UK Guide
http://www.legal500.com — The Legal 500
http://www.tcph.co.uk — The Training Contract and Pupillage
Handbook

Developments in the law and legal services market

http://www.lawgazette.co.uk — The Law Society's Gazette with
news and jobs aimed at solicitors.
http://www.legalweek.com — Online legal magazine featuring
legal news and information.
http://www.theguardian.com/law — The Guardian's law supplement.
http://www.thelawyer.com — Online legal magazine featuring
legal news and information.
http://www.thetimes.co.uk/tto/law — The Times' law supplement.

University, LPC and GDL Applications

http://www.lawcabs.ac.uk — Central applications website for the
GDL and LPC.
http://www.ucas.com — Central organisation for applying to universities in the UK.

Legal Careers Websites

http://www.allaboutlaw.co.uk — Legal careers website, which
aims to de-mystify the legal profession and the recruitment
process. The site features blogs from current trainees and law
students and some useful information for pre-university students
who are interested in a legal career.
http://www.aspiringsolicitors.co.uk — An organisation which
aims to increase diversity in the legal profession. This site offers
excellent careers advice, which, although targeted to aspiring

solicitors in under-represented groups, will be of interest and value to all aspiring solicitors.

http://www.chambersstudent.co.uk — A comprehensive source of information on legal careers and the recruitment process, including a detailed database of law firms, useful timetables for vacation scheme and training contract applications, and an explanation of key practice areas.

http://www.lawcareers.net — A comprehensive source of information on legal careers and the recruitment process, including interviews with recruiters and trainees, legal news, and an explanation of key practice areas.

http://www.prospects.ac.uk/p/sectors/law_sector.jsp — General information about the legal profession and careers advice.

http://www.targetjobs.co.uk/law — Comprehensive source of information on legal careers and the recruitment process. It includes useful advice on completing application forms and preparing for interviews and assessment centres, and has some interesting case studies on LPC students and trainee solicitors.

http://www.thelawyer.com/l2b — Student website attached to The Lawyer. This is a very valuable source which combines careers advice and insights with legal news features.

General Legal Interest

http://letr.org.uk/www.cityam.com — The online version of the free daily London business newspaper.

http://letr.org.uk/www.rollonfriday.com — A light-hearted site featuring news and gossip on the legal profession and aimed primarily at solicitors and aspiring solicitors.

Pro Bono and Volunteering Opportunities

http://www.ageconcern.org.uk/get-involved/volunteer — Age Concern.

http://www.amicus-alj.org — Amicus—assisting lawyers for justice on Death Row.

http://www.amnesty.org.uk — Amnesty International—worldwide human rights campaign group.

http://www.appropriateadult.org.uk — National Appropriate Adult Network—providing an "appropriate adult" for those under the age of 17 and adults who are considered to be mentally vulnerable during police interviews.

http://www.biduk.org — Bail for Immigration Detainees (BID)—an independent charity seeking to challenge immigration detention in the UK.

http://www.bunac.org/uk/workabroad/summercamp — Opportunities to work and volunteer abroad.

http://www.campamerica.co.uk — US summer camp experience.

http://www.citizensadvice.org.uk — The CAB website.

http://www.community-links.org — Community Links Advice Team—local charity in East London which includes advice on welfare benefits, housing and debt, employment law, private housing, and consumer law.

http://www.dls.org.uk — Disability Law Service—providing advice to disabled and deaf people.

http://www.dsc.org.uk — The Directory of Social Change—information about working in the voluntary sector.

http://www.enactusuk.org — Student, academic and business leaders working together using entrepreneurism to transform lives of people in need.

http://www.freerepresentationunit.org.uk — The Free Representation Unit (FRU)—providing free legal representation for Employment Tribunals, Social Security appeals in the Social Security and Child Support Appeals Tribunals and some immigration and criminal injury compensation cases.

http://www.gov.uk/government/get-involved/take-part/volunteer — Government volunteering site.

http://www.howardleague.org — The Howard League for Penal Reform—the oldest penal reform charity in the UK.

http://www.innocencenetwork.org.uk — Innocence Network UK (INUK).

http://www.jerseycharities.org — Membership organisation for Jersey charities.

http://www.joininuk.org — Connecting volunteers to sports related initiatives.

http://www.justice.org.uk — Justice—the human rights organisation.

http://www.lawcentres.org.uk — The Law Centres Network—not-for-profit legal practices offering free legal advice and representation to disadvantaged people.

http://www.lawworks.org.uk — LawWorks—a charity providing free legal help to individuals and community groups who cannot afford to pay for it and cannot access legal aid.

http://www.liberty-human-rights.org.uk — Liberty—the human rights organisation.

http://www.reprieve.org.uk — Reprieve—fighting for people on Death Row.

http://www.star-network.org.uk — Student Action for Refugees (STAR)—a national network of student groups working to improve the lives of refugees in the UK.

http://www.studentprobono.net — Joint initiative by Queen Mary University of London and LawWorks to promote student pro bono work.

http://www.tradingstandards.gov.uk — The Trading Standards Institute website.

http://www.victimsupport.org.uk — Victim Support—national charity for victims and witnesses of crime in England and Wales.

http://www.volunteering.org.uk — Volunteering opportunities in England.

http://www.volunteerscotland.net — Volunteering opportunities in Scotland.

http://www.volunteering-wales.net — Volunteering opportunities in Wales.

Special Interest and Other Useful Websites

http://www.aml.org.uk — The Association of Muslim Lawyers
http://www.blacksolicitorsnetwork.co.uk — Black Solicitors Network
http://communities.lawsociety.org.uk/women-lawyers — Women Lawyers Division
http://www.cps.gov.uk — The Crown Prosecution Service (CPS)
http://www.gov.uk/government/organisations/ministry-of-justice — Ministry of Justice
http://www.gls.gov.uk — Government Legal Services (GLS)

http://www.justice.gov.uk — The Ministry of Justice
http://www.lapg.co.uk — The Legal Aid Practitioners Group
http://www.lawcf.org — The Lawyers' Christian Fellowship
http://www.lawsociety.org.uk/lawyerswithdisabilities — The Law Society Lawyers with Disabilities Group
http://www.lawsociety.org.uk/juniorlawyers — The Law Society Junior Lawyers Division
http://www.localgovernmentlawyer.co.uk — Local Government Lawyer
http://www.primecommitment.org — Prime Commitment (broadening access to the profession)
http://www.societyofasianlawyers.co.uk — The Society of Asian Lawyers
http://www.suttontrust.com/programmes/pathways-to-law — Pathways to Law

BOOKS FOR LAW STUDENTS

C. Barnard, J. O'Sullivan and G. Virgo, *What about Law?*, 2nd edn (Hart Publishing, 2011)

E. Finch and S. Fafinski, *Employability Skills for Law Students* (Oxford University Press, 2014)

E. Finch and S. Fafinski, *Legal Skills*, 4th edn (Oxford University Press, 2013)

S. Foster, *How to Write Better Law Essays*, 3rd edn (Longman, 2012)

J. Holland and J. Webb, *Learning Legal Rules*, 7th edn (Oxford University Press, 2010)

N. J. McBride, *Letters to a Law Student*, 3rd edn (Pearson, 2013)

G. Slapper, *How the Law Works*, 3rd edn (Routledge, 2013)

L. Webley, *Legal Writing*, 3rd edn (Routledge, 2013)

G. Williams, *Learning the Law*, 15th edn (Sweet & Maxwell, 2013)

S. Wilson and P. Kenny, *The Law Student's Handbook* (Oxford University Press, 2007)

BOOKS FOR GENERAL LEGAL INTEREST

T. Bingham, *The Rule of Law* (Penguin 2011)
R. Susskind, *Tomorrow's Lawyers: An Introduction to Your Future* (OUP, 2013)

BOOKS ON PREPARING FOR INTERVIEWS

M. Eggert, *Perfect Interview* (Random House Books, 2008)
M. Eggert, *Perfect Answers to Interview Questions* (Random House Books, 2007)

BOOKS ON PREPARING FOR THE LNAT

R. Hutton, G. Hutton and F. Simpson, *Passing the National Admissions Test for Law,* 3rd edn (Law Matters Publishing, 2011)
G. Petrova, *Practise and Pass: LNAT (Practise & Pass Professional)* (Trotman, 2011)
M. Shepherd, *Mastering the National Admissions Test for Law*, 2nd edn (Routledge Cavendish, 2013)